S0-BDQ-421

Premiere Pro Editing Workshop

Marcus Geduld

CMPBooks

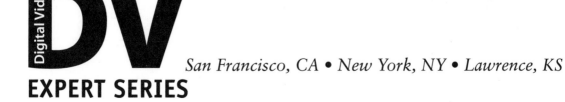

San Francisco, CA • New York, NY • Lawrence, KS

Published by CMP Books
an imprint of CMP Media LLC

Main office: 600 Harrison Street, San Francisco, CA 94107 USA
Tel: 415-947-6615; fax: 415-947-6015

Editorial office:
4601 West 6th Street, Suite B, Lawrence, KS 66049 USA
www.cmpbooks.com
email: books@cmp.com

Designations used by companies to distinguish their products are often claimed as trademarks. In all instances where CMP is aware of a trademark claim, the product name appears in initial capital letters, in all capital letters, or in accordance with the vendor's capitalization preference. Readers should contact the appropriate companies for more complete information on trademarks and trademark registrations. All trademarks and registered trademarks in this book are the property of their respective holders.

Copyright © 2004 by CMP Media LLC, except where noted otherwise. Published by CMP Books, CMP Media LLC. All rights reserved. Printed in the United States of America. No part of this publication may be reproduced or distributed in any form or by any means, or stored in a database or retrieval system, without the prior written permission of the publisher; with the exception that the program listings may be entered, stored, and executed in a computer system, but they may not be reproduced for publication.

The programs in this book are presented for instructional value. The programs have been carefully tested, but are not guaranteed for any particular purpose. The publisher does not offer any warranties and does not guarantee the accuracy, adequacy, or completeness of any information herein and is not responsible for any errors or omissions. The publisher assumes no liability for damages resulting from the use of the information in this book or for any infringement of the intellectual property rights of third parties that would result from the use of this information.

Senior Editor: Dorothy Cox
Managing Editor: Gail Saari
Cover Layout Design: Damien Castaneda

Distributed in the U.S. by: Distributed in Canada by:
Publishers Group West   Jaguar Book Group
1700 Fourth Street   100 Armstrong Avenue
Berkeley, CA 94710   Georgetown, Ontario M6K 3E7 Canada
1-800-788-3123   905-877-4483

For individual orders and information on special discounts for quantity orders, please contact:
CMP Books Distribution Center, 6600 Silacci Way, Gilroy, CA 95020
Tel: 1-800-500-6875 or 408-848-3854; fax: 408-848-5784
email: cmp@rushorder.com; Web: www.cmpbooks.com

ISBN: 1-57820-228-0

To my lovely wife, Lisa. A geek can marry a beautiful girl.

ACKNOWLEDGEMENTS

Thanks to Richard Harrington, Chris Phrommayon, Ben Kozuch, the folks at CMP Books, Dan Brown, and the American Diabetes Association. I would also like to thank my many students at Future Media Concepts (www.fmctraining.com), who, by asking the right questions, teach me which topics need special attention and explanation.

Footage used in many of the screenshots is courtesy of the American Diabetes Association (www.diabetes.org), production by RHED Pixel (www.rhedpixel.com).

Contents

Introduction

What Is Premiere Pro?

Premiere Pro is a nonlinear editing application. Competing nonlinear editors include Apple's Final Cut Pro and Avid Xpress DV. All of these programs are used to edit video. In the "old days," before computers came on the scene, editors had to work with physical film or tape. To change something that happened 20 minutes into the tape, the editor had to fast-forward through the first 20 minutes in a linear fashion: minute 1, minute 2, minute 3 … minute 20. Computer-based nonlinear applications allow editors to instantly jump forward 20 minutes. Then (if they want), they can jump backwards 5 minutes, jump forward 1 hour and 17 minutes, or jump backwards 3 seconds. In short, every moment of a video is instantly accessible without having to wind through tape or film.

In addition to being nonlinear, all computer-based editors are nondestructive. This means that they don't alter any files on your hard drive, nor do they alter any videotape in your camera.

Before you can edit in Premiere, you must first capture video from a camera or tape deck. This process involves hooking up the camera to your computer and copying the video from the camera into files on your hard drive. These files will generally be Windows Media files or QuickTime files.

Because Premiere is nondestructive, it never adds, deletes, or alters anything in these files. Instead it just helps you build a set of instructions specifying which order to play the files in and how much of each file to play. This is similar to how a slideshow works. You can place slides in any order in the slide projector's carousel, and if you place them in different orders each time you show the slides, you'll create many different slideshows. Still, no matter how you order the slides, you're not actually altering them.

In the same vein, you could put a piece of masking tape over the top half of a slide. When the projector showed that slide, you'd then only see the bottom half (the tape would be blocking the top half). But the top half would still be there. It wouldn't be deleted. It would just be hidden, under the tape.

Because Premiere can't do any damage (being nondestructive) and because it gives you easy access to any moment in your video (being nonlinear), it encourages playfulness, improvisation, and interactivity. Nothing that's done can't be easily undone. So if an idea pops into your head, you might as well try it.

HOW DO YOU USE PREMIERE?

That's the topic of this entire book, but the big picture can be summarized in three steps:

1. Import video, audio, and still images.

2. Arrange those items in whatever order you'd like them to play back.

3. Output the "playback" as a new file.

During step 2, there are many other things you can do to add pizzazz to the final output: you can add effects and transitions; you can adjust the audio, making it sound better; you can create titles; and you can even create simple animations.

But while all of these bells and whistles are great fun, Premiere's main function is to help you edit video. Editing is about choosing the order in which video or audio plays back, how much of it plays back, and for how long it plays back. You will have to make these three decisions for each shot (each bit of video) you cut into your sequence. That's what an editor does.

WHAT DOES AN EDITOR DO?

An editor—the human kind, not the computer kind—tells stories. These stories might be fiction or nonfiction. Storytelling is about what happens now, how long it happens for, and what happens next.

Most people think that the writer and director tell the story. But during production for most films and videos, there is a third collaborator who is equally important: the editor. It's the editor's job to take the raw footage supplied to him by the director and shape it into a coherent, compelling, original story.

The writer pens the original dialog or outline; the director works with the actors, performers, interviewers, or presenters to make sure they produce interesting performances.

He then passes these performances to the editor. They may take the form of the 50 takes (repeat filmings) of the same shot. The editor must decide which one of these 50 takes to use in the finished sequence. He must also decide whether to use the whole shot, half of it, or just a second of it. And he must decide what other shots go before it or after it.

If one actor says, "Hello," and the other says, "How are you?" it's the editor who decides whether there's a pause between the two lines or whether they come after each other in rapid succession. It's the editor who decides how long the viewer should be looking at one actor and when the sequence should cut to the other actor. It's the editor who decides whether to use the sad "hello" shot, the happy "hello" shot, the far-away "hello" shot, or the close-up "hello" shot.

In many ways, it's the editor who tells the story.

WHO USES PREMIERE?

Nowadays, video is everywhere: on the back of seats in airplanes, on screens in elevators, on cell phones, on sides of buildings in New York City, in PowerPoint presentations, and, of course, on television and the web. Who uses Premiere? It seems like everyone does.

Medical professionals use it to film procedures. Security analysts use it to organize evidence for court. Administrative assistants use it to make corporate presentations. Web designers use it to make videos that will be inserted in their HTML or Flash designs. Independent film makers use it to make features. If you try to list all the people who might be using Premiere, you've forgotten about some of them.

WHY PREMIERE?

The competing programs are really good too. It's hard to find much to complain about in Final Cut Pro or Xpress DV. But if you're using a PC, Premiere gives you the biggest bang for your buck. It's a full-featured nonlinear editor that costs hundreds of dollars less than its competitors.

Premiere Pro isn't just the next upgrade to Adobe Premiere 6.5. When Adobe made Premiere Pro, they decided to junk the old program and completely rewrite Premiere from the ground up. So Premiere Pro is a brand-new program, with all the latest features and a well thought out, easy-to-use interface—and Premiere Pro 1.5 has been refined still more. Compared to some of the competition, the learning curve is small. So with a little bit of instruction (provided in this book), you'll be up and running, making movies.

If you use other Adobe software, such as After Effects, Photoshop, Illustrator, Audition, or Encode, you'll appreciate Premiere's familiar interface and how well it integrates with the other Adobe programs.

How to Get Started

Read through this book. Then, if you want, practice editing with the footage on the (included) DVD. But you won't really learn Premiere until you use it to tell your own story. So grab a camera and film something, capture the footage into your PC, start a Premiere sequence, and start making editing decisions. It's that easy. It's that hard.

Chapter 1

System Setup

Few activities stress your PC more than video editing. For instance, it takes 3.6 megabytes (MB) to store one second of video (in the DV format). You may not have a gut sense of how much that is, but you can compare it to the capacity of a floppy disk, which is 1.4megabytes. This means that you'd need almost three floppy disks to store a second of video. To store a minute of video on floppy disks, you'd need 163 of them (see Figure 1.1). You'd need 9,772 of them to store an hour!

No one uses floppy disks to store video. Even so, the requirements of video can stagger even large hard drives. Captured DV

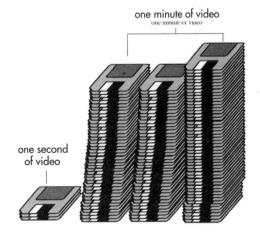

1.1 What if you tried to store video files on floppy disks?!

takes up about one gigabyte (GB) of space for every 5 minutes of footage. So if you filled up an entire 100GB drive with video, you could store 500 minutes. That may seem like a lot, but it's not strange to capture 20 minutes of footage for every 5 minutes that winds up in the finished video.

RAM is your computer's temporary memory (as opposed to the hard drive, which is its permanent memory), and it needs to be able to "think about" an entire video frame at once. One frame—if it's merely being displayed—takes up about 1MB of RAM, which doesn't sound like all that much. But once you start adding effects and transitions to that frame (or superimposing one frame on top of another), the RAM requirements shoot way up. And your computer isn't just thinking about that frame. It also needs to use some RAM to keep Premiere itself running. Any other applications you're running, even if they're just open and you're not currently working in them, also take up RAM—that includes your antivirus software and your screensaver (see Figure 1.2).

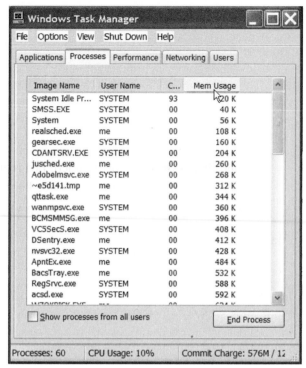

1.2   Every open application uses RAM, even if it's minimized.

Adobe claims that Premiere Pro will run on systems with just 256MB of RAM. And it will. It will run. You will be able to start it and click on its various buttons and tools. But with 256MB of RAM, don't be surprised if your computer locks up, crashes, or runs slower than a snail. You will be much happier with 1GB of RAM, which is actually the amount Adobe recommends.

Remember that software vendors like Adobe need to sell as many copies of their applications as possible. They test their programs on many machines, and if their programs run on those machines—just run, not run well—they will tell you that it's okay to use their programs on similar machines. But in the real world, where time is money and continual crashes and general sluggishness lead to missed deadlines, it's best to jack up the system a bit. When reading the following recommendations (most of which come straight from Adobe's literature), remember that it's best, when possible, to go with the recommended configuration rather than the minimal one.

PC REQUIREMENTS

What kind of computer do you need in order to run Adobe Premiere Pro?

- **Processor:** You'll need at least an 800MHz Intel Pentium III processor. But if your computer is that slow, then you'd better have a lot of patience as well. When working with digital video, the faster your computer, the better its performance, and the happier you'll be. Adobe recommends at least a 3GHz Pentium 4 processor.

- **Operating System:** Adobe Premiere Pro requires at least Windows XP (either Home or Professional Edition) with Service Pack 1.

- **RAM:** The bare minimum amount of RAM is 256MB, but as with processor speed, the more you have, the better your performance. Adobe recommends having at least 1GB of RAM.

- **Hard Drive(s):** You'll need at least 800MB of hard drive space just to install the software. But for storing all of your media files, you'll probably want a *lot* more. When working with DV, you can expect 1GB of hard drive space to store about 5 minutes of footage. Many editors have an additional hard drive dedicated solely to storing their video files. Since video editing requires hard drives to do a lot of work, you don't want to run the risk of overburdening the same drive that runs the application and Windows. So, if possible, get yourself another hard drive that has a rotational speed of at least 7,200rpm and an average seek time of 9 milliseconds (ms) or less, and store your footage on that drive. Adobe recommends either internal ATA or IDE drives, or high-speed external Ultra2 SCSI drives. Many FireWire drives that use the Oxford 911 or 922 chipset may also suffice, but they are not officially supported by Adobe. USB drives are too slow to use for video editing.

 Finding the Drive: Just because you've bought an additional drive to store your video doesn't mean Premiere will automatically store your video on that drive. After all, how can Premiere know which drive your want to use? To tell Premiere where to save your video, choose **Edit>Preferences>Scratch Disks** from the menu. Click the **Browse** button next to the **Capture Video** setting, and select your media drive. You may also want to select this drive for **Capture Audio**, the **Preview Options**, and **Conformed Audio** (see Figure 1.3).

- **Computer Monitor:** Although Adobe Premiere Pro will run with a mere 1,024×768 display, you really won't be able to work comfortably unless you have a monitor that supports at least a 1,280×1,024 resolution (see Figure 1.4). Make sure you

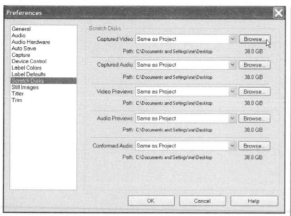
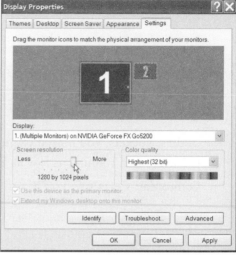

1.3 To select a media drive, choose Edit>Preferences>Scratch Disks, then click the Browse button.

1.4 Right-click the desktop, select Preferences, and then, on the Settings tab, set your display resolution to 1,280×1,024. *(above right)*

have the latest graphics drivers installed as well, otherwise you may experience jerky playback.

- **Video Card:** You may also want to purchase a good video card. Your computer already has a video card. It's the contraption that allows your computer's processor to speak to your monitor. But really good cards can help speed things up by doing most of the video processing themselves, leaving your main computer processor free to think about other things besides painting pixels on the screen. Many cards have built-in effects and transitions, which will speed up your work when you apply these effects in Premiere. Cards can also have additional features, like the ability to split the video signal to multiple monitors.

   Before buying a card, make sure you check with its vendor and verify that it's compatible with Adobe Premiere Pro. One popular card is the Parhelia by Matrox, which is designed specially for editors. (There are other cards that are designed and optimized for 3D animators and gamers). In addition to speeding up display performance, the Parhelia allows you display your video on up to three monitors at once (two computer monitors and one external NTSC or PAL monitor).

- **IEEE 1394:** The desktop digital video revolution can be accredited to development of IEEE 1394. This is the connection you need in order to capture digital video into your computer. (You need an IEEE 1394 socket on your computer—it looks a little like the USB socket.) IEEE 1394, named by the Institute of Electrical and

Electronics Engineers, is also known by a few different nicknames (since "I-triple-E 1394" is too much of a mouthful to pronounce). Its most common nickname is FireWire, but you may also see it referred to as i.LINK, OHCI, DV25, or simply DV.

Though many PCs now ship with FireWire, not all do. But before fretting that you don't have it, remember that it might not be called FireWire on your machine. You're also fine if you have IEEE 1394 or i.Link. If you're sure you don't have any of these sockets, you'll need to purchase a FireWire card. These are relatively inexpensive, often running as low as $20.

- **Camcorder:** Certainly, you'll also need a digital video camcorder or deck with a FireWire connection to attach to your computer. If you can afford it, buy both a camcorder and a deck. Try to avoid using your camcorder for rewinding, fast-forwarding, playing, and transferring video to your computer; limit its use for shooting purposes only. Video decks are designed for frequent playback of tapes, whereas camcorders are not. So to increase the lifespan of your camcorder, consider using a separate deck for input and output.

- **Video Monitor:** Also, whenever possible, you should edit with an external video monitor because computer screens do not accurately represent how your movie will look on television.

  In professional editing shops, these external monitors are called NTSC monitors or PAL monitors. They are basically very high-end television sets. If you can't afford one, you can get by with a standard color TV, as long as that TV can accept input from a computer (and you'll also need a video card that can output a signal to an external TV or monitor—see the previous section about video cards on page 4).

Another option is to keep your camcorder or deck connected to your computer while you're editing and also connect your TV to your camcorder. Premiere can route the video signal from your computer through your camcorder into your TV. This is an inexpensive alternative to purchasing a video card that can output to a TV or external monitor.

And when you're ready to advance your skills, you may opt for an editing keyboard (such as one from http://www.bella-usa.com), a DVD burner, a 5.1-channel audio card for surround sound, or a real-time video card for enhanced effects work. (Sample system configurations will be discussed later in this chapter on page 7.) Check Adobe's website for a list of third-party products that are compatible with Adobe Premiere Pro (see Figure 1.5).

1.5 Adobe's website lists third-party products that are compatible with Premiere Pro.

MAKING THE CONNECTION

Since digital video relies mostly on FireWire technology, connecting your equipment is fairly simple:

1. For best results, connect all of your equipment while it is turned off. With a FireWire cable, connect your computer's IEEE 1394 port to the DV in/out (I/O) port of your camcorder or deck.

2. If your camcorder or deck has an analog video output, such as a yellow RCA or S-Video port, then you can connect it to a television monitor to see a better representation of your edited work.

3. Likewise, if your camcorder or deck has an analog audio output, such as a minijack or white and red RCA ports, then you can connect these to your television monitor or to speakers.

4. Turn on all of the equipment (with camcorder in VCR mode), and make sure to turn the computer on last. The reason why you want to turn the computer on last is because if your computer doesn't recognize any of your equipment, such as an external hard drive, then you may have to reboot the computer in order for the drive to mount properly. So save yourself five minutes and get it right the first time: turn the computer on last.

If you ever need to connect or disconnect your DV equipment while your computer is turned on, make sure you don't do it while Adobe Premiere is running. Quit the application, connect or disconnect your equipment, and then relaunch Premiere.

INSTALLING PREMIERE PRO

Log into Windows as a user with administrator privileges and insert the Premiere Pro installation CD into your CD drive.

Install Adobe Premiere Pro as you would most other Windows applications. Just follow the onscreen instructions. If you're upgrading from an earlier version, you won't need to have that old version installed. Adobe recommends first deleting the older version by using the **Add or Remove Programs** option in the Windows Control Panel. When installing the upgrade, however, you will be asked to enter your old serial number. In fact, you can even use a serial number from version six for the Mac if you're upgrading from a Macintosh system.

You should also be logged in as an administrator when running Premiere; otherwise some of its features may not work properly.

When you finish the installation, Premiere will display the Activation screen, which will ask you to contact Adobe and tell them you've installed Premiere (see Figure 1.6). If you don't contact them, you'll only be able to use the product for two days. Adobe has implemented this procedure to ensure you're not installing one copy of Premiere on multiple machines, which would violate your license agreement. If your PC is connected to the Internet, you can activate automatically in a few seconds. But you also have the option activating by phone. If you're temporarily without a web or phone connection, don't worry. You have two days to use the product before you'll need to activate it.

SAMPLE CONFIGURATIONS

Basic DV System

- **Processor:** 2GHz or faster
- **RAM:** 1GB or more
- **Hard Drive:** One additional large internal drive for media files
- **Computer Monitor:** At least one 1,280×1,024 display
- **Video Input/Output:** FireWire card, standard on most systems
- **Video Devices:** One-chip MiniDV camcorder
- **Video Monitor:** Standard television with RCA inputs

Advanced DV System

- **Processor:** 3GHz or faster single or dual processors
- **RAM:** 1.5GB or more

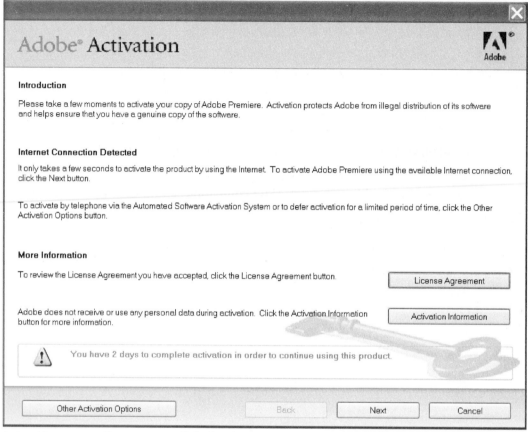

1.6   After you install it, Premiere will display the Activation screen.

- **Hard Drive:** Several large internal drives for media files
- **Computer Monitor:** At least two 1,280×1,024 displays
- **Computer Devices:** Adobe Premiere Pro editing keyboard
- **Video Input/Output:** Real-time DV card for capture and effects processing; DVD-R burner
- **Video Devices:** Three-chip MiniDV, DVCAM, or DVCPRO camcorder and deck; stereo SVHS deck with S-Video and RCA input
- **Video Monitor:** Broadcast CRT video monitor with blue-only filter
- **Audio Monitors:** Stereo speakers with one-eighth inch or RCA inputs

Professional DV/D1 System

- **Processor:** 3GHz or faster single or dual processors
- **RAM:** 2GB or more
- **Hard Drive:** Large external SCSI drive array for media files
- **Computer Monitor:** At least two 1,280×1,024 displays
- **Computer Devices:** Adobe Premiere Pro editing keyboard
- **Video Input/Output:** Uncompressed video card for capture and effects processing (not yet qualified for Premiere Pro); DVD-R burner
- **Audio Input/Output:** Multichannel ASIO-compatible sound card and audio mixer for surround sound work
- **Video Devices:** Three-chip MiniDV, DVCAM, or DVCPRO camcorder and deck with component video and XLR audio; DigiBeta camcorder and deck with component video and XLR audio; stereo SVHS deck with S-Video and RCA input
- **Video Monitor:** Broadcast CRT video monitor with component input and blue-only filter; external waveform monitor and vectorscope

    Audio Monitors: 5.1-channel surround sound speakers with XLR or one-fourth inch inputs

WRAPPING UP

Now that Premiere is up and running, your camcorder is connected to your PC, and your head bone's connected to your neck bone, you're ready to edit video. Almost. Before you can begin sculpting those raw shots into an Academy Award-winning production, you'll have to first set up a project file (the subject of Chapter 2) and import some video (the subject of Chapter 3, starting on page 33).

Chapter 2

Starting a Project

YOU DON'T IMPORT FOOTAGE; YOU LINK TO IT

Now that you've installed Premiere, it's time to dive in and start a project. Project files, which are saved with a .prproj extension, are the main organizational elements in Premiere. With a project file open, you can import footage that has already been saved on your hard drive. You can also capture footage directly from your camera and import it into your project file. Whether you import or capture, the footage isn't actually embedded in your project file. Instead, the project file contains links to your footage—similar to shortcuts on your desktop that link to programs but aren't actually those programs. If you delete a shortcut to Microsoft Word from your desktop, you haven't deleted Microsoft Word from your hard drive—just a pointer to it (see Figure 2.1).

2.1 Like shortcuts on your desktop that point to actual applications, imported clips link to video files on your hard drive.

Footage files are generally huge in terms of file size. But because they're not embedded, the project files are quite small. In fact, you can usually fit a project file on a floppy disk. This is amazing, considering that a project file may contain a two-hour movie. Project files are small because they don't contain the footage used in the movie. They just include all of your editing decisions (start with this bit of footage, then cut to that bit of footage, etc.)

When you're working within your project file, it *appears* as if the footage is actually embedded in it. You can play the footage, create sequences in which the footage appears with other footage, apply special effects, color correction, and transitions to the footage, etc. Premiere creates the illusion that you're manipulating the footage itself, whereas you're only manipulating pointers to the footage on your hard drive. This method, in addition to keeping the file size small, ensures that you can never damage your actual footage. Everything you do in Premiere is nondestructive. For instance, if you decide to "delete" the last five minutes of some footage, Premiere makes it look as if you've deleted it. However, the missing footage is just hidden, and it can always be restored.

In general, you can forget that you're not working with the actual footage when you're inside a Premiere project. But it's important to think about it if you're planning on deleting, moving, or renaming the footage files. If you do so, Premiere won't be able to find them. And if you ever give someone one of your project files, you'll have to give them your large footage files too, or the project will be pretty useless to them.

The actual video (audio or still image) files on your hard drives are called *footage files* or *media files*. The stand-ins (a.k.a *links* or *pointers*) for them within Premiere are called *clips*.

Note

Finding Files: If you move a group of media files from their original location to another folder or drive, Premiere will get somewhat confused. The next time you start Premiere, it will try to locate the files. When it can't find them, it will pop up an import window in which you can show Premiere where you moved the files (see Figure 2.2). You have to select only one of the moved files. Premiere will then be able to find the rest of them by itself. This technique assumes that when you moved the files, you moved them all to the same place. If you scattered them all over the place, in different folders and drives, Premiere will prompt you to locate each one separately.

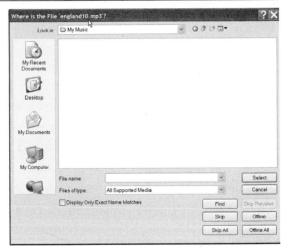

2.2 If you move or rename a media file, Premiere will prompt you to find it.

SEQUENCES

Within the project file, you create sequences (see Figure 2.3). Sequences are what we generally think of as movies (or videos). A sequence contains a group of clips, edited together to tell a story. You can create more than one sequence in the same project file. For instance, if you're creating a commercial, you might want to create two versions of it, a 1-minute version and a 30-second version. Because both versions will use the same footage, it will make sense to store both sequences in the same project file. You can also embed sequences inside sequences with a process called *nesting*, which is discussed in Chapter 6 on page 156.

When you've finished editing a sequence, you can output a sequence directly to tape or use a process called *rendering*. Rendering a sequence creates an actual video file, which will be huge like the footage files on your hard drive. Chapter 12 on page 297 covers the rendering process.

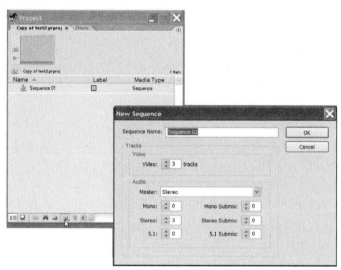

2.3   When you start a new project, it automatically contains one sequence. You can create additional sequences by clicking the New button at the bottom of the Project window.

Show Me the Money

If you're still confused about the relationship between clips and media files, it might help you to think about how paper money used to relate to gold bars. Back in "the old days," a dollar bill represented an actual amount of gold.

If you had a dollar in your pocket, in a sense that meant you owned a dollar's worth of gold. But you didn't carry the gold around with you; it would have been too heavy. Instead, the gold was stored in a bank. The dollar bill was a stand-in for the actual gold. If you gave the dollar bill to someone else, you symbolically transferred ownership of the gold from yourself to that other person.

Thus you could "move the gold" without actually moving the gold. And if you irresponsibly burnt the dollar bill, only the stand-in would be destroyed. The gold would still be safe in the bank.

CREATING A NEW PROJECT

In a Nutshell: Assuming you're making a video which will eventually be shown on a standard television:

1. Start Premiere Pro.

2. Click the **New Project** icon on the **Welcome** screen (see Figure 2.4).

3. For NTSC video (US and Japan), choose the **Standard 48kHz** preset in the *DV-NTSC* folder; for PAL video (Europe), choose **Standard 48kHz** in the *DV-PAL* folder.

4. At the bottom of the **New Project** screen, choose a location and a file name for your new project.

5. Click the **OK** button.

2.4   The Welcome screen allows you to open an old project file or create a new one.

When creating a project, you'll have to select certain options (about the video and sound quality for your project). These settings affect your video and audio while you are editing. For instance, if you choose one of the NTSC Standard presets (groups of settings), your video will be 720 pixels wide and 480 pixels high—*while you are editing it in Premiere.* You can later choose to export it at a smaller size if you wish. However, since many decisions you make while you're editing will impact the final output, you should be thinking about the final output when you choose your project settings.

If you're creating a standard video file—one that will be played back on a normal TV—starting a project is easy. When you start Premiere, the first screen you'll see is the **Welcome** screen, which allows you to open an old project file or create a new project file. Premiere lists recent projects down the left edge of the **Welcome** screen. You can click a project name to open it. If you don't see the project you want to open in that list, click the **Open Project** icon (the folder), which will allow you to browse to any project file on your hard drive.

To create a new project, click the **New Project** icon. If you close out of the **Welcome** screen and want to start a new project, choose **File>New>Project** from Premiere's menu. To open an old project, choose **File>Open Project** to navigate your hard drive and find a project file or **File>Open Recent Project** to choose project files from a list. Premiere only allows you to edit one project file at a time, so if you try to create or open a project file

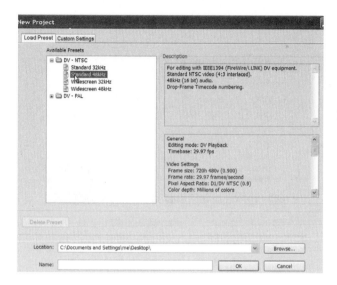

2.5 Pick a preset template from the New Project dialog window.

while you already have one open, Premiere will prompt you to save changes to the currently open project before allowing you to work on another one.

After you've clicked the **New Project** icon or chosen **File>New Project** from the menu, Premiere displays the **New Project** dialog window (see Figure 2.5). This window allows you to choose from some templates that make setting up standard video projects a cinch.

If you want to create a video that will be displayed on the NTSC system, which is how standard TV is displayed in the US and Japan, choose the **Standard 48kHz** preset by clicking its name. This preset is stored in the *DV-NTSC* folder. If the folder is closed, you can open it by clicking the plus sign to its left. Once the folder is open, the plus sign turns to a minus sign. Clicking the minus sign will close the folder, hiding its contents.

Note

Warning: If you choose the Standard 32kHz project setting, all of your DV audio, which was recorded by your camera at 48kHz, will be downsampled (degraded) to 32kHz.

It you want to create a video that will be displayed on the PAL system, used in Europe, open the *DV-PAL* folder and select the **Standard 48kHz** option.

After you select one of these two options, you'll need to select a folder on your hard drive where Premiere can store your project file. Click the **Browse** button in the lower-right corner of the window to navigate anywhere on your hard drive(s) and pick a location. You can click an existing folder to select it, or you can click the **Make New Folder** button to create a new folder. If you choose this option, you should select an existing folder first, because the new folder will be created inside that existing folder. For instance, if you choose click the *My Documents* folder and then click the **Make New Folder** button,

Kilohertz and Resampled Audio

48kHz (or 48 kilohertz) refers to the audio quality of the final project. As you may know, sound doesn't start and stop; it flows continuously. Anything that flows continually is called analog. Computers can't handle analog information. Computers are digital, which means that they can only think in discreet units. To play or record sound on a computer—and to be sure it sounds good—the original continuous sound must be sampled many times each second. This means that when you're recording sound into your computer, your computer isn't continually recording. It's starting and stopping, starting and stopping. Each little start and stop is a sample (see Figure 2.6). The more samples per second, the more the sound will seem to be continuous, even though it's not. If your sound was recorded at 1kHz, that would mean your computer took 1,000 samples of it each second (1,000 starts and stops). So 48kHz, the standard for DV, means that as the sound was recorded, the computer or camera sampled it 48,000 times per second.

original analog sound

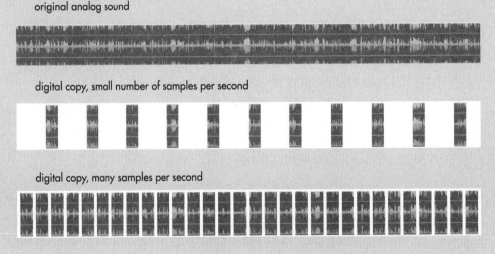

digital copy, small number of samples per second

digital copy, many samples per second

2.6   Analog sound is continuous, but digital sound must be sampled. The more samples per second, the more digital sound will sound like analog sound.

Setting your project at 48kHz assures you that no 48kHz sound (the sound recorded by DV cameras) will be downsampled (degraded) to a lower quality. What happens if you create a 48kHz project file (so that your DV sound will be protected) but then you import some lower-quality sound files, maybe some 32kHz MP3 files? Premiere will resample the lower-quality sound files so that they conform to the 48kHz setting for your project. Premiere will also resample higher-quality sounds, downsampling them to 48kHz.

This resampling will allow you to sync up all of your sounds within the same sequence, but in order to resample, Premiere will have to create copies of your sound files. (Remember, Premiere is nondestructive, so it will never alter your original files.) When you work with these sound clips within Premiere, you'll be linking to the resampled files instead of the originals. The exception to this will be 48kHz sound files, which (assuming the project is set to 48kHz), don't have to be resampled.

By default, Premiere saves its resampled audio files in the same folder as your Project file. This means that if you've bought a special disk drive for your big audio and video files, you'll may want to tell Premiere to use that drive when it saves resampled audio files. You can do so by choosing Edit>Preferences>Scratch Disks from the menu (see Figure 2.7). Click the lowest Browse button to choose a new location for resampled audio files.

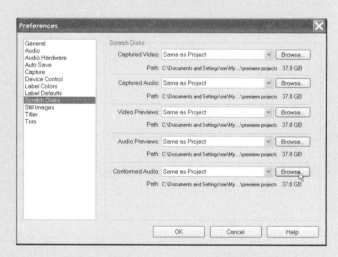

2.7 To pick a location for resampled audio files, choose Edit>Preferences>Scratch Disks from the menu.

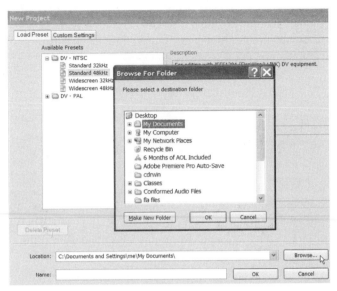

2.8 If you want to store your project file in a new folder, click the New Folder button in the File Browser.

Premiere will create a new folder within your *My Documents* folder. Click **OK** when you're done creating or choosing a folder (see Figure 2.8).

Finally, you'll need to give your project file a file name, which you can do in the bottom text field in the **New Project** window. When you're done naming the file, click the **OK** button, and Premiere's main interface will open, including a default sequence. You can now import footage files and begin editing.

CUSTOMIZING

If you're not making a video for a standard television

In the **New Project** dialog, you can choose from several presets for PAL or NTSC video. But if you're creating something a little out of the ordinary, you can create a custom project (one that doesn't conform to NTSC or PAL standards) by clicking the **Custom Settings** tab at the top of the **New Project** window. You might want to do this if you're creating video for the web or for a CD-ROM. NTSC and PAL video must play at specific frames rates and have specific dimensions, but there are no standards for videos playing back on a computer (as opposed to a TV screen), so for web and CD projects, you can customize as much as you'd like.

The **Custom Settings** tab contains four categories of customization options, including **General**, **Capture**, **Video Capturing**, and **Default Sequence**. To display a category's options, click its name in the window's left pane (see Figure 2.9).

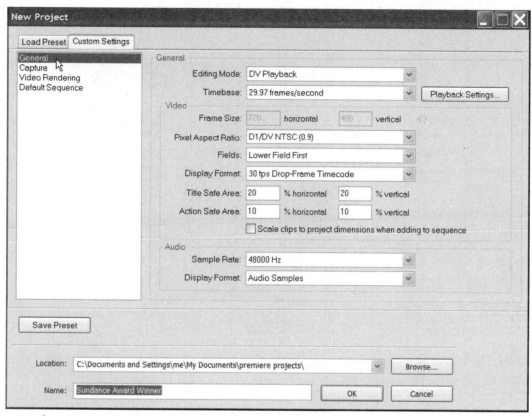

2.9 The Custom Settings tab contains four sets of customization options. To pick one, click its name in the left window pane.

Custom Settings

The **Custom Settings** tab contains dozens of customizable settings that are explained clearly in Premiere's online help. It's called "online help," but the help files are stored on your PC. You don't need to be connected to the Internet to read them. To access in-depth information about all the customizable settings, choose **Help>Contents** from the menu. Premiere will open the contents of its help system in your default web browser. In the left browser pane, click the **Working with Projects** option. Then, in the right pane, click the bottom option: **Specifying Project Settings** (see Figure 2.10).

The most common customization you're likely to want to make is to the dimensions of the video you're making. For instance, if you want to make a small video for the web (maybe 320×240), you'll have to customize, because all of the DV presets are full screen, although you can always create a full-screen project and then export it at a smaller size. (For export options, see Chapter 12 on page 295.) To customize width and height, click the **Custom Settings** tab of the **New Project** window and select the **General Settings**.

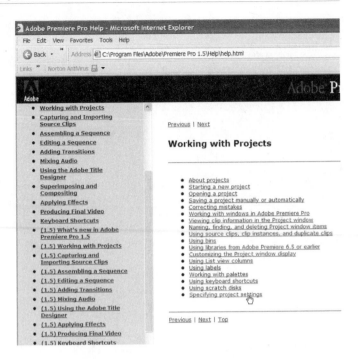

2.10 To learn more about custom project settings, choose Help>Contents>Working with Projects>Specifying Project Settings.

At the top of the **General Settings** options, change the **Editing Mode** from **DV Playback** to **Video for Windows.** If you have a sophisticated video card installed in your PC, you may have other options for **Editing Mode.** Feel free to choose your card's options to make the most of its special display capabilities and speed up your work in Premiere. When using **DV Playback,** you can't alter the dimensions, because DV video has specific preset dimensions. But once you choose the **Video for Windows** option, you can alter the **Frame Size** settings, which are grayed out when the **Editing Mode** is set to **DV Playback** (see Figure 2.11).

2.11 You can't customize the frame size if the editing mode is set to DV Video Playback. DV has a preset frame size.

Display format

NTSC video runs at 29.97 frames per second (29.97 pictures are taken by your camera and flashed on your TV screen every second). For the sake of convenience, Premiere pretends that NTSC frame rate is 30 frames per second (fps). This could create some timing problems if you're editing a full-length video. To deal with this discrepancy, most editors

More about Custom Settings

DV Restrictions

Perplexed because you can't adjust the width and height? Bamboozled because you can only set the frame rate to one of two choices, 29.97 (NTSC) and 30 (PAL)? This is because the default editing mode is **DV Playback**. Which means that, if you want, you can connect your DV camera to your computer while you're editing and watch your progress in your camera's monitor. If Premiere is going to play back in your camera, it can't allow you to customize settings that your camera can't handle. DV cameras can only handle images that conform to the DV standard.

External Monitors

Why would you want to view your editing decisions on your camera's tiny screen instead of your computer's larger monitor? You wouldn't. But most cameras can connect directly to a television set. So if you connect your camera to your computer and your computer to your television, you'll be able to watch your work on your TV while you edit, allowing you to see the final output more accurately (assuming it's intended for television). If you don't care about previewing through your camera, you can switch the **Editing Mode to Video for Windows**, which will allow you to customize the frame rate and the width and height.

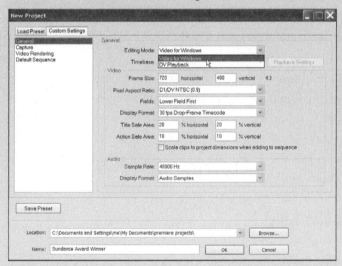

2.12 If you don't care about routing video through your DV camera, you can change the Editing Mode to Video for Windows, which will allow you to customize the frame size and frame rate.

Assuming you've connected your camcorder and TV, you can preview through your TV by choosing **Project>Project Settings>General** from the menu and then clicking the **Playback Settings** button. Then check the **Play Video on DV Hardware** option. To learn about the other playback settings, see the online help section: **Editing a Sequence>Previewing a Sequence>Previewing On Another Monitor**.

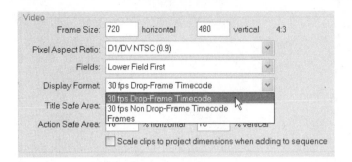

2.13 To ensure that Premiere's timing matches real-world timing, set Display format to 29.97 Drop-frame Timecode.

work in what's called 29.97 fps Drop-frame Timecode. This sounds scary, but don't worry: no frames are dropped. This is just a numbering system in which each frame is given a unique number. Using Drop-frame Timecode, every now and then a *number* (not a frame) is dropped. This is similar to the way some buildings apparently don't have a 13th floor. Of course, they do have a 13th floor. It's just numbered 14. By dropping some frame numbers, Premiere can assure you that when it says you're two hours into your sequence, you *are* two hours into your sequence. The alternative is 29.97 Non Drop-frame Timecode, in which each frame is numbered sequentially—but then Premiere time will not match up to real-world time (see Figure 2.13).

Scale clips to project dimensions when adding to sequence

What if you import video or stills that are bigger or smaller than your project's width and height? If you check this option, all imports will be squashed or stretched to fill the screen (see Figure 2.14). If you leave this option unchecked, images will import at their original size. This means that they may only fill up part of the screen. Or they may be much bigger than the screen, in which case you'll only see part of them (see Figure 2.15). You can then animate the image moving around in the screen, to simulate panning around in a large image. For more information about motion effects, see Chapter 9 on page 211.

24fps (video that looks like film)

Standard video runs at either 29.97 ps (NTSC: U.S. and Japan) or 25 frames per second (PAL: Europe). Film runs at 24fps. This is one of the reasons why film and video look so different—differing frame rates. Because the film look is popular, more and more camcorders are able to shoot at 24fps. If you have such a camera, you can use it to get that film look, even if you're final output will be for television.

In such a case, Premiere will have to convert the 24 fps to 29.97fps (for NTSC). This process is called *pull down*.

2.14 If you check the Scale clips... option, Premiere will squash (or stretch) oversized (or undersized) images so that they fit the screen. (above and right)

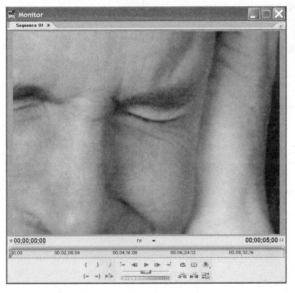

2.15 Leave the Scale clips option unchecked if you don't want Premiere to resize images. (left)

1. To instruct Premiere to pull down footage, try the following:

2. In the **New Project** window, select the **Custom Settings** tab.

3. In the **Timebase** field, select **23.98 frames/second**.

4. In the **Display** format field, select either **24fps Timecode** or **Frames**.
   This will only affect how time is measured in Premiere; it won't affect the final output. **24fps Timecode** will measure time as follows:

   * The first frame will be called 00:00:00:00 (from right to left, 0 hours, 0 minutes, 0 seconds, and 0 frames).

   * The second frame will be called 00:00:00:01.

   * The third frame will be called 00:00:00:02, and so on.

The next frame after 00:00:00:23 will be 00:00:01:00, because at 24fps, 24 frames equals 1 second. If you choose **Frames** as the display format, each frame will simply be numbered sequentially: 0, 1, 2, 3, 4…

5. If you're using **DV Playback** as your editing mode, click the **Playback Settings** button.

6. In the **DV Playback Settings** dialog, select either the **Interlaced Frame Pull Up** option or the **Repeat Frame Pull Up** option. The **Interlaced** option will look much better, but will tax your PC's resources much more than the **Repeat Frame** option.

If you've spent a long time customizing project settings, you should probably save your work as a new preset. That way, if you ever create another project like this one, you won't have to go through the customization steps all over again (see Figure 2.16).

To save your settings, click the **Save Preset** button at the button of the **Custom Settings** tab of the **New Project** window. Premiere will prompt you to name your customization and write an (optional) short description of it. Then, next time you start up Premiere, your customized settings will be listed in the presets area, along with the default PAL and NTSC presets (see Figure 2.17).

2.16 If you continually make the same customizations, try saving your custom settings as a preset.

2.17 You can access saved presets from the New Project window.

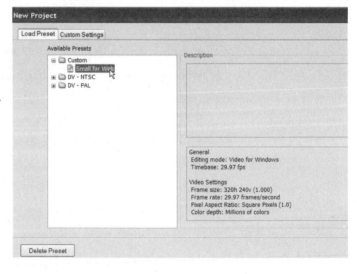

GDI versus Direct3D

GDI stands for Graphic Display Interface. It's the standard method used by PC to display graphics on a computer monitor. Some video cards can draw on the screen using a faster method, called Direct3D. Premiere generally does a good job detecting whether or not you have one of these cards, but if you have a Direct3D card, and you suspect Premiere isn't using it (or if you want to turn off Premiere's use of Direct3D), choose **Project>Project Settings>General** from the menu. Click the **Playback Settings** button, and then select either the GDI option or the Direct3D option at the bottom of the **DV Playback Settings** window.

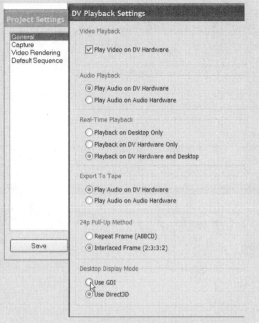

2.18 For GDI settings, choose Project>Project Settings>General from the menu, and then click the Playback Settings button.

Changing Settings: You can change some settings even after you've started a project by choosing **Project>Project Settings** from the menu.

INTERFACE

Once you've opened an old project or created a new one, Premiere will display its main interface, which includes a default sequence, already open and ready for your creative hand. Premiere's default interface displays four floating windows: the **Project** window, the **Monitor** window, the **Timeline** window, and the **Tools** palette. All of these windows, except the tool palette (which is the thin vertical strip, containing a bunch of icons), have their names printed across their tops (see Figure 2.19).

2.19 Premiere's default interface: the Project window, the Monitor window, the Timeline window, and the Tools palette.

If you accidentally (or purposefully) close a window, you can get it back by choosing its name from the **Window** menu (see Figure 2.20).

The **Project** window will contain all of the footage clips, illustrations, and sound files that you import or capture. Currently, it should only list one item: *Sequence 01*. This is the default sequence that is automatically created for you when you start a new project. Sequences are listed in the **Project** window along with imported footage, because you can use sequences as if they were imported footage. In other words, just as you can edit imported footage into *Sequence 01*, you can edit *Sequence 01* into *Sequence 02*. This process, called *nesting*, is covered in Chapter 6 on page 156. To help keep your work organized, you might want to right-click *Sequence 01* in the

2.20 To reopen a window you've closed by accident, select its name from the Window menu.

Project window and choose **Rename** from the pop-up menu (see Figure 2.21). Give your sequence a meaningful name, like *Star Wars: Episode VII*. (You might as well think big!)

The **Monitor** window contains two monitors, the **Source Monitor** and the **Program Monitor**. In the **Source Monitor**, you can audition footage that you may want to add to the sequence—but you're not yet sure whether or not you really want to add it or, if sure, how much of it you want to add. In other words, it's a preview monitor. The **Program Monitor**, on the other hand, displays your sequence as it exists so far, and it's intimately tied together with the **Timeline** window (see Figure 2.22).

The **Timeline** window is a graph of your sequence's progress through time. Towards its top is a time ruler, with tick marks that represent increments of time. Also in the **Timeline** is the **Current Time Indicator**, a blue triangle which, by default, is located at the beginning of the time ruler. You can drag the **Current Time Indicator** right and left in the time ruler to view later or

2.21 Right-click a sequence name to rename it.

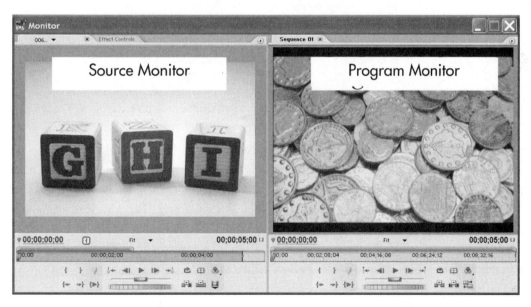

2.22 The Monitor window contains two monitors: the Source Monitor (for auditioning clips) and the Program Monitor (for viewing sequences).

2.23 The Timeline window and both monitors contain Current Time Indicators that you can drag to view a specific frame. The Timeline and Program Monitor Indicators are linked together; the Source Monitor's Indicator is independent.

earlier times in your sequence. The **Program Monitor** will display whatever point in time on which you park the **Current Time Indicator.**

The **Source** and **Program Monitors** have their own **Current Time Indicators,** which are also draggable. The **Program Monitor's Current Time Indicator** is tied to the **Timeline's Current Time Indicator.** Drag one and the other one moves too. The **Source Monitor's Current Time Indicator** is not linked to either of the other **Current Time Indicators** (see Figure 2.23). Instead, it allows you to drag through footage you're contemplating adding to the sequence.

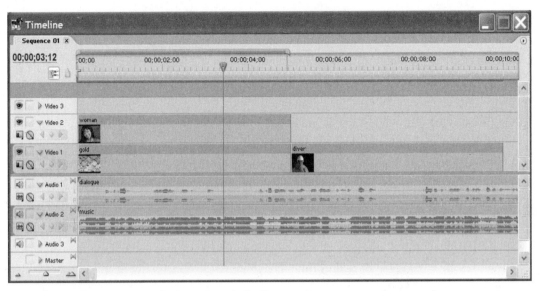

2.24 The Timeline contains multiple tracks, which allow you to composite video or audio.

The **Timeline** also contains multiple tracks, which allow you to stack multiple video and audio footage items on top of each other, to make video or audio *composites* or *collages* (see Figure 2.24). In other words, you can play multiple sounds at the same time or superimpose many images together into one composite image (e.g., titles on top of a background image).

The **Tools** palette contains tools that allow you to finesse footage once it's been added to the sequence. There are tools to delete parts of the footage and tools to bring deleted parts back. There are tools to slow down or speed up footage (see Figure 2.25).

The basic editing technique, outlined in Chapters 3 and 4, involves auditioning clips by dragging them from the **Project** window to the **Source Monitor**, adding them or parts of them to the sequence by dragging them to the **Timeline**, and then viewing the sequence in the **Program Monitor**. After adding several footage

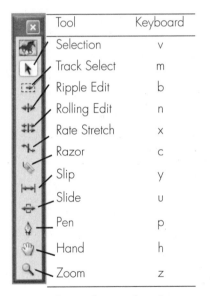

Tool	Keyboard
Selection	v
Track Select	m
Ripple Edit	b
Rolling Edit	n
Rate Stretch	x
Razor	c
Slip	y
Slide	u
Pen	p
Hand	h
Zoom	z

2.25 To finesse footage that's been added to a sequence, use the tools on the Tools palette.

items to the **Timeline,** you can finesse them using the tools on the **Tools** palette. Finally, you will save your sequence as a computer video file (e.g., a Windows Media or Quick-Time file) or print it directly to tape. These output options are explored in Chapter 12 on page 295.

But before you can begin editing, you'll need to learn how to capture and import, which is discussed in the following chapter, Chapter 3.

SAVING

As in any computer program, it's important to frequently save changes to your "document" so that if there's a crash or a power outage, you won't lose data. To save changes to your project file, use the keyboard shortcut **Control+S** or choose **File>Save** from the menu.

Premiere also has an autosave option, which defaults to saving changes every 20 minutes. You can change this default by choosing **Edit>Preferences>Auto Save** from the menu (see Figure 2.26).

2.26 To adjust Premiere's autosave option, choose Edit>Preferences>Auto Save from the menu.

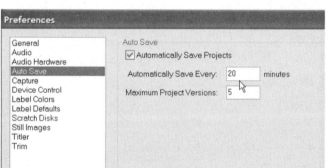

Unlike most other programs, when Premiere autosaves, it doesn't update your open file. To update that file, you need to do an explicit save, using **Control+S** or **File>Save.** **Autosave** saves a copy of your file to a specific folder on your hard drive: *My Documents/ Adobe/Adobe Premiere Pro/7.0/Adobe Premiere Pro Auto-Save.* So if you have a crash and you need to recover your project file, try opening it from that folder.

If you choose the **Edit>Preferences>Auto Save** option again, you can set the maximum project versions saved by **Auto Save,** which is set to 5 by default. This means that each time **Auto Save** saves (every 20 minutes by default) it saves a new copy of your file to the *Auto Save* folder—until it reaches the maximum project versions number. Once it does, it will start overwriting older copies.

UNDO

At any point during the editing process, if you make a mistake, simply press **Control+Z** (**Edit>Undo**) to undo the mistake. If you made the mistake three steps ago, press **Control+Z, Control+Z, Control+Z** to go back three steps. You can undo many, many times, limited only by the amount of RAM (memory) on your PC.

To see a list of all the undoable steps, choose **Window>History** from the menu. In the **History** window, your actions are listed in sequential order from top to bottom (see Figure 2.27). You can revert to earlier states by clicking an action. Any actions below the one you clicked will be undone.

Even people who know about the undo command tend to struggle to find a way erase problems. This proves that the hardest thing about using undo is remembering that it exists in the first place. If you can beat it into your brain, your work will improve: just press **Control+Z, Control+Z, Control+Z**...until your sequence is back the way you want it. If you accidentally back up too far, use **Control+Shift+Z** (**Edit>Redo**) to redo the last step you undid.

2.27 The History palette lists all of the undoable actions.

WRAPPING UP

Did all this talk of kilohertz and timecode make your head spin? Never fear. We'll soon be moving on to the real job of editing, which is telling a story. In fact, the whole point of dealing with all this technical mumbo jumbo at the beginning is to allow you to forget about it while you're editing. There's only one more hurdle to cross before true editing can begin. You must first get some video into Premiere, which is the subject of the next chapter.

Chapter 3

Capturing and Importing

IMPORT OR CAPTURE?

Before you can create anything in Premiere, you'll need to bring source material into the program. To "get stuff in," you'll either import or capture. If the material is already a computer file, stored somewhere on your hard drive, you can import it. Premiere allows you to import most standard video file types, such as Windows Media and Quicktime. It also allows you to import standard audio file types, such as MP3 and WAV files. Or you can import still images: standard image files types, such as TIFF and JPEG, as well as files from Photoshop and Illustrator.

If the material you want to import is not on your computer—if it's in your camera or on your tape deck—you'll have to capture it. Capturing turns the video and/or audio footage into computer files, stored on your hard drive. It also creates clips in the **Project** window, that act as stand-ins for the computer files.

We talk about capturing or importing files into Premiere, because that's an easy way to speak. But keep in mind that when you import, you're not really importing anything. You're creating clips, which are virtual stand-ins (similar to desktop shortcuts) to the actual media files on your hard drive. These clips are quite small in size, even if they link to four-hour-long videos (which themselves are huge files on your hard drive). So though your project may contain many hours of clips, the project file—which contains them all—

will probably be small enough to fit on a floppy disk. That's because the source video and audio isn't contained within your project file. Clips in the project file just link to source files on your hard drive.

When you edit in Premiere, you'll work with the clips instead of the source files. You won't notice a difference. When you edit two clips together with a crossfade between them, it will seem as though you're manipulating the actual source files. But you won't be. Instead, you'll be creating a set of instructions specifying how much of each clip you want to play, when you want it to play, and what you want to play after it's done playing.

The great advantage here is that everything you do is nondestructive. You can import or capture 20 minutes of footage and delete the first 10 minutes. In Premiere, it will *appear* as if 10 minutes are missing. But if you navigate to the actual source footage on your hard drive, you'll find that the entire 20 minutes is still there, untouched. Premiere has just created an instruction *not* to show the first 10 minutes of the footage when you play the clip. It has just hidden the footage. And you can always unhide it.

PRECAPTURE PROJECT SETUP

Bins (a.k.a. folders)

Before capturing or importing, it's a good idea to create some bins in the project window. Bins are similar to folders on your hard drive: they are used to organize clips, and their icons look like little folders. But be aware that bins are not *actually* folders on your hard drive. They are organizational structures that only exist within your project file (see Figure 3.1). Likewise, you might think of each page in an MS Word file or each slide in a MS PowerPoint file as a separate entity, but they are all stored within a single file.

You can capture and import without creating bins. If you do, all of your material will be stored in one default bin. But if your project contains dozens of video clips, audio files, and still images—as many projects do—you'll thank yourself in the end if you take the time to organize your material. Organization is a personal matter. One editor might create three bins called *Video, Audio,* and *Stills.* Another editor might create bins called *Scene 1 Footage, Scene 2 Footage,* etc. How you organize is up to you, and it should take the form of whatever structure makes it easiest and fastest for you to find the clips you need when you need them.

To create a new bin, click the **Bin** button at the bottom of the **Project** window. Then type an appropriate bin name and press **Enter** on your keyboard.

To delete a bin, click it and press **Delete** on your keyboard. If you delete a bin, the material inside a bin will also be deleted. But remember, the clips in the bin are not the actual files, they are just stand-ins, like desktop shortcuts. If you delete a clip, the actual source file will still remain, taking up space on your hard drive.

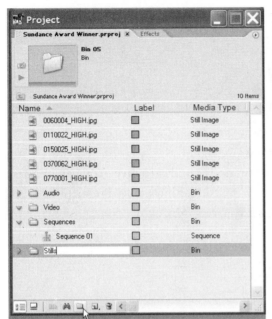

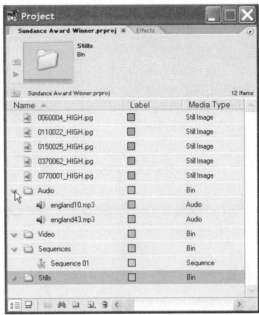

3.1 Premiere's basic organizational structure: bins in the Project window.

3.2 Click the triangle to open or close a bin.

To open a bin, double-click it or click the little triangle to its left (see Figure 3.2). Click the triangle again to close it. Open bins reveal their contents; closed bins don't.

To move clips from one bin to another, select the clips in one bin and then drag them into another bin. You can select multiple clips by clicking each one while holding down the **Control** key on your keyboard. Or you can click one clip and then **Shift**+click another clip. Both clips and any clips between them will become selected. To remove a clip from the group of all selected clips, **Control**+click it. To move an entire group of selected clips into a new folder, drag one of the selected clips into the new folder. The others will follow (see Figure 3.3).

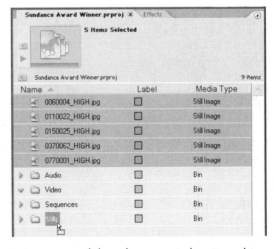

3.3 Drag and drop clips to move them into a bin.

 When selecting clips, click them once. **Note** Don't double-click them. Double-clicking a clip loads it into the **Source** monitor—a process discussed fully in Chapter 4.

Bin Confusions

If you double-click a bin, the contents of that bin will take over the whole **Project** window, and you won't be able to see clips in any other bins. To return to the view of everything, click the **Up One Level** button, above the bin and clip list (see Figure 3.4). Clicking the triangle by a closed bin will reveal its contents without hiding other bins and clips.

If a bin is selected when you create a new bin, the new bin will become a sub-bin of the selected bin. If you do this by accident, drag the sub-bin out of the selected bin (see Figure 3.5).

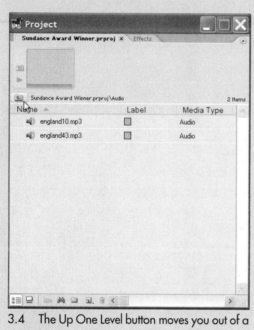

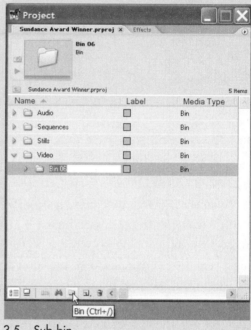

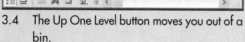

3.4   The Up One Level button moves you out of a bin.

3.5   Sub-bin.

IMPORTING

Importing is easy. Choose **File>Import** from the menu, navigate to the file you want (it can be a video file, a sound file, or a still-image file), select the file, and click the **OK** button. You can use this technique to import video files, audio files or still-image files (see Figure 3.6).

If you want to import multiple files at once, choose **File>Import** and then navigate to a folder on your hard drive that contains all the files. If you want to import all the files in that folder, select the folder and click **OK**. If you want to import some of the files inside the folder, navigate inside the folder, and **Control**+click each file to select it (see

3.6 Choose File>Import from the menu to import video files, audio files or still images. (left)

3.7 Control+click multiple files to select them.

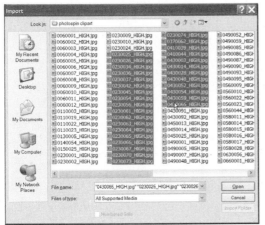

3.8 Click one file, then Shift+click another to select both files and any files between them.

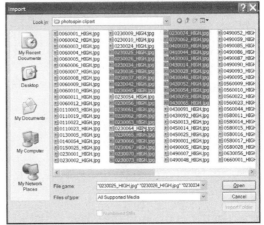

3.9 Remove files from the selected group by Control+clicking them.

Figure 3.7). Or you can click one file and **Shift+**click another file. Both files and any files between them will become selected (see Figure 3.8). **Control+**click any selected files that you'd like to deselect. When you're done selecting files, click **OK** to import (see Figure 3.9).

If you want to import files into a specific bin, click the bin to select it *before* choosing **File>Import** from the menu. Any clips you import will be imported into the selected bin.

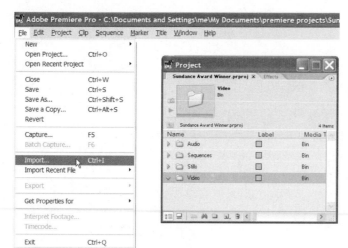

3.10 To import files into a specific bin, click the bin to select it before choosing File>Import from the menu.

The exception to this is when you import a folder. Premiere imports folders as new bins, named after the folder, with a clip inside for each file within the original folder (see Figure 3.10).

You can also import files or folders by dragging them from the desktop into the **Project** window. If you want files to go into a specific bin, drag them directly to that bin.

Importing Video: Premiere will import the following video file formats: AVI, MOV, MPEG/MPE/MPG, Open DML, and WMV.

Importing Audio: Premiere will import the following audio formats: AIFF, AVI, MOV, MP3, WAV, and WMA.

Importing Still Images: Premiere will import the following still image formats: AI, BMP/ DIB/RLE, EPS, FLC/FLI, GIF, ICO, JPEG/JPE/JPG/JFIF, PCX, PICT/PIC/PCT, PNG, PRTL, PSD, TGA/ICB/VST/VDA, and TIFF.

Preparing still images for import
Widths and heights

If your video is eventually going to be displayed on a TV, it must conform to some standards. These standards vary from country to country. For instance, in the U.S., televised video conforms to the NTSC standard, which mandates a specific screen size. The European PAL system mandates a different screen size. This is one of the many reasons you can't play a European video in an American VHS deck (and vice versa).

When you prepare still images in programs such as Photoshop, you should make those images very specific sizes if you want them to fill the entire video screen. In a

Sorting and Searching Bins

If you open your **Project** window really wide and click the **List View** button at the bottom of the **Project** window, you'll see many columns of information about your clips. To sort a column, click its heading (e.g., **Media Duration**). Click a column heading a second time for a reverse sort (see Figure 3.11).

If you've imported hundreds of clips and can't find the one you want, click the **Binoculars** button at the bottom of the **Project** window to run a custom search (see Figure 3.12).

3.11 Widen the Project window and click the List View button to see many columns of information about your clips.

3.12 Click the Binoculars button to search for a clip.

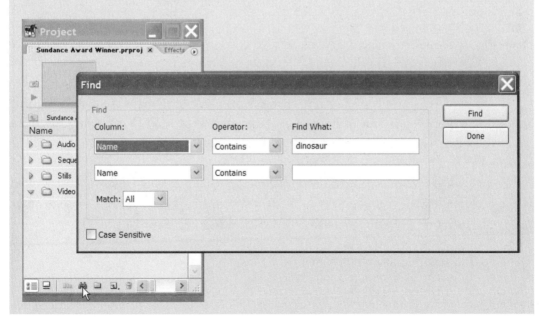

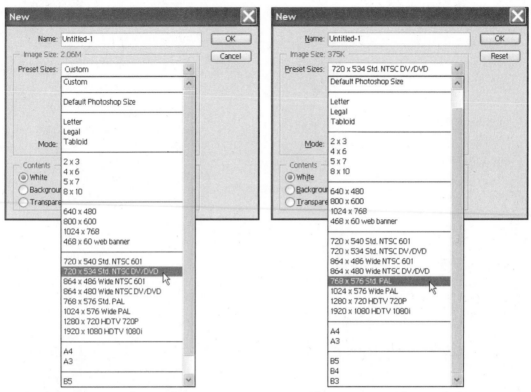

3.13 When creating a still image for import into an NTSC DV video, make it 720 pixels wide by 534 pixels high.

3.14 When creating a still image for import into a PAL DV video, make it 768 pixels wide by 576 pixels high.

nutshell, you should create your images at 720 pixels wide by 534 pixels high if you're planing to import the images into a NTSC project and merge them with footage shot with an DV camcorder (see Figure 3.13).

If you're preparing images for a PAL project, you should prepare them at 768 pixels high by 576 pixels high (see Figure 3.14). Note that Photoshop has presets for these image sizes, that you can choose from the dialog window that pops up when you choose **File>New** from Photoshop's menu.

This is a gross oversimplification of a complex topic. If you'd like to know more about preparing still images for video, a great resource is *Photoshop CS for Nonlinear Editors*, by Richard Harrington, published by CMP books (see Figure 3.15).

Still Image Widths and Heights

If NTSC-DV is 720×480, why should you prepare your still images at 720×534? Because the pixels in still images created on a computer (or scanned into a computer) are square, whereas images captured by video cameras are rectangular. 720×534 is the square pixel equivalent to the rectangular-pixel dimension of 720×480. Some people mistakenly think they're doing themselves a favor by creating still graphics at 720×480, but when they import these graphics into Premiere, they notice distortions. This is because Premiere must stretch the square pixels into rectangles. But if you start with a 720×534 image, everything will work out right.

PAL video suffers from the same square/non-square pixel issue. Whereas standard PAL DV dimensions are 720×576, you should prepare stills for PAL at 768×576.

If you've upgraded to Photoshop CS, you can actually work with and view non-square pixels right in Photoshop.

You can also import images that are much bigger than your project's width and height. You might do this because you want to "pan" around in an image, revealing different parts of it at different times—a common technique in many documentaries. Or you might want to "zoom" in on part of an images— say, a person's eyes. You can't really zoom in Premiere, but you can scale an image up, which looks as if you're zooming. But you should never scale a small image up until just part of it (e.g., the eyes) fill the screen, because a scaled-up image looks blocky and fuzzy. Instead, you should start with a really big image, scale it down, and then animate it, scaling up to its orig-

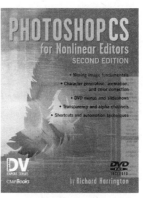

3.15 Photoshop CS for Nonlinear Editors, by Richard Harrington, CMP books. ISBN 1-57820-237-X

inal size. You can bring images into Premiere that are up to 4,000 pixels wide by 4,000 pixels high. To learn how to pan around in large images, or to learn how to scale them to simulate zooms, see Chapter 9.

It's possible that when you import an oversized image, Premiere will squash and distort it so that it fits within the frame size of your project. If this happens to you, it's because you somehow changed a preference. To undo the damage, choose **File>Project Settings>General** from the menu. In the dialog window that appears, *un*check the **Scale Clips to Project Dimensions** option.

Importing still images
How long will they stay on the screen?

Even though still images are still, they still must exist for a certain length of time within the video sequence you create in Premiere. You can set a default length for your stills, but you can always override this default for any specific still in your sequence. To set a default duration, choose **Edit>Preferences>Still Image** from the menu. Type the number of frames you'd like your image to span in the **Default Duration field**. Video in America and Japan runs close to 30 frames per second, so if you'd like an image to last one-half second, enter 15 frames. In Europe, video runs at 25fps, so a two-second still in a European video should span 50 frames. In any case, don't fret this decision too much, because you can always override it using trimming tools (see Figure 3.16 and Chapter 5).

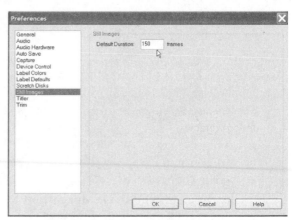

3.16 Setting a default still-image duration: Edit>Preferences>Still Image.

Photoshop files

If you import Photoshop files (files with a PSD extension on the end of their file names), you can access some special import options. Complex Photoshop files tend to be layered, like a stack of images on top of each other. When importing a layered Photoshop file, you can choose to import the layers all merged together into a single image, or you can choose to extract one layer and import it in by itself.

Premiere automatically detects when you're trying to import a layered Photoshop file. When you choose **File>Import** from the menu and select such an image, Premiere responds with the **Import Layered File** dialog window, in which you can choose to merge all the layers together or to import a specific layer (see Figure 3.17).

When importing a layer, you can choose import it at the document size (whatever width and height you set up in Photoshop when you created the file) or you can crop the layer to the size its visible pixels. In other words, if your Photoshop document is 800×600 but you're importing a layer that only has a 200×300 rectangle in it, you can crop the image to 200×300.

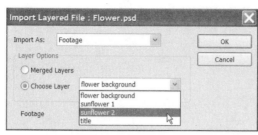
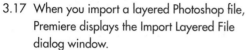
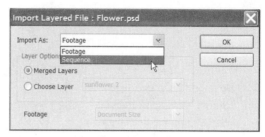

3.17 When you import a layered Photoshop file, Premiere displays the Import Layered File dialog window.

3.18 Importing a layered Photoshop document as a sequence.

You can also import a layered Photoshop file as a sequence, in which case each layer will import as a separate clip in the **Project** window, and Premiere will also create a sequence for you, using all of the layers (see Figure 3.18).

If you double-click the sequence in the **Project** window, it will open, and you'll see each layer inhabiting its own track in the **Timeline** (see Figure 3.19).

Importing a file sequence

Some animation programs, such as Adobe After Effects, can export each frame as a separate image file. These files might be named *frame1.tiff, frame2.tiff, frame3.tiff*. If you have a folder full of these images, you can import them into Premiere as a single animated movie. After choosing **File>Import**, navigate to the first file in the sequence (e.g.,

3.19 Each Photoshop layer becomes a track in the Timeline.

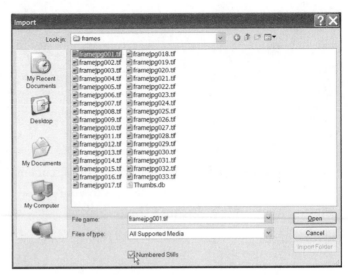

3.20 To import an image sequence, choose File>Import from the menu, select the first image in the sequence, check the Import Numbered Stills option, and click OK.

frame1.tif) and select it. Then, before you click **OK**, select the **Import Numbered Stills** option in the **Import** window (see Figure 3.20).

Premiere can import animation sequences in the following formats: AI, BMP/DIB/ RLE, Filmstrip, GIF, PICT/PIC/PCT, TGA/ICB/VST/VDA, TIFF, PSD. Note that if your images are layered Photoshop or Illustrator files, you'll need to flatten them before importing them as frames in an animation sequence.

AAF, OMF, and EDL

No, those aren't the names of the three witches from MacBeth. AAF stands for Advanced Authoring Format, OMF stands for Open Media Framework, and EDL stands for Edit Decision List. You can import all three of these beasties into Premiere. Each of these formats was developed to allow editors to exchange editing decisions and multimedia files without having to worry too much about what sort of computers are involved or what sort of program was used. In theory, you could start editing in Avid Xpress DV, resume editing in Final Cut Pro, and then finish editing in Premiere—as long as you used one of these formats. In practice, it's usually not quite that simple, because each editing program has its own quirks and features. For instance, a Premiere-only transition will not translate into an Avid and vice versa. Still, these formats work well enough for exchanging basic editing decisions.

Note that Premiere can also export in these formats. To learn more about exporting, see Chapter 12 on page 295. Premiere's online help contains quite a bit of in-depth information about AAF, OMF, and EDL.

CAPTURING

Device control

When people connect camcorders and decks to computers, the video generally travels through a specialized cable called IEEE 1394 (pronounced *I triple-E 1394*), often known by the brand names FireWire and i.LINK. If you own a device that can be hooked up to your computer using one of these cables, Premiere can control the device for you. This saves you from having to operate both Premiere and your device at the same time. You just tell Premiere what you want it to do, and Premiere takes care of the rest.

After you've connected your camera to your PC, set your camera to VCR mode rather than to Record mode (because you're playing back, not filming). The method of doing this differs from camera to camera, so you'll have to check your camera's manual.

Finally, you need to tell Premiere what kind of camera or deck you're using by choosing **Edit>Preferences>Device Control** from the menu.

From the **Device** pop-up menu, choose **DV Device Control**, and then click the **Options** button, select the **Device Brand** (the company, e.g., Panasonic), and the **Device Type** (i.e., the specific model) (see Figure 3.21). If you don't find your device listed, you should contact your camera or deck vendor and tell them you're trying to use your device with Premiere Pro. They may tell you to choose a similar device in Premiere. You can also click the **Go Online for Device Info** button. If your machine is connected to the Internet, you'll be whisked online to Adobe's website, where you may find some help.

Premiere will now try to access your camera or deck. If it succeeds, it will print **Success** at the **Device Option's** status display. If the display reads **Offline**, Premiere was unable to access your device. Check your cables and try again.

Logging

After you've set up your device, you can play your video through and mark all of the segments you'd like to save as clips. Each segment you mark will become a clip in your **Project** window.

Check the Cable

When all goes well, IEEE 1394 makes a wonderful servant. But if you can't seem to capture video, always check the cable. We tend to suspect Premiere, our camera and our computer of causing problems. If we're right, these problems can be complicated and costly to fix. But a damaged cable is cheap and easy to replace. Also, make sure your cable is securely plugged in to both the computer and the camera. Loose cables can thwart capturing.

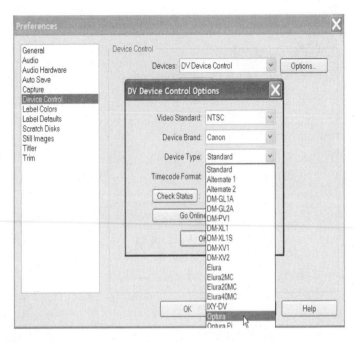

3.21 To allow Premiere to control your camera or deck, choose Edit>Preferences>Device Control from the menu, enable DV Device Control, click the Options button and tell Premiere your device's brand and type.

But you won't actually record any media to your hard drive. Your clips will be *offline* clips, because they will refer to media that isn't online—i.e., not on your computer yet, because it's still in your camera. It's as though you've watched a video and made a note for Premiere on a piece of scrap paper about which sections of the tape you'd like it to transfer onto your computer. You didn't want Premiere to transfer the sections while you were watching, because that would take time. Logging allows you to fast forward (or rewind) through long sections of tape that you want captured later. You can say, "Start capturing *here!*" then fast-forward for a while, then play at normal speed to find a specific point on the tape, and say, "End capturing *here.*"

Later you can tell Premiere to batch capture your offline clips. Batch capturing is a lengthy process, but it's automated, so once Premiere has started, you can go get coffee, take a walk, or even go to bed. When you wake up, Premiere will have saved all of your

Capture while You Work

Instead of taking a nap, you can (if you want) continue to edit while Premiere is batch capturing. For instance, you could edit scene 1 while Premiere captures the footage for scene 2. If you do this, there's a slight chance that Premiere might loose some frames during the capture. To avoid this, try not to do any taxing edits while Premiere is capturing. Taxing edits include effects and complex audio processing. Also, the more RAM you have on your machine, the less likely you are to lose frames.

Help with camera problems

When trying solve device problems, it's easy to fall between the cracks into Tech Support Limbo. Adobe didn't create the camera; Panasonic (or whoever) didn't create Premiere. Neither vendor created your PC. So who do you turn to for help? Your best bet, when all else fails, is the web. Someone else, somewhere in the world, has the same camera and has encountered the same problem. If you're lucky, he or she may have solved it and written up the solution. Try searching the following sites for relevant information. If searching fails you, try politely posting a question. When you post, add as many details as you can, including make and model of camera, details about your computer (brand, processor, etc.) and the version of Premiere Pro you're using:

- http://www.creativecow.net/index.php?forumid=3
- http://groups.google.com/groups?group=adobe.premiere.windows
- http://www.adobeforums.com/cgi-bin/webx?14@@.1de9c1bf

3.22 Web sites like Creative Cow may offer the help you need.

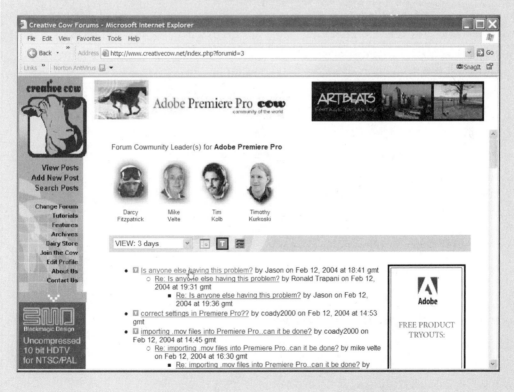

segments as files on your hard drive and associated each one to one of your formerly offline clips. The action of marking segments for a later batch capture is called *logging*.

Here's how to log segments of video for a later batch capture:

1. Choose **File>Capture** from the menu and then click the **Logging** tab in the **Capture** window (see Figure 3.23).

2. At the top of the **Capture** window, tell Premiere whether you want to capture just video, just audio, or both video and audio (see Figure 3.24).

3. Click a bin in the large white area next to the text that reads **Log Clips To**. Premiere will store your clips in this bin. If, at any time, you want to store a clip in a different bin, just click that bin. The next clip you log will be stored in that bin (see Figure 3.25).

4. Next, tell Premiere the tape's name.
    The name you type here should also be written on the actual tape itself, maybe in black magic marker. Remember that while you log, you won't actually be capturing any video to your hard drive. You're just telling Premiere which segments to grab when it captures later, at which time it will tell you to insert whatever tape you tell it about now. It will be easy to find that tape if the name written on it matches the name Premiere displays (see Figure 3.26).

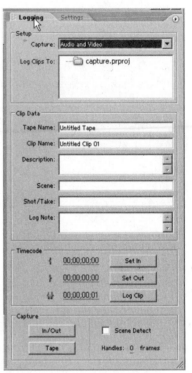

3.23 To begin logging, choose File>Capture from the menu; then click the Logging tab in the Capture window.

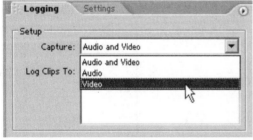

3.24 Tell Premiere whether you want to capture video, audio, or both.

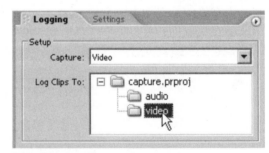

3.25 Choose a bin.

5. Now preview your tape using the controls in the **Capture** window (see Figure 3.27).

As you play, look for segments that you'd like to save as clips. To learn more about the preview controls, see the sidebar "The Many Ways of Playing, Pausing, and Navigating to a Specific Frame" on page 50. Regardless of how you play, reverse-play, fast-forward, or rewind, your goal is to find the starting frame of a segment you'd like to capture. Say your tape starts with 10 minutes of a tiger in the zoo and then cuts to a polar bear pacing around in his cage. After the polar bear, the tape cuts again, this time to a gorilla. You're interested in capturing the polar bear, so you need to move the tape to around the first frame at which the polar bear appears, just after the end of the tiger segment.

6. When you find the starting frame of the segment you want to capture, click the **Set In Point** button. This marks that frame as the beginning of what you want to capture (see Figure 3.28).

7. Then play, shuttle, jog, or enter timecode that will get you to the last frame of the segment you want to capture.

   Don't worry about being exact. Just get in the ballpark. And try to capture a little more than you think you need, either by moving a few frames past the end you want, or by setting a **Handle** value on the **Settings** tab of the **Capture** window. If you already set a handle value when you marked your in point, you don't need to do anything. The one handle value instructs Premiere to capture extra frames before the beginning and after the end.

8. When you find the ending frame of the segment, mark it by clicking the **Set Out Point** button (see Figure 3.29).

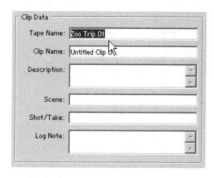

3.26 Tell Premiere the tape's name.

3.27 Preview the tape using the "VCR" controls in the capture window.

3.28 Set In Point button

3.29 Set Out Point button

The Many Ways of Playing, Pausing, and Navigating to a Specific Frame

▷ To play the tape, click the **Play** button.

◁ To play the tape backwards, click the **Play Reverse** button.

❚❚ To pause the tape, click the **Pause** button.

▮▷ To move the tape forward one frame, click the **Forward One Frame** button.

◁▮ To move the tape back one frame, click the **Back One Frame** button.

▪ To stop the tape, click the **Stop** button.

◀◀ To rewind the tape to the beginning, click the **Rewind** button.

▶▶ To fast forward the tape to the end, click the **Fast-forward** button.

If the tape is stopped and you fast forward or rewind, the tape will race to the beginning or end at full speed. If the tape is playing, and you fast forward or rewind, the tape will play backwards or forwards in fast motion.

You can also drag the shuttle control to the left to play backward or the right to play forwards. The further you drag the shuttle from the center, the faster the tape will play.

Or you can drag the jog wheel to the left or to the right, to play forwards or backwards with finer control.

Now that you've marked an in and an out point, you've defined the segment you want Premiere to capture. In the **Capture** window, Premiere displays the in and out point timecodes below the monitor, in the center. To the right it displays the duration of the segment you marked (how much time elapses between the in point and the out point). To the

The Many Ways of Playing, Pausing, and Navigating to a Specific Frame cont'd

You can also preview using the keyboard:

Frame by frame forward	**Right Arrow** key or **Shift**+Numeric Keypad **6**
Frame by frame backward	**Left Arrow** key or **Shift**+Numeric Keypad **4**
Go to the start of the video	**Home** key or **Shift**+Numeric Keypad **7**
Go to the end of the video	**End** key or **Shift**+Numeric Keypad **1**
Play/Pause	Spacebar

Finally, you can click the timecode at the left and type in a specific time that you'd like to move the tape to. Timecode is a frame-numbering system in which each frame has a unique id-number which represents how far into the video that frame is from the start of the video. For example, frame 01;02;15;08 is 1 hour, 2 minutes, 15 seconds, and 8 frames into your video. Timecode is similar to the normal way we represent time (hours:minutes:seconds), except that there's an extra unit at the end—frames (hours;minutes;seconds;frames).

When typing timecode, you can leave out the punctuation, and you only need to type the significant digits from right to left. For instance, if you want to navigate to the frame that is 10 seconds into your video, click the timecode and type *1000* (10 seconds and 00 frames). If you want to go to 5 minutes and 12 seconds, type *51200* (5 minutes, 12 frames and 00 seconds). A common mistake is to type *10* when you want to go to 10 seconds. Remember, the last two digits are frames, not seconds; so 10 means 10 frames into the video. 10 seconds is 1000.

Or you can type an offset. For instance, if you type *+30*, the tape will fast-forward 30 frames. If you type *−220300*, the tape will rewind 22 minutes and 3 seconds.

| ▼ | +30 | ▷¦ 00;02;42;21 00;02;44;25 ¦ | 00;00;02;05 ⬇ |

▼ 00;02;43;28   In addition to typing timecode, you can hold down on the timecode and drag to the left or the right. This action, called *scrubbing*, will rewind or fast-forward the tape, similar to the shuttle.

left, Premiere displays the timecode of the current frame showing in the monitor (see Figure 3.30).

▼ 00;02;42;21   ¦ 00;02;42;21 00;02;44;25 ¦   00;00;02;05 ⬇

3.30 Premiere displays timecodes for the in and out points in the center of the monitor; on the right it displays in-to-out duration; on the left it displays the timecode for the currently displayed frame.

Handle

If you've done your job well during the filming, you shouldn't have to be too exact in locating a starting frame. Hopefully, you filmed more polar bear than you need. This will allow you to start somewhere near the beginning without having to nitpick over finding a specific frame. Also, if you know you're going to need three minutes of polar bear in your video, you should try to capture a little more than that—maybe three minutes and 30 seconds. Of course, if you've only filmed three minutes, you can't capture any extra. This extra footage is called *handle*. During the editing stage, you'll use handle to give you some leeway in case you want to need to make your finished sequence a little longer than you originally though you would.

In fact, handle is so important that you can even force Premiere to capture a little more footage than you specify: automatic handle. At the bottom of the Settings tab of the **Capture** window, click or scrub the Handle value to enter the number of extra frames you'd like Premiere to capture. If you're capturing NTSC video, it runs at close to 30 frames per second, so if you enter a

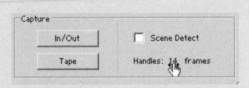

3.31 At the bottom of the Capture window, you can tell Premiere to automatically capture handle.

Handle value of 150 frames, you'll capture 5 extra seconds. PAL video runs at 25 frames per second, so you need to type *125* if you want to capture five extra seconds of footage. If you take the time to specify handle, you don't need to worry about finding an earlier start frame than you need. Just find the exact start frame you need—or a frame close to it. Premiere will capture some extra frames before it (see Figure 3.31).

Don't try to be exact at this stage. When in doubt, capture too much. Don't worry if you get a little bit of tiger mixed in with your polar bear. You'll be able to fix all those problems later, when you edit.

At this point, you should name your segment by typing something appropriate—like "polar bear"—in the **Clip Name** text field (see Figure 3.32). If you'd like some additional information to travel along with the segment, type that info in the **Description** field. For instance, you might note that the lighting was bad when you shot the clip. This information might be useful later when you're trying to decide whether to use this footage or the footage of your uncle Ralph instead. (After all, the lighting is better in his segment, and he looks a little bit like a polar bear.)

Finally, click the **Log Clip** button to store your in and out point (see Figure 3.33). Premiere won't capture the clip now—that will happen during the batch capture phase—but it will remember the segment that you marked.

Repeat this process for each segment of the tape you want to capture: find the beginning of the segment, mark an in point, find the end of the segment, mark an out point, type a name for your clip and any comments you'd like, and click the **Log Clip** button.

You don't need to log the segments in the order than they appear on the tape. If after logging the polar bear, you realize that you really should capture an earlier tiger segment too, no problem. Just rewind the tape, mark the segment, type a name, and then click the **Log Clip** button.

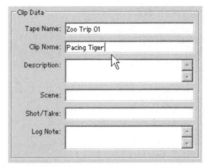

3.32 Name the clip.

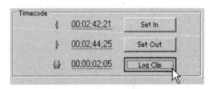

3.33 Click the Log Clip button.

You can even change tapes during a logging session. Just remember to type a new tape name after you insert a new tape into your camera or deck. During the batch capturing stage, Premiere will remember which segment is on which tape. When it needs a new tape, it will stop capturing and ask you to insert that tape.

Some cameras and decks display timecode as they play back tape. If you have one of these cameras, you can bypass Premiere's interface for much of the logging process. Just watch the tape on your device and write down the in and out points that define the segments. When you've finished, start Premiere, and choose **File>Capture** from the menu. On the **Settings** tab, tell Premiere whether you want to capture audio, video, or both audio and video, select a bin, and log your first segment by clicking the in and out point values (next to the **Set In** and **Set Out** buttons) and typing in the timecodes for that segment. Type a name and optional description; then click the **Log Clip** button. Repeat this process for each segment, entering the timecodes you wrote down earlier, while you were watching the tape. You camera or deck does not need to be plugged into your computer during this process.

You can even type your timecode information into a spreadsheet or text file and then import it into Premiere. For information on how to log clips this way, see **Help>Capturing** and **Importing Source Clips>Batch-Capturing Video**.

Batch capturing

In a Nutshell

1. Plug your camera into your computer and insert the tape that contains your footage.

2. Open a bin and select the clips within it that you'd like to capture.

3. Choose **File>Batch Capture** from the menu.

Now that you've logged your clips, you've finished doing the hard part. It's time to let Premiere do some of the dirty work. Close out of the **Capture** window, if it's still open, and open the bin that contains all of the clips you'd like to capture.

Clips are little icons that store the information you entered when you were logging. Each clip contains the in point, out point, tape name, etc., that you entered in the Settings tab of the Capture window. In a way, clips are like card-catalog items in a library that tell you how to find a specific book. Clips tell Premiere how to find a specific segment on a tape. Once Premiere has captured the footage as files on your hard drive, the clips will act as stand-ins for those files. You will edit using the clips instead of the actual files. That way, if you make a mistake, you won't be affecting anything serious. Similarly, you could arrange card-catalog cards in the order you'd like to read your books. At the moment, though, your clips are offline clips, meaning that they point to footage that is on tape, rather than on your hard drive.

Once you've opened your bin, you need to select the clips that you want Premiere to capture. To select them, **Control**+click each clip you'd like to add to the capture group. Or you can click one clip, say the clip at the top of the bin, and **Shift**+click another clip, say the clip at the bottom of the bin. Premiere will add both clips to the selection group, as well as all clips in between (see Figure 3.34).

Now plug your camera or deck into your computer. If you logged the clips by typing the time-code into the **Settings** tab, you may have to set up **Device Control** at this point.

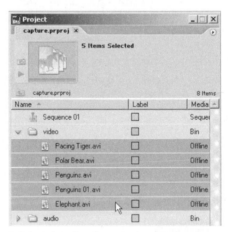

3.34 Select the clips you want to batch capture.

Choose **File>Batch Capture** from the menu. Click **OK** in the dialog window that pops up. Premiere will then ask you to insert a tape. Do so and click **OK**. Your work is now done, unless some of your clips are on other tapes, in which case, Premiere will eventually stop capturing and ask you to insert them (see Figure 3.35).

If you have a sudden urge to stop the capturing process, press the **Stop** button in the **Capture** window or the **Esc** key on your keyboard. You can resume capture at any time by reselecting the clips in the bins (the ones that aren't already captured) and choosing **File>Capture** from the menu. Don't worry if you accidently select some clips that have already been captured. Premiere will ignore them.

After clips have been captured, their icons will become the first frame of their associated files. To see larger thumbnails, click the **Icon View** button at the bottom of the **Project** window. To see smaller icons, click the **List View** icon to its left (see Figure 3.36).

Select a clip (by clicking it once, not double-clicking it) to see a larger thumbnail and some information at the top of the **Project** window. You can click the little **Play** button below the larger thumbnail to play the clip. Click the same button again to stop the clip playing. Or you can drag the slider to view frames throughout the clip's duration. To set a different frame as the thumbnail image, move to that frame using **Play** buttons and the slider, and then click the **Set Poster Frame** button (see Figure 3.37).

3.35 After you select File>Batch Capture from the menu, Premiere will ask you to insert the tape. Do so and click OK. Premiere will do the rest.

3.36 For larger clip icons, click the Icon View button at the bottom of the Project window.

3.37 At the top of the Project window, you'll see information and a large thumbnail representing the selected clip. To choose an new icon for that clip (or drag the slider) to a specific frame and then click the Set Poster Frame button.

Manual capturing

Instead of batch capturing—which delays the actual transfer from camera or deck to computer until after you've logged all of the clips—you can use the following techniques to capture footage immediately.

1. Enter the same information on the **Capture** window's Settings tab that you enter when you're logging a clip for batch capturing, including tape name, bin, and clip name.

2. Play the tape using the controls in the **Capture** window and use the **Set In** and **Set Out** buttons to mark a segment.

3. Click the **In/Out** button (instead of the **Log Clip** button) on the **Settings** tab. Premiere will immediately capture the footage as a file on your hard drive and create an associated clip in the bin you selected (see Figure 3.38).

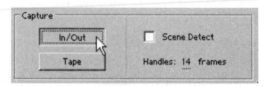

3.38 Click the In/Out button to force Premiere to capture immediately.

Even simpler: use the controls in the **Capture** window to move the tape to the starting frame of a segment segment you want to capture. Type a tape name and clip name into the appropriate fields on the **Settings** tab, and click the **Record** button in the **Capture** window. When the tape reaches the end of the segment, click the **Stop** button (see Figure 3.39).

3.39 After moving the tape to the first frame you want to capture, click the Record button. Click the Stop button when you want to stop recording.

Consider setting a **Handle** value to force Premiere to capture a little bit of extra footage before using either of these capture techniques.

What can go wrong?

Batch capturing the beginning of the tape: As the first 30 seconds or so of your tape plays, your deck may be trying to lock onto and read the timecode. Accurate timecode is vital for batch capturing, yet the process may go awry at the beginning of the tape. Rather than risking this, try manually capturing the first 30 seconds of tape. Then switch to logging and batch capturing for the rest of the segments.

A better solution is to only shoot test footage at the beginning of the tape. Start your real filming a little further into it, and then you won't need to worry about capturing the beginning at all. The same issues may plague the final 30 seconds of the tape, so you may want to stop filming before you get to the very end.

Pausing the tape: If you pause your camera or deck while filming, you risk damaging or restarting the timecode on the tape. You can tell Premiere to create a new clip each time it comes across one of these rifts in time. Premiere thinks of them as the beginnings of new scenes.

Click the **Scene Detect** button in the **Capture** window before logging or capturing any clips. If a Premiere encounters a timecode error in the middle of the segment, it will split the segment into two files and two associated clips during capture, using the location of the error as the split point (see Figure 3.40).

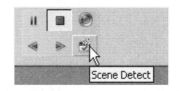

3.40 To force Premiere to create a new clip each time there's a timecode-break on the tape, click the Scene Detect button.

Depending on the way your camera works, you may be able to avoid this problem by continuing to film a few extra seconds after you've finished a shot (rather than pressing pause or stop immediately). Then you can pause or stop your camera. When you're ready to film the next shot, rewind back into one of those extra frames in the previous shot. Then begin filming.

You run out of space on your hard drive: Video and audio files take up a lot of disk space, and when you're out of room, you're out of room. You can buy bigger hard drives, or you can delete files from your existing hard drives. By default, Premiere saves captured footage to the drive and folder as where you've saved the project file. To change this default to a drive with move space, choose **Edit>Preferences>Scratch Disks** from the menu. For more about project preferences, see Chapter 1.

Recapturing

If you work on many editing projects, at some point you'll run out of space on your hard drives. At that point, you'll either have to buy new drives or delete footage files from the drive you have, to make room for new footage files (or you can archive the files to some kind of external storage media, like a CD-ROM or DVD-ROM disk). Deleting footage sounds scary, but it's actually pretty common. You're always safe as long as you save your project files and the original source tape(s). To maximize the lifespan of your source tapes, keep them in their cases, and store them in a climate-controlled environment.

The project files are much more important than the captured footage files, because the project stores all of your editing decisions, which may have taken you hours, days, or weeks to finish. The footage files are just copies of stuff from the tape, which you can recapture at any time. This is good news, because footage files take up tons of disk space, whereas project files are so small, they can fit on a floppy disk. In fact, it's worthwhile backing up your project files onto floppy disks, CDs, or some other kind of external storage.

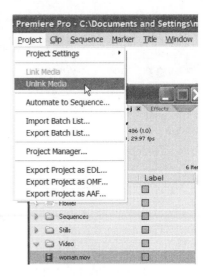

Even if you've deleted all of the footage files, their associated clips will still remain in their bins. These clips store the in and out points needed to locate their associated footage on the original tape. But before you can recapture, you must tell Premiere that the footage is missing.

3.41 If you want to recapture media files, select their associated clips and choose Project Unlink media from the menu. Then repeat the batch capturing process.

1. Open the project and the select the clips that you want to recapture.

2. From the menu, choose **Project>Unlink Media** (see Figure 3.41).

3. In the dialog window that appears, select the **Media Files Are Deleted** option.

4. Then, with the clips still selected and your camera or deck connected to your PC, choose **File>Batch Capture** and go through the **Batch Capturing** process.

Capturing audio

Alas, Premiere can't capture audio directly from a CD. In order to do that, you need to use another program, such as Apple's iTunes (which runs on a PC) or Adobe Audition. In Audition (or whatever program you use), you must convert the CD tracks into audio files, such as MP3s or WAVs. Once the tracks are stored as files, you can bring them into Premiere by choosing **File>Import** from the menu.

Premiere can import audio from video tape, using the normal capture procedures described in this chapter. In the **Capture** window's **Settings** tab, specify whether you want to capture audio only or audio and video. If you capture both audio and video, Premiere will represent them as a single clip. Later, during the editing process, you can unlink the audio from the video to use the two components separately. For more information about linking or unlinking audio and video, see Chapter 10.

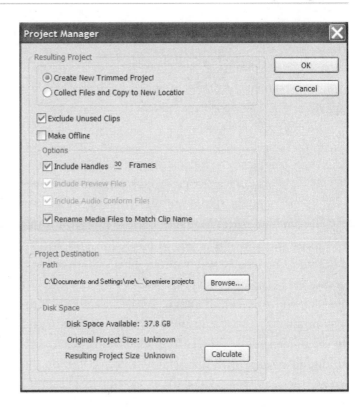

3.42 Project Manager.

Finally, you can record audio directly into Premiere through a microphone or other device plugged into your PC's sound card. For more information about this procedure, see Chapter 10.

Project Manager

With all of these video, audio, and still files floating about, you can easily get disorganized when you're working on a complex project. For instance, you might import music from one folder, sound effects from another folder, illustrations from a third folder, still photos from a fourth folder, and video from a fifth folder. In this scenario, your media files would be scattered all over your hard drive or maybe over several hard drives. If you later needed to archive the footage onto a DVD or some other kind of storage medium, how would you know where to find it all?

Never fear: Premiere's **Project Manager** is here to rescue you. The **Project Manager** copies your entire project and all of its associated media files to a new folder of your choice. That's one folder, not five. The new copy of the project will be referencing the new copies of the media files—not the old ones scattered all over your hard drive. Once you've run the **Project Manager,** you can easily archive your project by moving that one new folder onto a DVD (see Figure 3.42).

Note **Exception:** The only items that won't be copied into this folder are fonts you use in Premiere titles. This is important to consider if you're ever going to edit the project on a different PC—one that might not have the same fonts installed as the ones on the original PC. If you've used any nonstandard fonts, copy them manually from your *Fonts* folder (a subfolder of the Windows folder) onto the DVD too. You'll also have to manually install these fonts onto the new PC—dragging them into that PC's *Fonts* folder.

To run the **Project Manager,** choose **Project>Project Manager** from the menu.

You can then choose one of two main options: **Create a Trimmed Project** or **Collect Files and Copy to New Location.** The second of the two options is the simplest. It just copies every file, as is, to a new folder of your choice. The first option, **Create a Trimmed Project,** will only copy footage you've actually used to the new folder. This means that if you originally captured 25 minutes of polar bear but only used 3 seconds of it in your Premiere sequence, the **Project Manager** will only copy the three used seconds into the new folder. In other words, the **Trimmed Project** option does not include handle. This should greatly decrease the copies' file sizes, but it will limit your editing decisions should you ever reopen the copy of the project file.

You can cheat a little by using setting the **Include Handles** option. If you set this to 30 frames, Premiere will copy more than three seconds to the new folder. It will copy three seconds and 30 frames. So you'll then have 30 frames of handle to work with, which is better than nothing. But you still won't have access to your original 25 minutes. Of course, you can always recapture that footage.

Before closing out of the **Project Manager,** make sure you click the **Browse** button and choose or create a new folder for your copies. Then click the **OK** button to set the **Project Manager** to work.

WRAPPING UP

If you thought video editing was just cutting footage together, this chapter should have changed your mind. Editors deal with video, yes. But they also must import many formats of audio and still image files. Once all these media types are imported and living happily in the **Project** window, they become the bricks with which you build your movie. Are you ready? If so, flip over to the next chapter and learn how to edit your clips together into a sequence.

Chapter 4

Building a Rough Cut

USING THE MONITOR WINDOW TO ASSEMBLE A SEQUENCE

By default, the **Monitor** window sports two viewscreens, the **Source Monitor** on the left and the **Program Monitor** on the right (see Figure 4.1).

4.1   The Monitor window contains a Source Monitor and a Program monitor. Footage courtesy of the American Diabetes Association (www.diabetes.org). Production by RHED Pixel (www.rhedpixel.com).

In the **Program Monitor**, you can play through your sequence as it exists so far. Of course, if you haven't added any footage to your sequence yet, there won't be anything to see. In the **Source Monitor**, you can audition clips (video footage, still images, or sounds chosen from the **Project window**) that you're thinking about adding to your sequence. You can play a clip in the **Source Monitor** and mark the portion of that clip that you want to edit into your sequence. For instance, you might load a long clip into the **Source Monitor** of a kid playing baseball. As you watch the clip, you might notice that most of it just shows the kid standing around, holding his bat, not doing much of anything. Then for a few seconds, he swings the bat as the ball whizzes by his head. Then more standing around, while he waits for a second pitch. Most of that footage is boring, so you don't want to add it to your sequence. The only part you want is that brief swing-of-the-bat moment. So you mark that portion of the clip and add it to your sequence. Then you can watch your sequence in the **Program Monitor**. Usually, the first step in making a sequence involves doing this source/program dance repeatedly:

1. Add clip A to the **Source Monitor**.

2. Mark the section that you want use.

3. Add it to your sequence.

4. View your sequence in the **Program Monitor**.

Then repeat these steps for clip B, clip C, and so on, until you've assembled a rough cut of your sequence.

A rough cut is so named because it's only an approximation of the final, polished results you hope to achieve. Your goal at this point is merely to make a general outline of your sequence. You shouldn't spend hours in the **Source Monitor**, painstakingly going through each clip for the perfect part to use. You'll have plenty of time to refine later. For instance, if you have five minutes of Washington Monument footage, and you know you only want to add five seconds of this to your sequence, resist the urge to examine the footage frame by frame in the **Source Monitor**. Just find any five-second segment and add it to the sequence. Later on, you can exchange that segment for a better segment. Your goal at this stage is to put together a sequence as quickly as possible. Similar advice is often given to writers: don't fret over each word as you write your first draft. Just get it down on paper. You will have plenty of time to refine it later.

Here's the basic procedure: To add a clip to the **Source Monitor**, double-click it in the **Project** window. (Either double-click its small icon to the left of its name or its large thumbnail at the top of the **Project** window.) You can also drag it from the **Project** window by its icon to the right of its name or by its larger thumbnail at the top of the **Project** window and drop in into the **Source Monitor**, but double-clicking is faster. You can then

One Frame Back   One Frame Forward   Current Time Indicator

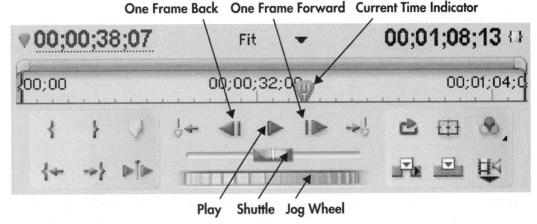

Play   Shuttle   Jog Wheel

4.2   The Source Monitor viewing controls.

use the VCR-like controls below the **Source Monitor** (shown in Figure 4.2) to view the clip.

> **Insert the Whole Clip:** You can also drag from the **Project** window directly to the **Timeline** or **Program Monitor**, but that will insert the entire clip into the sequence—and you might want to trim part of it off before including it, which is best done in the **Source Monitor**.

5.   Click the **Play** button to play the clip.

Click it a second time to pause the clip once it's playing. Click the button to the right of the **Play** button to move one frame forward. Click the button to the left of **Play** to move one frame backward. Drag the shuttle to the right

4.3   Timecode.

or the left to move forward or backward at the speed of your mouse drag. Drag the **Jog** control to the right or the left to move slowly through your video. Drag **Current Time Indicator,** the rounded triangle on the ruler line, to a specific frame. Click the **Timecode** display shown in Figure 4.3 to type a specific time you'd like to jump to. After typing, press **Enter.**

Timecode, a special format for marking video time, uses eight digits (e.g., 01;33;18;02). The left two stand for hours, the next two stand for minutes, the next two stand for seconds, and the final two stand for frames. So 00;00;02;15 marks 0 hours, 0 minutes, 2 seconds, and 15 frames into your clip. When you type timecode, you only need to type the significant digits from right to left. For instance, if you want to jump to 35 frames into a clip, you only need to type *35*. You don't need to type 00;00;00;35. If you want to jump to one second and two frames into your clip, you need to type only *102*. You don't need to type the semicolons. Premiere interprets 102 to mean 1;02. Premiere always interprets number below 100 as frames, so 99 means 99 frames, but 100 means one second and zero frames. Beginners often make the mistake of typing 10 when they want to move 10 seconds into their clip. But 10 means 10 *frames*. To move 10 seconds into your clip, type *1000*, which Premiere interprets as 10;00—10 seconds and 0 frames.

You can also scrub the timecode display. Scrubbing is a little hard to explain, but it's fun to do, so read the following description and then play around until you get it. To scrub the timecode, point to it with the mouse, then hold down the mouse button and drag left or right. The timecode will act as though it's a slider control, and you'll move in time through your source clip. When you scrub, be careful not to click and release the mouse. That's what you do when you want to type in timecode, as explained previously. When you want to scrub timecode, you just hold down the mouse button and drag.

You'll find that there are a variety of controls in Premiere that you can scrub. Scrubbable controls are always indicated by a dotted underline, like the one underneath the timecode. So if you see an underline, try scrubbing. If you use Adobe After Effects, you'll be happy to know that underlined values are scrubbable in that program too. Once you get the hang of scrubbing, you'll find it so intuitive and easy that you'll want to call Adobe and urge them to add it to all of their programs—it would be great to be able to scrub in Photoshop.[1] In addition to scrubbing, you can also click any underlined value to type in a new value.

Note that the **Program Monitor** also has VCR buttons underneath it (see Figure 4.4). These serve a different purpose than the ones below the **Source Monitor**. They are for playing back (and moving through) completed (or partially completed) sequences. When you start a new project, you don't yet have any footage in your sequence. So these buttons won't do anything.

Once you decide which segment of your clip you want to use, you need to mark it. In this chapter, I will use the word *segment* to mean a portion of a longer clip. Say that your clip is 25 seconds long, and you want to use the segment that starts at second 3 and ends at second 12. To mark this segment, move to its start—second 3 (00;00;03;00)—using any of the buttons mentioned earlier: **Play, Frame by frame, Shuttle, Jog**, etc.

1. Click the **Mark In** button (see Figure 4.4).

---

1. In Photoshop CS and Illustrator CS, try selecting some text and then scrubbing the icons on the Character palette (e.g., the icon to the left of the Font Size adjuster).

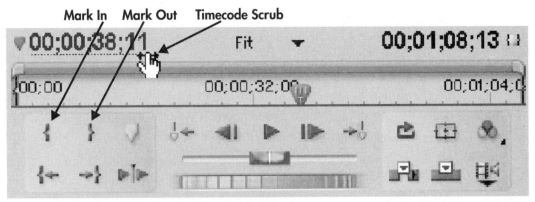

4.4 Scrubbing timecode and setting in and out points.

3. Before adding this segment to your sequence, you must decide whether you want to add both audio and video, just the audio, or just the video.

4. Click the **Take Audio and Video** button repeatedly to toggle through the three options shown in Figures 4.5–4.7.

   • Use both video and audio

   • Use only video

   • Use only audio

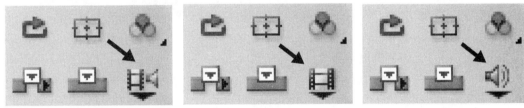

4.5 Take audio and video. 4.6 Take video only. 4.7 Take Audio only.

Finally, before you can add your segment to the sequence, you need to choose which track (or tracks) it will go in. If you look at the **Timeline**, you'll notice that it consists of several rows, called tracks, labeled **Video 1**, **Video 2**, **Video 3**, **Audio 1**, **Audio 2**, and **Audio 3**. Depending on what sort of project you're working on, you may see more or fewer tracks. Tracks are somewhat like layers in a Photoshop document. If you want to superimpose a title over some video, you'd put the video in the **Video 1** track and the title above it in the **Video 2** track. In **Audio 1**, you might put voiceover narration. You might put music in the **Audio 2** track and sound effects in the **Audio 3** track. If your source clip contains both video and audio, you'll need to place it in two tracks on the **Timeline**—one

Audio Only

If you load an audio clip into the **Source Monitor**—or set the **Take Audio and Video** button to use only audio—you will see audio waveforms in the **Source Monitor** instead of a video image (see Figure 4.8). Audio waveforms are squiggly lines that graph the level (volume) changes of the audio as it progresses through time. The taller the squiggle, the louder the sound. Mono sounds will have one waveform; stereo sounds will have two (one for each speaker).

You can set in and out points on audio clips just as you can for video clips. Use the waveform as a guide (see Figure 4.9). For instance, if you want to set the in point right before a drum beat, it should be pretty easy to tell when the beat occurs by looking for a spike in the waveform. Of course, you can also play the clip to hear the sound.

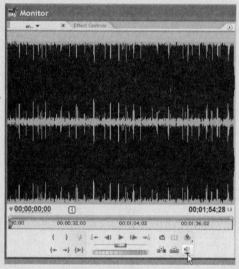

4.8   Audio waveforms in the Source Monitor.

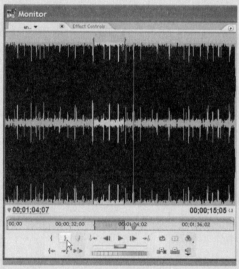

4.9   In and Out points marked for an audio clip.

video track and one audio track—that is, assuming you choose to use both the clip's video and audio.

If you're just starting a sequence and there's nothing in your **Timeline** yet, you probably won't care much where your segment goes. But care or not, you still need to make a choice. It usually makes sense to lay your rough cut down in **Video 1** (and **Audio 1**, if your clips contain audio). To select a track, click the track's name in the **Timeline**, as shown in Figure 4.10 (e.g., click the name **Video 1**).

Now you're ready to add the segment to your sequence. You've marked the in and out points, you've chosen which elements you want to add (video, audio, or both), and you've

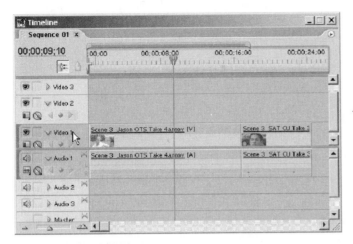

4.10 To target a track, click its name in the Timeline.

selected target tracks in your **Timeline**. To add the segment to your sequence, try one of the following techniques:

- Drag the image in the **Source Monitor** and drop it in the **Program Monitor**.

- Drag the image from the **Source Monitor** into the **Timeline**.

- Click the **Insert** button.

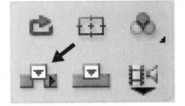

4.11 The Insert button

If you use the second technique—dragging from the **Source Monitor** to the **Timeline**—you can skip selecting tracks first. Simply drag the segment to the track in which you want it to go (see Figure 4.12).

If you watch the **Program Monitor** as you drag, you'll notice that it has split into two images. The image on the left displays the final frame (the out point) of the segment you're dragging. The image on the right displays the sequence frame that will follow your segment, should you drop it at this point. By watching the two images, you can gauge the transition between the new segment and what follows it in the sequence.

If you press the **Insert** button instead of dragging, Premiere will add new segments so that they start at the location of the **Current Time Indicator** in the **Timeline**. As you add new segments—by using the **Insert** button or dragging to the **Program Monitor**—Premiere will automatically move the **Current Time Indicator** to the end of that segment in the **Timeline**. That way, the *next* segment will be added immediately after it. You can mess things up by moving the **Current Time Indicator**. Because new segments get inserted at the location of the **Indicator**, if you move the **Indicator** unintentionally, Premiere may insert

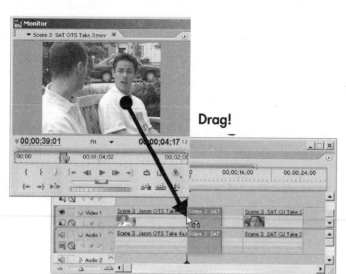

Drag!

4.12 Dragging a segment from the Source Monitor to the Timeline.

your next clip somewhere unexpected. If you drag the segment (rather than using the **Insert** button), the segment will start wherever you drop it.

There are several ways to move the **Indicator**, intentionally or unintentionally, including dragging it in the **Timeline** and moving its little cousin below the **Program Monitor**. The **Program Monitor Indicator** and the **Timeline Indicator** are linked together: move one, and the other one moves. You can also move it by adjusting any of the **VCR, Shuttle, Jog,** or **Timecode** controls in the **Program Monitor** or the timecode in the **Timeline**.

If you do make a mistake and cut in a segment in the wrong place, don't panic. Just press **Control+Z**, which will undo your last action. You can press **Control+Z** multiple times to undo your last several actions. And if you absolutely hate the keyboard, you can also find the **Undo** command on the **Edit** menu. But it's worth memorizing the keyboard shortcut, because it works in almost every program. You can **Control+Z** to undo in Premiere, Photoshop, After Effects, Illustrator, Microsoft Word, etc.

When you're done building your sequence, use the **Play** button on the **Program Monitor** to play it back.

THREE-POINT EDITING

As you make your first pass through a sequence, building it from scratch, you can work as outlined previously, marking segments and adding them on to the end of your sequence. Your sequence will grow longer and longer until you finish it.

But at some point, you will probably want to go back and add footage at an earlier point. When you do this, you will need to decide whether you want to insert the footage *in between* items that are already in the **Timeline** or whether you want to *record over* footage already in the **Timeline**. These two techniques are called *insert* and *overlay*, respectively.

Assembling a quick rough cut

When starting a new sequence, you'll probably want to add a series of segments one after the other. The easiest way to do this is by using the **Insert** button (rather than dragging). When you add new segments to a track, they have to start at some point in time. When you press the **Insert** button, the segment will start at the location marked by the **Current Time Indicator**. After adding a segment by pressing the **Insert** button, the **Current Time Indicator** will automatically move to the end of that segment, which means that you're all set up for adding your next segment. You can quickly add segments by repeating this procedure:

1. Load a clip into the **Source Monitor**.

2. Mark in and out points.

3. Target a track.

   (You'll only have to do this for the first segment you add. The rest will continue to drop into this track, unless you target another track).

4. Press the **Insert** button.

You can speed up even more by using the following keyboard shortcuts:

- Spacebar to play/pause
- **I** to add an in point
- **O** to add an out point
- **Comma** key to insert

Additional keys that may help you are the **J**, **K**, and **L** keys (which will play backwards, stop, and play forwards, respectively), and the arrow keys, which will move you forward and backward frame by frame. These keys will only control the **Source Monitor** if the **Source Monitor** is selected. Pressing **Control+Tab** repeatedly will cycle you through each window, selecting each one in turn. Once the **Monitor** window is selected, you can toggle between the **Source Monitor** and the **Program Monitor** by pressing **Control+`**. That's the tick mark key, which is to the left of the **1** key on most keyboards. When the **Source Monitor** is selected, you'll see thin blue bars directly above and below the image in it.

OVERLAY

When you make an overlay edit, you mark three points. This is why an overlay is a type of three-point edit: you mark an in point, an out point, and a third point, which can be either an in point or an out point. When marking these points, you are concerned about two things: how much of the source clip you want to use and where in the sequence you want it to go. You'll tell Premiere of your intentions by using in and out points. Once you've completed the overlay, you'll notice that the source segment has recorded over part of the sequence. This is the whole point of an overlay. If you want to add a segment without recording over part of the sequence, you'll have to do an insert edit (covered on page 77). Since overlays record over preexisting footage, your sequence won't grow any longer after an overlay. In other words, if you cut in a three-second segment using overlay, it will record over three seconds in the **Timeline**, replacing an old three seconds with a new three seconds—so your sequence will stay the same length as it was before.

Overlays are great when you're locked into a specific duration. For instance, you might have a five-minute sequence laid down in your **Timeline**. You want to add some new footage, but your sequence can't run longer than five minutes. Overlays solve this problem by recording over old footage with new footage.

Though there are several different kinds of overlays, the basic technique is as follows:

4.13 The Overlay button.

1. Load a clip into the **Source Monitor** and mark the part of that clip you want to use (the segment).

2. Mark the place in the sequence where you'd like the segment to go.

3. Click the **overlay** button (see Figure 4.13).

When you mark the clip and the sequence, you will use a total of three points, an in and an out point in one of the two monitors and an in *or* an out point in the other monitor. Note that both monitors have **Mark In** and **Mark Out** buttons beneath them. To add in or out points in the **Source Monitor**, click the appropriate buttons on the **Source Monitor** side. To mark in or out points in the sequence, click the appropriate buttons on the **Program Monitor** side. Make sure you mark only three points (an in and an out on one side and an in *or* an out on the other side).

When you finish marking, before you cut your segment into the sequence, remember to tell Premiere whether you want video, audio, or both by clicking the **Take Audio and Video** button until it toggles to the option you want. Also, select the track or tracks in the **Timeline** where you want the segment to go by clicking the track names (**Video 1**, etc.).

A more complete set of overlay steps would be:

1. Load a clip into the **Source Monitor** and mark the part of that clip you want to use (the segment).

2. Mark the place in the sequence where you'd like the segment to go.

3. Toggle the **Take Audio and Video** button to the option you want.

4. Select the track in the **Timeline** where you want your segment to go.

5. Click the **Overlay** button.

There are four possible combinations of points you may choose to use. As an editor, your job will be to choose which combination to use to complete the task at hand.

Source: in and out points, Program: in point

Use this combination when it's vital that your segment starts and ends on specific frames of the source clip, and it's also important that the segment gets placed so it starts at a very specific point in the sequence (see Figure 4.14).

For instance, say you are auditioning a clip of a clown in the **Source Monitor**. He's standing around looking bored. All of the sudden, a pie flies into the shot and splats onto the clown's face. Instead of getting mad, the clown runs his fingers through the pie, scraping some off his nose, and then sticks his fingers in his mouth. You want the portion that begins when the pie first enters the picture and ends as the clown gets hit in the face. You don't want to use the standing around before the pie, nor do you want to use the pie tasting that comes after. So you mark an in point on the first frame in which you can see the pie. You mark an out point on a frame that shows the pie splattered on the clown's face.

In the sequence (in the **Timeline** and **Program Monitor**), a little boy sneaks up to the clown, holding a pie behind his back. Then he jumps up into the air and hurls the pie at the unsuspecting clown. All of this is filmed from fairly far away (a long shot), and you'd like to cut the clown close-up as the pie leaves the boy's hands. So at the frame where this happens, you mark an in point on the **Program** side. That's your way of telling Premiere that you want to cut in the **Source** segment so that it starts there (at the in point in the sequence). Premiere will line the **Source** segment's in point up with the sequence's in point. When you click the **Overlay** button, Premiere will record over the sequence footage of the

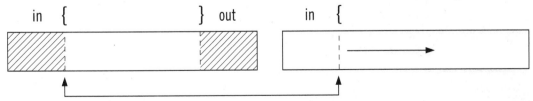

4.14 Source: in and out, Program: in.

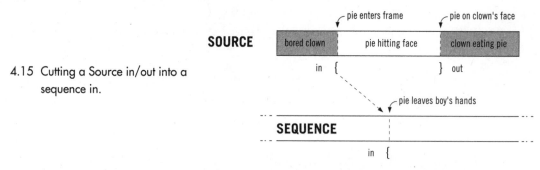

4.15 Cutting a Source in/out into a sequence in.

pie leaving the boy's hands and replace it with the close-up of the pie hitting the clown's face. The close-up will end at your marked out point (the pie on the clown's face), at which point the sequence will cut back to the long shot, showing the clown and the boy at a distance, post-pie (see Figure 4.15).

Source: in and out points, Program: out point

Use this combination when it's vital that you pull a portion from the **Source** clip and splice it into the sequence so that it *ends* at a specific sequence frame (see Figure 4.16).

For instance, say that in the **Source Monitor** you're auditioning a shot of a window, seen from outside a building. At first, nothing is happening inside. Then a woman runs by, screaming. She's chased by a masked man carrying a cleaver. They both run past the window, and once again there's nothing much to see. So you mark in and out points on the Source side, selecting just the segment when the man and woman run by.

Also in the sequence, a teenager watches his neighbor's house through binoculars. At first he looks bored, but then he looks surprised and shocked. He throws down the binoculars and runs to call the police. You want to cut the window-chase into this shot so that it *ends* as he throws down his binoculars. So you mark a frame right as he's about to do so. This time, you'll mark the frame with an out point.

When you overlay, Premiere will line up the two out points, so that just after the man and woman leave the window, the sequence will cut to the teen throwing down his binoculars (see Figure 4.17).

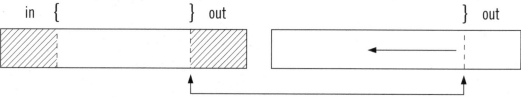

4.16 Source: in and out. Program: out.

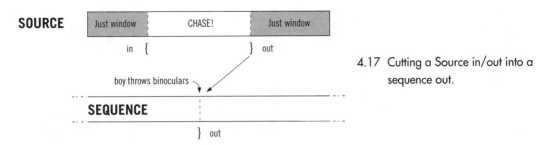

4.17 Cutting a Source in/out into a sequence out.

Source: in point, Program: in and out points

Use this combination when you're trying to replace a specific portion of the sequence. Having marked the start and end of the duration you want to replace (with in and out points), you will then mark an in point in the **Source Monitor**, indicating that you want to replace a sequence segment *starting* at this in point (see Figure 4.18).

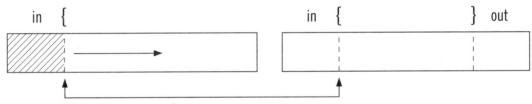

4.18 Source: in, Program: in and out.

Suppose your sequence in the **Program Monitor** shows the CEO of a company talking about his plans for the future. He talks about reorganizing the HR department; then he talks about firing 1,000 employees; then he talks about buying a new photocopier for the legal department. Since the firing comment is pretty shocking, you'd like to replace it with a shot of the interviewer, so that you can see his reaction.

The CEO says, "…in addition to my plans for the HR department, I've decided to fire 1,000 employees, effective as of tomorrow morning. They will be asked to leave the building immediately, and they will not be receiving any severance pay. I've also got this great idea about photocopiers…"

You mark an in point in the sequence immediately after he says "fire 1,000 employees" and an out point right after "severance pay." This is the portion of the sequence that you want to replace with the reaction shot.

You then load the reaction clip into the **Source Monitor** and mark the point at which the realization of the firing is just starting to dawn on the interviewer's face.

When you overlay, Premiere will line up this in point with the sequence in point. As you watch the sequence, you will see the CEO as he talks about the HR department. When he mentions the firing, the sequence will cut to the interviewer's shocked face.

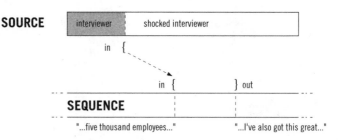

4.19 Cutting a Source in into a
sequence in/out.

Then, as he talks about photocopiers, the sequence will cut back to the CEO (see Figure 4.19).

Source: out point, Program: in and out points

Use this combination when you want to replace a portion of your sequence with a **Source** clip that *ends* at a specific frame (see Figure 4.20).

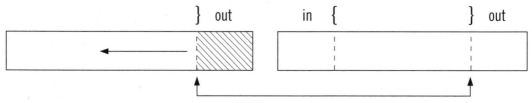

4.20 Source: out, Program in/out.

Suppose in your sequence that the lead singer of a boy band rips his shirt off and throws it at the audience. He then grabs the microphone and begins to croon a little off-key. Suddenly, his shirt flies back onto the stage and hits him in the face.

The shirt-ripping is dramatic; you decide to keep it. And the moment he gets hit in the face is priceless—it definitely has to stay. But the crooning in the middle is kind of boring. So you mark it for replacement. You mark a sequence in point right after he begins crooning. You mark a sequence out point right before he gets hit in the face with his returning shirt.

Then you load a clip of the audience into the **Source Monitor.** You cue it until you find a shot of a girl tossing the singer's shirt back onto the stage. At the moment the shirt flies from her hands, you mark an out point.

When you overlay, Premiere will line up the source out point with the sequence out point. As you watch your sequence, you will see the singer rip off his shirt and throw it; then the sequence will cut to the audience, where you'll see a girl clutching his shirt and then tossing it back. At this point, the sequence will cut back to the singer, just in time for you to see him getting decked by his own shirt (see Figure 4.21).

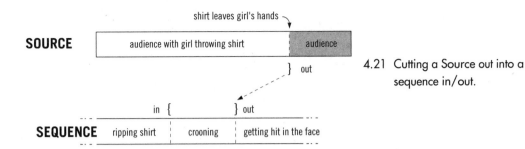

4.21 Cutting a Source out into a sequence in/out.

Notice that in each of these examples, you give up a certain amount of control. In the first and third examples, you control the duration of the segment and when that segment cuts into the sequence, but you don't control at which point it ends in the sequence. Premiere determines the end by the duration of the source clip.

As this is somewhat confusing, an analogy might help: say you're shopping for a new sofa. You find the perfect one and measure it. It's seven feet long. (You could say that its duration is seven feet.) After it's delivered to your house, you need to decide where it's going to go. You decide that it would look really nice if its left edge was lined up with an arm chair. So you know how long your sofa is (seven feet), and you know where it's going to start (at the arm chair), but you can't control where it's going to end. It's going to end seven feet away from where it starts. You may want it to end near the TV, but if the TV is 10 feet away, you're out of luck (see Figure 4.22).

You could, of course, line its *other* end—its right side—up with the TV, but then you'd lose control over its start. It will now start seven feet away from the TV, which will be a bit far from the chair. So you need to ask yourself, Which is more important, that the

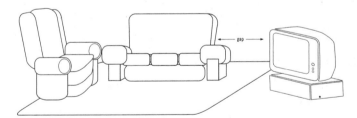

4.22 What is more important: lining the sofa up with the armchair or the television?

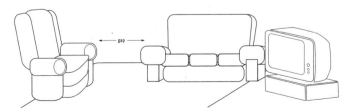

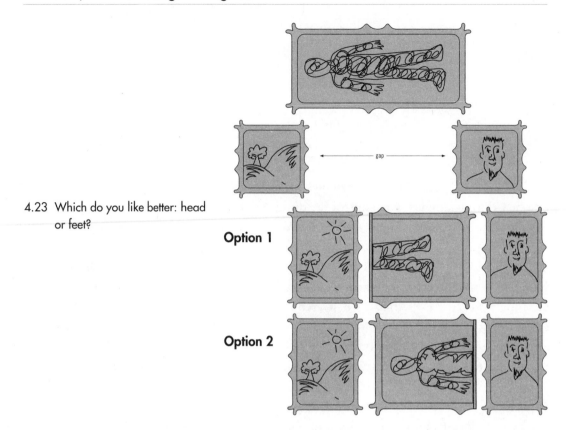

4.23 Which do you like better: head or feet?

Option 1

Option 2

sofa start at the chair or that it end at the TV? If it's vital that it stretch from the arm chair to the TV, you'll have to buy a longer sofa (giving up control over the length of the sofa).

One more analogy: Imagine you're the director of an art gallery, and you've just sold two paintings. You now have a six-foot gap on your wall where those paintings used to be. The only painting you have to fill that gap is a large portrait of a reclining nude—her head facing the left side of the canvas and her feet facing right. Unfortunately, the portrait is 18 feet long. You can't possibly fit it in a six-foot gap. So you decide to cut part of the painting off to make it fit. (Surely the artist won't mind.) You could line the nude's feet up with the right side of the gap (see Figure 4.23). You'll lose her head, but the painting will fit. Or you could line her head up with the left side of the gap. You'll have to cut off her feet, but once again the painting will fit where you need it to fit. Which is more important to you, the head or the feet?

You've now waded through a long description of three-point editing. I hope you now understand it conceptually. It's vital that you do understand these concepts, because three-point editing is a major part of an editor's job. It's the meat of the job. The rest is all gravy. If you're having trouble getting it, reread this section until it makes sense and try

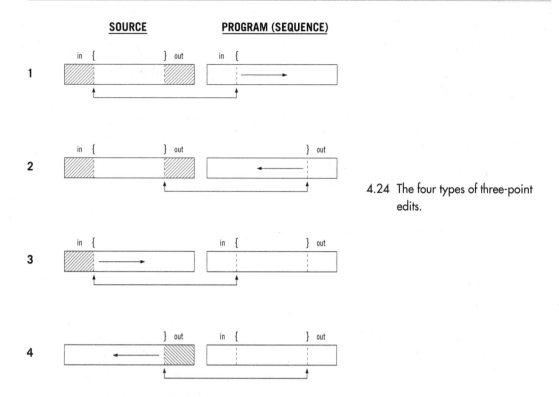

4.24 The four types of three-point edits.

these techniques out with your own footage. Figure 4.24 recaps the four possible ways of arranging your three points.

INSERT

When you make an insert edit, you splice the segment into your **Timeline** in such a way that all of the original **Timeline** footage is maintained. You don't record over anything. Let's say that in your **Timeline**, you have a shot of eggs being cracked followed by a shot of the yolks and whites in the mixing bowl. You would like to insert a close-up of the cook's face in between these two shots. Your end goal is cracking eggs / close-up / mixing bowl. You want Premiere Pro to move mixing bowl (and everything after it) to the right on the **Timeline**, leaving a gap between it and cracking eggs. You intend to drop the close-up into that gap. Of course, the end result will be that your sequence will get longer.

1. Begin your insert edit the same way you began your earlier overlay edits: load the close-up into the **Source Monitor** and mark a segment of it with in and out points. These in and out points are two of the three points you'll need to mark before completing the insert.

2. Now you need to switch over to the **Program Monitor,** where you will mark your third point, either an in point or an out point.

The in and out points on the **Source** side indicate the segment—the portion of the clip that you want to add to the sequence. The in or out point on the **Program** side indicates where you want that segment to go. If you mark an in point, your segment will start at that in point. If you mark an out point, your segment will end at that out point.

Another example: Suppose that you already have laid down a shot the cook cracking an egg on the side the bowl. You then cut to the yolk and white in the bowl. In between these shots, you want to cut in a close-up of the egg being cracked.

1. In this case, you load the close-up into the **Source Monitor** and mark in and out points around the segment you want to use.

2. Switching to the **Program Monitor,** you use its **VCR** controls (or its **Jog, Shuttle,** or **Timecode** controls) to cue the sequence to the exact point at which you want to insert the close-up. In this case, you cue to the last frame of the cook cracking the egg.

3. Mark an in point, using the **In Point** button below the **Program Monitor.** You now have your three points: in and out on the **Source** side and in on the **Program** side.

4. Select **Video Only, Audio Only,** or **Video and Audio** on the **Source** side to indicate what parts of the **Source** clip you want to add to the sequence.

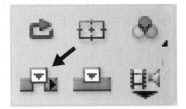

4.25 The Insert button.

5. Select **Video 1** track in the **Timeline** to indicate that you want Premiere Pro to insert the close-up in that track, which is where all your other segments are sitting.

6. Finally, click the **Insert** button (see Figure 4.25).

Premiere Pro will insert your segment, pushing all the video after it to the right. Your **Timeline** will grow longer by exactly the duration of your segment. If you're cutting in a three-second segment, your sequence will grow three seconds longer than it was before the insert.)

You can also insert by holding down the **Control** key and dragging a segment from the **Source Monitor** to the **Timeline.** Make sure you release the mouse button *before* releasing the **Control** key. If you release the **Control** key first, or if you don't hold down the **Control** key, you'll perform an overlay.

Note that the segment's in point (that you previously marked in the **Source Monitor**) is lined up with the sequence's in point (which you marked in the **Program Monitor**). When your three-point edit involves two in points—one on the **Source** side and one on the **Program** side—they will always line up in the sequence.

This is one kind of three-point edit, but there are many other kinds—the same kinds that you encountered in the **Overlay** section on page 70. The only rule is that you use three points. You have tremendous leeway as to where those points go and what kind of points they are. Possibilities include the following:

- **Source**: in and out, **Program**: in
- **Source**: in and out, **Program**: out
- **Source**: in, **Program**: in and out
- **Source**: out, **Program**: in and out

As an editor, part of your job will be to figure out which type of three-point edit to use in various situations.

REMOVING FRAMES FROM THE SEQUENCE

We've gone through several ways to add segments to a sequence, but what about removing segments? To do this, you can choose one of two kinds of edits: a lift or an extract. When you lift a segment, you delete some of the footage in the **Timeline**, leaving a gap behind, which, presumably, you'll fill later—otherwise when you play your sequence, you'll just see darkness during that section (see Figure 4.26).

When you extract a segment, you remove footage from the **Timeline**, and Premiere closes up the gap, shortening the duration of your sequence (see Figure 4.27).

Since lifts leave a gap of the same length as the removed segment, they don't shorten or lengthen your sequence.

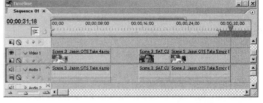

4.26 Lifting a segment from the Timeline.

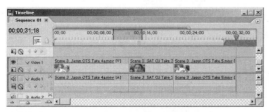

4.27 Extracting a segment from the Timeline.

1. Whether you lift or extract, you begin by setting in and out points on the **Program** side to mark a span of your **Timeline,** the span you want to remove.

   You can use the **Program Monitor** in point and out point buttons, or you can use the **I** and **O** keys on the keyboard (see the section on keyboard shortcuts on page 83), as long as you've first activated the **Program Monitor** by clicking it. If you don't activate the **Program Monitor,** you risk adding in and out points on the **Source** side, where lifts and extracts won't do anything. Alternately, you can click the **Timeline** to activate it. Since the **Timeline** and the **Program Monitor** are tied together, clicking either one achieves the same result.

2. Mark as much or as little of the **Timeline** for removal as you want.

   The segment that you mark doesn't have to span just a single clip. You can include multiple clips. Just make sure your in and out points surround them. You can even remove part of a clip by marking just that part with in and out points. You can set an in point halfway into one clip and an out point halfway into the next clip. When you lift or extract, Premiere will remove half of both clips.

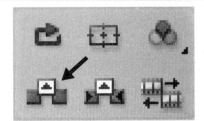

4.28 The Lift button

3. Select the **Timeline** track you want to affect. Click the track's name to select it (e.g., click **Video 1**).

4. Finally, click the **Lift** button to remove the footage from the **Timeline** and leave a gap behind (see Figure 4.28). Or click the **Extract** button to remove the footage and have Premiere close up the gap (see Figure 4.29).

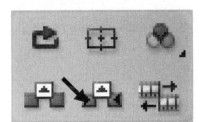

4.29 The Extract button

CLOSING GAPS

If there's a gap in your **Timeline,** left behind by a lift edit or some other action, you can quickly close it up by right-clicking the gap and choosing **Ripple Delete** from the pop-up menu. Premiere will remove the gap and shift all of the subsequent footage to the left, shortening the duration of the sequence, as in Figure 4.30.

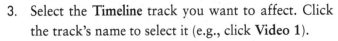
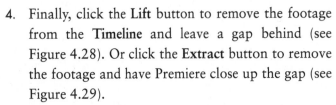

4.30 To close a Timeline gap, right-click it and choose the Ripple Delete option from the pop-up menu.

Deleting an entire clip from the Timeline

If you want to delete an entire clip (not part of a clip or a span that starts partway through one clip and ends partway through another clip), the easiest way is to click it in the **Timeline** and then press **Delete** on the keyboard. When clicking the clip in the **Timeline**, just click it once to select it for deletion. Don't double-click it. Double-clicking a **Timeline** clip loads it back into the **Source Monitor**.

Replacing parts of the sequence with new footage

You already know how to replace parts of the sequence by performing overlays. Overlays "tape over" parts of the sequence with whatever segment you've marked in the **Source Monitor**. Here are a couple of tips that will speed things up for you.

When you want to replace a specific part of the sequence, mark in and out points on the **Program** side, specifying the portion of the **Timeline** you'd like to replace, and select the track you want to affect. Then mark either an in point or an out point in the **Source Monitor** and perform an overlay.

If you want to replace an entire clip in the sequence, right-click that clip and choose **Marker>Set Sequence Marker>In and Out around Selection** from the menu. Or you can press the **Forward Slash** (/) key on the keyboard. Premiere will select the entire clip. Then you need only mark a third point in the **Source Monitor** and perform an overlay.

You can even mark a gap in the **Timeline**. Just click the gap to select it, select the appropriate track and choose **Marker>Set Sequence Marker>In and Out around Selection** from the menu. Or you can press the **Forward Slash** (/) key on the keyboard. This is a great way to deal with the gap left behind by a lift edit.

You can also click the gap or clip to select it, right-click the time ruler at the top of the **Timeline**, and choose **Set Sequence Marker>In and Out around Selection** from the pop-up menu.

If you've selected multiple clips by **Shift**+clicking them, you can then press the forward slash (/) key on the keyboard to set in and out points around the selection.

ZOOMING IN THE TIMELINE

As you assemble your rough cut, your sequence may grow so long that you can't see all your **Timeline** on screen at once. You may have noticed the horizontal scrollbar along the bottom of your **Timeline**, which you can use to display portions of the **Timeline** that are hidden off screen. The **Hand** tool on the **Tools** palette does the same thing. If you select it and drag anywhere in the **Timeline**, you can scroll without having to use the scroll bar. Click the **Selection** tool—the black arrow—when you're done using the **Hand** tool.

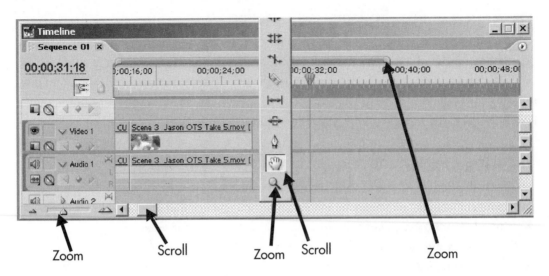

4.31 Zooming and scrolling.

But scrolling can take a long time, especially if you're editing a really long sequence. Often, a better option is zooming, which will allow you to look at a larger or smaller portion of your sequence on screen. Premiere gives you many ways to zoom (see Figure 4.31). Try any or all of the following:

- Slide the zoom slider to the left to zoom out and to the right to zoom in.

- Click the little mountains to the left of the **Zoom** slider to zoom out; click the bigger mountains to the right of the slider to zoom in.

- Drag the handles above the time ruler at the top of the **Timeline** to zoom in and out.

- Select the **Zoom** tool (the magnifying glass) on the **Tools** palette and click the **Timeline** to zoom in. **Alt**+click the **Timeline** with the **Zoom** tool to zoom out.

- Marquee select a portion of the **Timeline** with the **Zoom** tool to zoom in on that section. To marquee select, hold down the mouse button and drag the **Zoom** tool diagonally in the **Timeline**.

- Choose **Sequence>Zoom in** or **Sequence>Zoom out** from the menu.

- Press the equals (=) key on the keyboard to **Zoom** in and the minus (-) key on the keyboard to zoom out.

- Email Adobe and tell them that they haven't given us enough ways to zoom in and out of the **Timeline**.

Four-point editing

Though most of the time it's more helpful to mark only three points, you can mark in and out points on both the **Source** side and the **Program** side. Generally, when you do this, you'll either mark a **Source** segment that's too long or short to fill the marked region in the sequence. When you click the **Insert** or **Overlay** button, Premiere will pop up a dialog window, asking you how you'd like it to resolve this mismatch.

If the **Source** segment is too small, you can tell Premiere to ignore the in point in the sequence, in which case you'll really be performing a three-point edit, with in and out points in the **Source Monitor** and an out point in the sequence. Or you can tell Premiere to ignore the sequence out point, which will also amount to a three-point edit, this time with in and out points in the **Source** and an in point in the sequence.

Your other option is to allow Premiere to change the **Source** clip's speed so that it lengthens to fill the gap. Your clip will then play in slow motion when you view that part of the sequence in the **Program Monitor**.

If the source is too long, Premiere will offer to cut frames off the left side or the right side of the **Source** clip, so that it will fit between your in and out markers in the **Timeline**. You can allow Premiere to change your clip's speed. In this case, the clip will get shorter and run in fast motion.

SPEED TIPS FOR THREE-POINT EDITING

Real men don't eat quiche, and real editors don't use the mouse. Or at least they avoid the mouse whenever possible and use the keyboard instead. Why? Because working with the keyboard is faster, and for most editing jobs, time is money.

You can complete almost all three-point editing tasks without touching the mouse, using only keyboard shortcuts that are fairly easy to remember. Since you're reading this book, chances are you're just beginning as an editor. Why not *start* by using the keyboard commands, so that you learn them right away. If you start using them now, they'll be pounded into your head by the time you finish your first lengthy project.

Specific shortcuts will be divulged in the following sections.

Loading multiple clips into the source monitor

As you create a sequence, you may need to add a segment of clip A, a segment of clip B, and then another segment from clip A. In fact, when editing a dialog scene between two people, it's very common to cut back and forth between two clips, one focused on each actor as he or she speaks. It would be slow work if you had to keep going back to the **Project** window to reload the same clip, over and over. Luckily, you don't have to do this.

Premiere keeps track of all the clips you've loaded into the **Source Monitor.** You can reload these clips by clicking on the name of the currently loaded clip, at the top left of the monitor (see Figure 4.32). A menu will drop down, and you'll see a list of all the clips you've previously loaded. To reload one of these clips, just click its name.

4.32 From the menu at the top of the Source monitor, you can select any previously loaded clip.

If you know you've going to be working with a group of clips from the **Project** window, you can pre-load them all into the menu. Just hold down the **Control** key and click each clip you'd like to add. Or if you click one clip and then **Shift**+click another clip, which will select both those clips and any clips that are in between them. To remove a clip that you've accidentally added to the group, **Control**+click it.

Once you've selected a group of clips, drag any one of them into the **Source Monitor.** When you drag, all of the clips in the group will be loaded into the monitor, and you'll be able to access them through the menu.

Unfortunately, Premiere does not ship with a keyboard shortcut that allows you to toggle through all of the clips loaded into the **Source Monitor**—so you should add one yourself!

1. Select **Edit>Keyboard Customization** from the menu (see Figure 4.33).

2. In the **Keyboard Customization** window, select the **Window** option from the lower of the two dropdown menus.

3. In the **Commands** list, expand the **Monitor** and **Trim** windows group by clicking the triangle to the left of its name (see Figure 4.34).

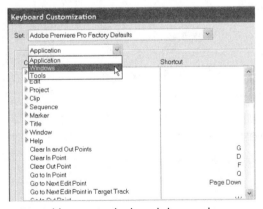

4.33 Add your own keyboard shortcuts by choosing Edit>Keyboard Customization from the menu.

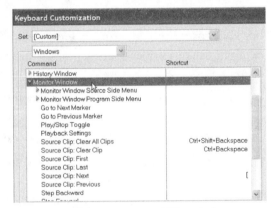

4.34 Expand the Monitor and Trim windows group.

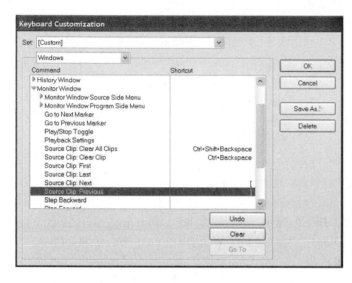

4.35 Type the bracket keys as shortcuts for Source Clip:Next and Source Clip: Previous.

4. Scroll down in the **Commands** list until you see the two commands called **Source Clip: Next** and **Source Clip:Previous**.

5. In the **Shortcuts** list (the column to the right of the commands list), click the area to the right of **Source Clip:Next**.

6. Type a] (right-facing bracket).

7. In the **Shortcuts** list, click the area to the right of **Source Clip:Previous**.

8. Type a [(left-facing bracket) (see Figure 4.35).

9. Click the **OK** button.

Now you will be able to toggle back through all of the clips loaded into your **Source Monitor** by pressing the left or right bracket keys. To learn more about keyboard customization, see Appendix A on page 311.

J, K, and L keys

These keys are the editor's best friends. L plays forwards, K stops, and J plays backwards. You can remember that J and L play in opposite directions by noticing that a J looks pretty much like a backwards L. The horizontal line at the bottom of the L indicates the forward play direction. The hook at the bottom of the J indicates the backward play direction.

Notice that on your keyboard, J, K, and L are in a row. So you can rest three fingers of your right hand on those keys, press L to play, and when you get to a frame where you want to set an in or out point, press K to stop. If you accidentally go too far, press J to play backwards until you find the frame you're searching for. Then press K to stop again.

After you do this a few times, you should be able to just rest your fingers on these keys and use them without looking at the keyboard (see Figure 4.36).

Pressing L repeatedly will let you play in fast motion. Each time you press **L**, Premiere will play faster and faster. Similarly, pressing **J** repeatedly will play in reverse faster and faster. Remember that keyboards repeat keys if you hold them down (if you're typing in your word processor, and you hold down the S key, you'll type SSSSSSSSSSSSSSSSSSSSSS.) So if you want to play at normal speed, just tap the L or J keys. Holding them down is just like pressing them repeatedly, which will cause Premiere to play faster and faster.

Pressing **Shift+L** will play in slow motion. Pressing **Shift+J** will play backwards in slow motion. So if you press **L** to find a specific frame but go too far, press **K** to stop. Then you

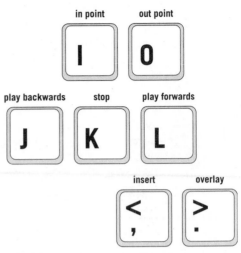

4.36 The most important editing keys are grouped about J, K, and L on the keyboard.

might want to press **Shift+J** to back up slowly, pressing **K** to stop when you find the exact frame you're looking for. And if the slow motion is not slow enough for you, you can press the **Left Arrow** key repeatedly to back up frame by frame and the **Right Arrow** key to move forward frame by frame. The **Home** key will rewind to the beginning of the active monitor; the **End** key will fast-forward to the last frame of the selected monitor.

You can also press the spacebar to play and then press it again to stop. The spacebar toggles between play and stop, so it's like the L key and the K key combined.

Control + the Tick Mark key: All of the keys mentioned so far will play, stop, or move the around in one of the two monitors, but which one? It all depends on which monitor you've most recently activated. You can activate a monitor by clicking it with the mouse. If you click the **Source Monitor** with the mouse and then press the spacebar or L key, the **Source Monitor** will play, assuming you've loaded a clip into it. If you click the **Program Monitor,** the same keys will play the sequence (assuming there is a sequence in your **Timeline**). **Control+`** (the tickmark key, which is just above the **Tab** key) will toggle you back and forth between the two monitors so that you don't have to use the mouse.

If your keyboard keys don't play either monitor, it's because your entire monitor window is deselected. Maybe you recently clicked the **Project** window. To select the monitor window, just click either monitor with the mouse (or press **Control+Tab** repeatedly to toggle-select each window until the **Monitor** window becomes selected. Then you can use the **Control+`** shortcut to toggle between them.

I and O keys: The I and O keys set in and out points (I for in, O for out) in the active monitor. Conveniently, **I** and **O** are next to each other on the keyboard and right above J, K, and L. These five keys are standards in all major nonlinear editing applications. So if you ever switch to Avid or Final Cut Pro, you may not know much about those applications, but you are guaranteed that **I** will set an in point, **O** will set an out point, and J, K, and L will play backwards, stop, and play forwards.

D, F, and G keys: To get rid of in and out points in the active monitor, press G. You can remember this if you think of **G** as the **Go Away** key. To get rid of just the in point, press D. To get rid of just the out point, click F. Notice that D, F, and G are in a row on your keyboard.

Q and the W keys: To go to the in point (to move the **Current Time Indicator** to the out point), press **Q**. To go to the in point, press **W**. These keys are also next to each other on the keyboard. One cool trick that you can do only with the mouse is to press the **Play In To Out** button (there's one for each monitor), which will just play from the in point to the out point (see Figure 4.37). This is a great way to evaluate whether

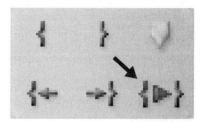

4.37 The Play In To Out button.

your current in and out points are really going to give you what you want. You can set a preference to map this button to a keyboard shortcut. For more information on keyboard preferences, see "Preferences" on page 317 in Appendix A.

Comma key and the Period key: The comma (,) key inserts and the period (.) key overlays. Notice that these keys are directly below the J, K, and L keys. So by using a small area of the keyboard, you can find frames, set in and out points, and then insert or overlay—all the necessary steps in performing a three-point edit.

A Quick Sequence

Putting all the keys together, here's how you can use them to quickly assemble a sequence:

1. Load a clip into the **Source Monitor**, which will also activate the **Monitor** Window; so you don't have to click it.

2. Then use J, K, or L to move to specific frames and set in and out points (or just an in or and out point), using **I** and **O**.

3. Press **Control+`** to toggle to the **Program Monitor.**

4. Once again use **J, K,** and **L** to move to a specifics frames and then **I** and **O** to set in and out points (or just an in point or an out point).

5. Click the **Take Audio and Video** button to choose the option you want. (To map this button to the keyboard, so you don't have to use the mouse, see "Keyboard Short-cuts" on page 311 in Appendix A).

6. Click a track name to select a target track.

7. Press the comma (,) key to insert or the period (.) key to overlay.

Taking Audio, Video, or Both: no shortcut: Unfortunately, you do have to toggle the **Take Audio and Video** button, but you probably won't have to keep remaking these choices each time you add a clip to your sequence. Just use the mouse to select default a choice, and then only make new choices when you have to. Or to learn how to assign keyboard shortcuts to these functions, see "Keyboard Shortcuts" on page 311 in Appendix A.

Control+= and Control+−: To target a track, you'll need to first select the **Timeline** win-dow. Press **Control+Tab** repeatedly to toggle-select windows until the **Timeline** is selected. Then you can use the keyboard to target a track. **Control+=** (the equal sign) will select the video track *above* the currently selected track (e.g., if **Video 1** is selected, **Control+=** will deselect that and select **Video 2**). **Control+−** (the minus—or dash—key, right next to the equal sign key) will select the video *below* the currently selected track. **Shift+Control+=** and **Shift+Control+−** will select audio tracks above and below the currently selected track.

Control+Z: Undo. This is the editor's *bestest* best friend. The hardest thing about **Undo** is remembering it exists. If you make a mistake, don't panic. Just press **Control+Z.** Press it several times, and you'll undo your last few steps.

Control+S: This is the universal keyboard shortcut for **Save.** Press these keys now and again so that if you have a power outage or a computer crash, Premiere will have saved your work up until then. True, Premiere has an autosave feature (see "Saving" on page 30 in Chapter 2), but it's not a bad idea to click **Control+S** every now and again, just so you can feel safe.

Memorize these shortcuts

As with most programs, Premiere comes with dozens of keyboard shortcuts that you can change or customize, as is explained in "Keyboard Shortcuts" on page 311 in Appendix A. You don't need to memorize all of them, but if you take the time to memo-rize the ones in Table 4.1, you'll whiz through your editing tasks like a speed demon. Try completing several projects with this table in front of you and force yourself to use these keys instead of the mouse, and by the time you're done, they'll be stuck in your brain.

Table 4.1   Premiere Keyboard Shortcuts

Key	Shortcut
J	Play backwards
K	Stop
L	Play forwards
J multiple times	Play backwards in fast motion
L multiple times	Play forwards in fast motion
Shift+J	Play backwards in slow motion
Shift+L	Play forwards in slow motion
Spacebar	Play/stop
Left Arrow	Move to next frame
Right Arrow	Move to previous frame
Home	Move to beginning of sequence or clip
End	Move to end of sequence or clip
Control+Tab	Toggle-select windows
Control+' (Tick)	Toggle between Source and Program monitors
I	Set in point
O	Set out point
/	Set in and out points around selected clip(s) or gap
D	Remove in point
F	Remove out point
G	Remove both in and out point
Q	Go to in point
W	Go to out point

Table 4.1   Premiere Keyboard Shortcuts (Continued)

Key	Shortcut
, (Comma)	Insert
. (Period)	Overlay
; (Semicolon)	Lift
' (Single Quote)	Extract
Control+=	Select higher video track
Control+−	Select lower video track
Shift+Control+=	Select lower audio track
Shift+Control+−	Select higher audio track
Control+Z	Undo
Control+S	Save
= (Equals)	Zoom into the Timeline
− (Minus)	Zoom out of the Timeline

Inserting and overlaying by dragging from the source monitor

If you absolutely loathe the keyboard, you can perform insert or overlays by simply dragging clips from the **Source Monitor** to the **Timeline**. In this case, you need to mark only in and out points in the **Source Monitor** to indicate the segment that you want to cut into the sequence. You don't need to mark any points in the **Timeline**, because you'll indicate where the segment goes by where you drag. You'll also indicate the target track by where you drag; so there's no need to click a track name if you choose to insert or overlay by dragging.

One thing you will have to remember to do before you drag is to toggle the **Take Audio and Video** button to the option you want, so that Premiere knows whether you want to cut in the video, the audio, or both.

After you've marked the segment in the **Source Monitor,** drag the segment where you want to place it in the **Timeline** to perform an overlay.

Control+drag the segment from the **Source Monitor** to the **Timeline** to perform an Insert. It seems there's no escaping the keyboard after all!

Using the Timeline Current Time Indicator as an in point

When inserting or overlaying, it's allowable to mark just two points in the **Source Monitor**—an in and an out point—and then park the **Current Time Indicator** in the **Timeline** where you want the segment to go. If no third point is marked in the **Timeline**, Premiere assumes that the **Current Time Indicator**'s position is an in point.

As always, toggle the **Take Audio and Video** button to the selection you want, select the appropriate track, and then press the **Insert** or **Overlay** button. Premiere will cut the marked segment of the **Source** clip into the **Timeline** starting at the location of the **Current Time Indicator.**

Creating subclips

Long clips can be difficult to work with. And a single long clip can only contain one segment at a time, because within that clip, you can only mark one in point and one out point. Sometimes it's convenient to work with shorter clips. You can create such short clips by loading longer clips into the **Source Monitor** and dividing them up into subclips. Premiere stores subclips back in the **Project** window, where they look and act like regular clips. You can load subclips into the **Source Monitor** just as you can load normal clips, by double-clicking them or by dragging them.

One instance in which you might want to create subclips is when your original clip starts with a shot of one person—let's say a lion tamer. In the same clip, there's a second shot, this time of the lion. You could separate the two shots into two subclips, one of the lion and the other of the lion tamer.

To create a subclip:

1. Load the original, longer clip into the **Source Monitor.**

2. Mark the segment that you'd like to turn into a subclip by setting in and out points.

   In the example of the lion and lion tamer, you'd mark an in point when the lion first appeared and an out point at the lion's final frame.

3. Finally, drag from the **Source Monitor** to the **Project** window (not to the **Timeline**) (see Figure 4.38).

Premiere will create a subclip in the **Project** window. Premiere will give the subclip the same name as the original clip, which is confusing. So you may want to rename your subclip by right-clicking it in the **Project** window and choosing the **Rename** option from the pop-up menu (see Figure 4.39).

4.38 You can create a subclip by dragging a marked segment from the Source monitor to the Project window.

Note that each subclip will contain all of the frames from the original clip, so in a way, subclips are just copies. But subclips contain a unique set of in and out points. So in the lion example, the subclip—which you might rename "*lion,*" to indicate that it focuses on the lion and not the lion tamer—contains both the lion *and* the lion tamer frames. But the lion segment is marked, ready for an insert or overlay, in the subclip. In the original clip, you're free to move the in and out points to new locations—for instance, around the lion tamer's frames. Any changes you make to in and out points in the original clip will not affect the in and out points in the subclip and vice versa.

Loading a clip from the Timeline to the Source Monitor

If you double-click a clip in the **Timeline**, Premiere will load that segment into the **Source Monitor**, showing

4.39 To rename a subclip, right-click it in the Project window and choose the Rename option from the pop-up menu.

you the in and out points that you set when you originally cut the segment into the sequence. This might lead you to the false belief that changing the in and out points in the **Source Monitor** will update them in the **Timeline**. Alas, this is not so. Generally, the purpose of loading a segment from the **Timeline** into the **Source Monitor** is because you want to insert a second copy of that segment somewhere else in the **Timeline**.

If you want to adjust in and out points for a clip already in the **Timeline**, you'll have to use trimming tools, which are explored in "Trim Tools" on page 101 in Chapter 5.

Automating to the sequence

Instead of assembling a sequence yourself, you can let Premiere do it for you. To begin, load all the clips you want to use into the **Source Monitor** and choose the segment that you'd like to use from each clip, marking that segment with in and out points (see "Loading a clip from the Timeline to the Source Monitor" on page 92). When you finish marking a clip, don't add it to the sequence. Instead, move on to the next clip and mark its in and out points. Keep marking in and out points until you've chosen segments from all of your clips.

Note that you can only mark one segment in each clip, because each clip can only have one in point and one out point. You can get around this limitation by creating subclips of any clips from which you want to use multiple segments. Each subclip can have its own in and out points.

When you're finished marking segments, click the **Icon View** button at the bottom of the **Project** window. Premiere will display a thumbnail image for each clip (see Figure 4.40). By default, the icon will be the frame at the clip's in point, which will be the first frame of the clip if you haven't explicitly set another in point in the **Source Monitor.** You can set another frame to appear as the icon, selecting the clip in the **Project** window, cueing the thumbnail at the top of the **Project** window

4.40 Icon View displays a thumbnail image for each clip.

to a specific frame, and then clicking the **Set Poster Frame** button. Note that Premiere will only display your choice of poster frame if it's a later frame than the in point. That is to say, Premiere will display whichever frame comes last, the poster frame or the in point.

You can put the clips in the order you'd like them to appear in the sequence by dragging them with the mouse.

When you're done ordering them, click the first clip and **Shift**+click the last clip. Premiere will select the two clips you clicked and all of the clips between them. Or you can select clips one by one by **Control**+clicking each clip you want to include (see Figure 4.41). If you include any unwanted clips by accident, **Control**+click them. **Control**+clicking a selected clip will remove that clip from the selection group.

Select the clips in the order you'd like them to appear, and make sure that only the clips you want in your sequence are selected.

The easiest way to determine which clip will go first, which clip will go second, and so on, is to select the clips in the order you'd like them to appear. So if you want clip B to appear first, followed by clip A and then clip C, **Control**+click **clip B**, then clip A, then clip C.

Once you're done selecting clips, click the **Automate to Sequence** button at the bottom of the **Project** window (see Figure 4.42).

Premiere will display the **Automate to Sequence** dialog window (see Figure 4.43).

By default, Premiere will cut the clips into the sequence in the order in which they're sorted in the **Project** window. To get Premiere to respect your selection order, choose the **Selection Order** option from the **Order** dropdown menu.

4.41 Select the clips you'd like to include in the sequence.

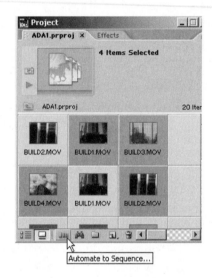

4.42 The Automate to Sequence button.

The **Method** option is an important consideration only if you already have clips in your sequence and you're using **Automate to Sequence** to add new clips. It's not important if you're adding clips to a new, empty sequence. Premiere wants to know if you want to Insert the new clips (the default), in which case it will shove all the old clips to the right to make room for the new ones. Or you can choose to overlay, in which case older clips will be "taped over" by the new ones. **Automate to Sequence** will add the new clips starting at the position of the **Current Time Indicator** in the **Timeline**.

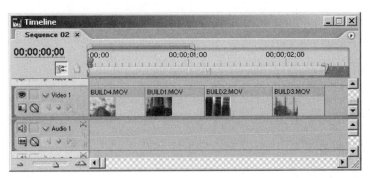

4.43 The Automate to Sequence dialog window. *(left)*

4.44 Clips added to a sequence by the Automate to Sequence option. *(below)*

Unless you change the default options, Premiere will overlap each clip with the next clip and add a crossfade transition between them. To learn more about transitions, see Chapter 6 on page 159. If you don't want Premiere to add a transition, set the **Clip Overlap** option to zero frames and uncheck the **Apply Default Video Transition** option.

Finally, if your clips contain both audio and video, you can use the **Ignore Options** to tell Premiere to use only the audio or only the video when it cuts the clips into the sequence. When you click **OK**, Premiere will edit your selected clips into the sequence (see Figure 4.44).

WRAPPING UP

It's hard to stress enough how quickly you should work while you assemble your rough cut. You'll want to get a sequence laid down in the **Timeline** so that you can move on to the really fun and creative part, which is trimming (discussed in the next chapter). To work as quickly as possible, memorize those keyboard shortcuts and don't obsess over details. It's an editor's job to obsess over details, but not at this point. At this point, you're creating the details. So stop reading now and throw something together. When you're finished, read on. In the next chapter, you'll learn how to turn lead into gold.

Chapter 5

Trimming

Now that you've finished assembling a rough cut, it's time to trim. While three-point editing is the nuts-and-bolts, assembly-line part of editing, trimming is the artistic part. As you trim, you'll refine your sequence, shaping it into a story. You'll make dozens of small decisions that will ultimately make your sequence uniquely yours. Another editor, armed with the same rough-cut sequence, would trim it very differently from you. Trimming is when you inject your personality into the sequence.

When you trim, you will often add back footage that you deleted during the three-point editing stage. How is this possible? To understand the process, you first need to get a handle on...*handles*.

HANDLES

Handles are the bits of video you cut off when you made your original three-point edit—the parts before your in point and after your out point. Though these parts seem to be deleted, they're not. They're merely hidden. And if you imagine the visible portion of your clip—the portion between the in and out points—to be a tea tray, the missing bits are like invisible handles on either side (see Figure 5.1).

A more common way of imagining footage is to think of it as a scroll, like a Torah. The visible footage, between the in and out points, is the unrolled portion of the scroll. The handles are the rolled up parts on either side, as in Figure 5.2.

97

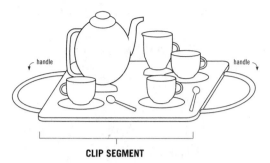

CLIP SEGMENT

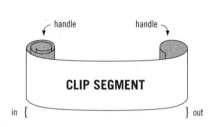

5.1   Like tea trays, clips can have handles on both sides.

5.2   You can think of a trimmed clip as a scroll. The rolled up parts are handles.

Real scrolls can be unrolled from either end to reveal more text—or they can be rolled up to hide more text. Similarly, you can add footage from a handle (footage that you "deleted" when you made your three-point edit) or remove currently displayed footage. No action is final or irrevocable. You can tinker as long as you like—adding more footage, changing your mind, removing, changing your mind again, adding back. Regardless of what you do, the segments in your sequence always refer back to their sources in the **Project** window. The sources always refer to *all* the footage. The clips in the sequence contain in and out points, which simply tell Premiere what portion of the source footage to hide and what portion to show. The hidden parts get "rolled up" as handles.

One more way to visualize handles is to think of them as grayed-out areas beyond in and out points. To add more footage (say, to the beginning of the clip), slide the in point to the left. You can think of it as unwinding the left end of a scroll, as in Figure 5.3.

To remove footage from the beginning of the clip, slide the in point closer towards the center of the clip, as in Figure 5.4.

And, of course, you can perform the same operations on the out point, moving it to the right to reveal more footage, as in Figure 5.5. Or move to the left to hide more footage, as in Figure 5.6.

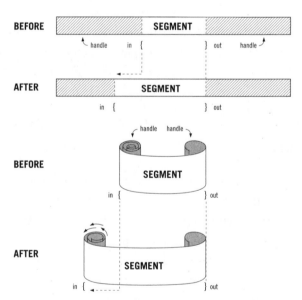

5.3   Sliding an in point to the left reveals more footage and shrinks the left-side handle.

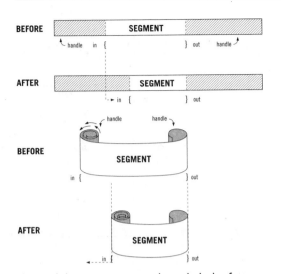

5.4 Sliding an in point to the right hides footage and adds more handle.

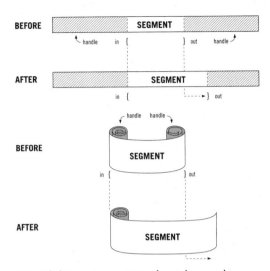

5.5 Sliding an out point to the right reveals more footage and shrinks the right-side handle.

Editors use the word *trimming* to describe the action of rolling or unrolling handles (moving the in/out points to hide or reveal footage). Note that in everyday speech, we use "trim" to mean making something shorter, as in trimming our toenails. But within the world of nonlinear editing, trimming can mean pruning away or adding back. Editors refer to removing footage as *trimming in,* because to do so you have to slide the in or out point *in* towards the center of a clip. *Trimming out* means adding back parts of the footage, because to trim out you have to slide an in or out point out, away from the center of the clip. Sometimes, you'll hear editors call the in point the

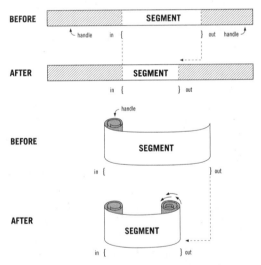

5.6 Sliding an out point to the left hides footage and creates more right-side handle.

head of the clip and the out point the *tail* of the clip. Keeping this in mind, can you translate the following editorese into English? "I'm going to trim out the tail of my clip." It means that the editor is going to slide the clip's out point to the right (like unrolling the right side of a scroll) to reveal more footage. The clip will be longer after the trim.

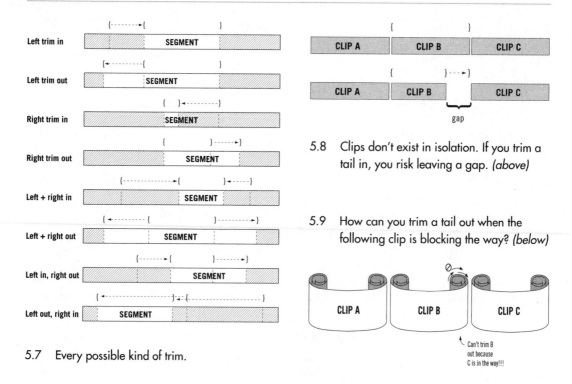

5.7 Every possible kind of trim.

5.8 Clips don't exist in isolation. If you trim a tail in, you risk leaving a gap. *(above)*

5.9 How can you trim a tail out when the following clip is blocking the way? *(below)*

There are four different types of trims: head trims in, head trims out, tail trims in, and tail trims out. You can also perform combination trims, in which both head and tail are trimmed in or out, or the head is trimmed one way and the tail is trimmed the opposite way (see Figure 5.7).

Clips don't exist in isolation. They are packed together, side by side, in a crowded timeline. When you trim a clip, you will inevitably affect its neighbors. For instance, if you trim a clip's tail in, you risk leaving a gap between it and the clip to its right, as in Figure 5.8.

Worse, what if you want to trim a clip's tail to the right, adding more footage at the end of the clip? Seemingly you can't, because the clip immediately to the right of it is blocking the way, taking up the space where the added footage would go (see Figure 5.9).

Luckily, Premiere's trim tools help you fix these problems. These tools include the **Selection** tool, the **Ripple Edit** tool, the **Rolling Edit** tool, the **Slip** tool, and the **Slide** tool, and they're all located on Premiere's **Tools** palette. In the following section we'll examine each of these tools in great detail. Learn them well. They are an editor's main arsenal.

TRIM TOOLS

After you make a rough cut using three-point editing techniques discussed in the previous chapter, you will probably want to refine your editing choices—adding a little here, removing a little there, reordering, and splicing in new material. You can make these refinements using the trim tools. The most basic trim tools is the **Selection** tool—the default black arrow tool that is selected for you if you don't click any tool button.

Selection tool

When you point to the tail of a clip with the **Selection** tool (see Figure 5.10), the mouse cursor changes to a bracketed trim symbol. Once you see this symbol, you can hold down the mouse button and drag to the left to trim in (shorten) the tail of the clip. For instance, if the clip shows a Yellow Cab zooming across the screen and then a bus also zooming, you might want to cut out the bus. Using the **Selection** tool, drag the tail to the left, until you no longer see the bus in the **Program Monitor**. It's as though you've rolled up a rug at its right side, hiding some of the pattern on its surface. If you change your mind and want to see the bus again, drag the tail to the right until you've brought back the bus footage. You've unrolled the rug.

What if you can't trim?

If Premiere doesn't let you drag to the right, it's because you've unrolled the clip all the way (once a carpet is all the way unrolled, you can't unroll it further). If you've added all of the original source footage, you can't extend the clip any longer—there's no more footage to add. Premiere indicates that a clip is fully extended by placing a small triangle at the upper-right corner of a clip's tail, if the tail is fully extended and/or at the upper-left corner of a clip's head, if its head is fully extended (see Figure 5.11).

Note that you can't see the triangles while the clip is selected (see Figure 5.12).

5.10 Selection tool.

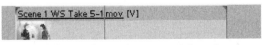

5.11 Small triangles in clip's upper-left and upper-right corners indicate a clips is fully extended (no handle).

5.12 Note that you can't see the triangles while the clip is selected.

If you find you can't trim out any more, try deselecting the clip by clicking another clip or a gray area on the timeline. Once the clip is no longer selected, you'll be able to see the triangles. Even if you do see a triangle, you can still trim in—shortening a clip. If you do so, the triangle will disappear. If you trim all the way out again, the triangle will reappear.

Don't trim the wrong clip!

Another possible gotcha is that it's very easy to accidentally trim the wrong clip: when using the Selection tool to trim, you point to the crack between two clips. You have to tell Premiere which of the two clips you want to trim, the clip to the left of the crack or the clip to the right of the crack. If you nudge your mouse a little to the left, the bracket cursor will point to the left, indicating that you're about to trim the left clip's tail. If you nudge your mouse a little to the right, the bracket cursor will point to the right, indicating that you're about to trim the right clip's head (see Figure 5.13).

Watch the Timecode

As you trim, take a look at the **Program Monitor**. It will display the new end frame if you're dragging in from the tail and the new start frame if you're dragging in from the head. Also note the numbers at the lower-right corner of the **Program Monitor**. Normally, this readout displays the position of the **Current Time Indicator**, telling you how far into the sequence the **Program Monitor's** currently displayed frame is. But while you trim, it

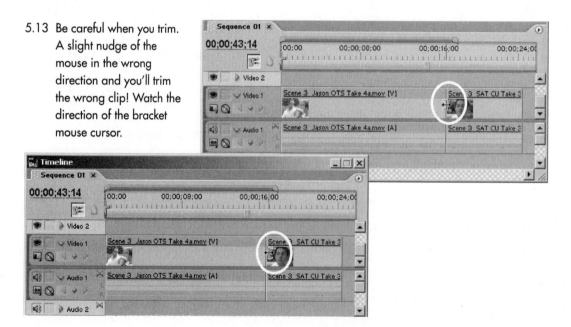

5.13 Be careful when you trim. A slight nudge of the mouse in the wrong direction and you'll trim the wrong clip! Watch the direction of the bracket mouse cursor.

tells you how many frames you're adding or removing. If you trim in, you'll see a minus sign to the left of the numbers, indicating that you're removing (subtracting) frames. If you trim out, you'll see a plus sign, indicating that you're adding frames. The numbers, separated by semicolons from left to right, indicate hours, minutes, seconds, and frames. So if you see +00;00;03;18, you've added 3 seconds and 18 frames. This numbering system is called *timecode*.

The timecode in the bottom right tells you the changing duration of the clip, so if a clip reads 00;02;11;25 before a trim, that means that the clip is (0 hours) 2 minutes, 11 seconds, and 25 frames long. If after a trim, it reads, 00;02;11;01, the clip is now (0 hours, 2 minutes, 11 seconds, and 2 frames long. You've trimmed 23 frames away. The numbers on the left should read –00;00;00;23.

Problems with the Selection tool

The **Selection** tool will not let you trim out (lengthen) a clip if another clip is in the way. You'll notice another **Selection** tool drawback if you trim a clip in: Premiere will leave a gap between the clip you trimmed and its nearest neighbor (see Figure 5.14). There are various ways of closing up or filling these gaps, but you can save time by using other editing tools that don't leave gaps in the first place.

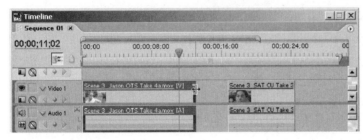

5.14 If you trim a tail to the left with the Selection tool, you'll leave a gap.

Other Selection tool tricks

But before we leave the **Selection** tool, note that it has some other uses besides trimming. For instance, you can use it to select a clip (hence the name "Selection tool") to indicate that you want to delete or move it somewhere else. Click a clip to select it. Premiere will highlight the clip to indicate that it's selected (see Figure 5.15).

Then you can press the **Delete** or **Backspace** key to delete the clip. Premiere will remove the clip and leave a gap in its place (see Figure 5.16). (The clip isn't really deleted. It's just removed from the **Timeline**. You can always find it in the **Project** window, load it back into the **Source Monitor**—where you'll notice that its most recent in and out points have been maintained—and edit it back into the **Timeline**.)

5.15 To select a clip, click it with the Selection tool.

5.16 Press the Delete or Backspace key on the keyboard to remove a selected clip.

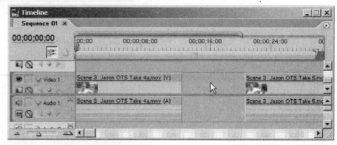

5.17 To move a selected clip to a new position, drag it with the Selection tool.

Or you can move a selected clip to a new position in the **Timeline** by dragging it there. But be warned that if you drag a clip on top of other clips, it will overwrite those clips (see Figure 5.17).

You can stop the clip from overwriting by holding down the **Control** key before you start dragging the clip and keeping the **Control** key held down until you drop the clip into its new location. **Control**+dragging inserts the clip instead of overwriting it. Just as with a three-point edit insert, other clips will be pushed to the right to make room for the clip you're dragging. To learn more about three-point editing, read "Three-Point Editing" on page 68.

If you hold down the **Shift** key and click multiple clips, you will select all of the clips you click, and Premiere will highlight them all. Then you can delete or move them using the methods discussed previously. To remove a clip from the selection group, **Shift**+click it a second time. You can also use the **Track Selection** tool, discussed later in this chapter on page 125, to select multiple clips (see Figure 5.18).

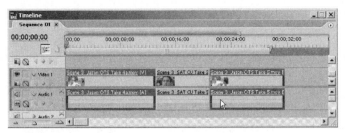

5.18 To select multiple clips, Shift+click them with the Selection tool.

Ripple Edit tool

Much more sophisticated than the **Selection** tool, the **Ripple Edit** tool allows you to trim one clip and affect all of the clips that follow after it, sending a *ripple* all the way to the end of the sequence (see Figure 5.19). As a result, those pesky gaps that you got with the **Selection** tool will no longer be a problem. Premiere will close them. Also, by using the **Ripple Edit** tool, you'll be able to trim out, even if other clips are in the way. Premiere will shove those clips over to make room for the footage you're adding.

Try using the **Ripple Edit** tool to trim in the tail of a clip. Select the tool, point to the clip's right edge and drag to the left (see Figure 5.20).

The **Ripple Edit** tool rolls up the right edge of the clip, as though it were rolling up a carpet. If you were using the **Selection** tool, this process would leave a gap to the right of the clip. But the **Ripple Edit** tool pulls all of the following clips along for the ride, closing up the gap. Since you've shortened one clip and dragged all the following clips to the left, you've made the entire sequence shorter than it was before you used the **Ripple Edit** tool.

5.19 The Ripple Edit tool.

You can also use the **Ripple Edit** tool to trim the tail of a clip out, which will unroll it, adding more footage, like unrolling a carpet (see Figure 5.21). Premiere will push all of the following clips to the right, to make room for the footage you are adding.

This action will cause the sequence's duration to change. To see exactly how many frames you're adding and how much longer you're making the entire sequence, watch the numbers on the lower left of the **Program Monitor**. As with **Selection** tool trimming, these show you how many frames you're adding or removing during a trim. The numbers at the lower-right display the changing duration of the clip, as you add or remove frames.

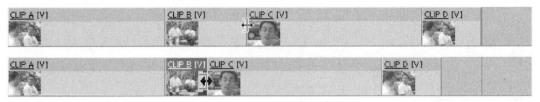

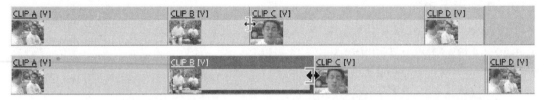

5.20   If you trim in a clip's tail with the Ripple Edit tool, clips to the right will move in, and the sequence will get shorter.

5.21   If you trim out a clip's tail with the Ripple Edit tool, clips to the right will move over to make room for the new footage.

While you're looking at the **Program Monitor**, you'll also notice that its display changes while you're using the **Ripple Edit** tool, as it does while you're using the rest of the trim tools discussed in this chapter. When performing a ripple edit, you always point your cursor to the edit (the crack) between two clips. The image on the left of the **Program Monitor** shows you the *final* frame of the left clip (its out point/tail). The image on the right shows you the *first* frame of the right clip (its in point/head). When you're editing, it's always important to think about how one shot is transitioning into another shot (see Figure 5.22). So these two views are vital. You want to see that you'll be cutting to the snarling panther immediately after the heroine screams. If she hasn't yet opened her mouth to scream, you'll trim out until you see her screaming.

Ripple Edit head trims: the big confusion

Most people understand what happens when you trim a clip's tail: dragging to the left shortens the clip and the rest of the sequence shifts downstream to close up the gap—the entire sequence gets shorter; dragging to the right lengthens the clip and the rest of the

5.22   Check the Program Monitor while using the Ripple Edit tool to see the tail of the left clip and the head of the right clip.

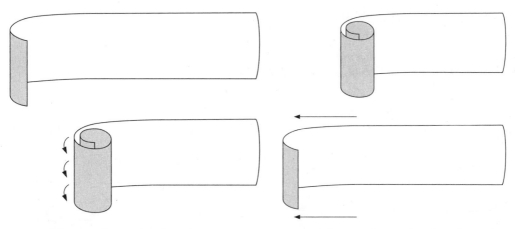

5.23 While using the Ripple Edit tool, trimming a
head to the right removes frames.

5.24 While using the Ripple Edit tool, trimming a
head to the left adds frames.

sequence shift upstream to make room for the new frames—the entire sequence gets longer.

Most people—even some pros—get confused when they trim a clip's *head* (left side, in point) using the **Ripple Edit** tool. At first, the result doesn't seem so puzzling: trimming to the right removes frames, while trimming to the left adds frames (see Figures 5.23 and 5.24).

Note that the exact opposite is true when you trim the tail. When you trim the tail to the right, the clip grows longer. When you trim to the left, it grows shorter (see Figure 5.25).

The first big confusion stems from the fact that we tend to think (wrongly) that trimming to the right lengthens and trimming to the left shortens. But that's only true for tail trimming. The opposite is true when you trim the head. (Again, imagine rolling and unrolling the left side of a carpet versus rolling and unrolling the right side of a carpet.)

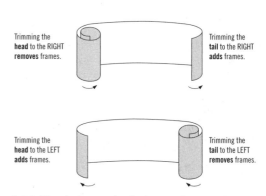

Trimming the **head** to the RIGHT **removes** frames.

Trimming the **tail** to the RIGHT **adds** frames.

Trimming the **head** to the LEFT **adds** frames.

Trimming the **tail** to the LEFT **removes** frames.

5.25 Head trims and tail trims act in opposite ways when you use the Ripple Edit tool.

The second big confusing—and the *bigger* of the big confusions—revolves around what happens to all the other clips in the sequence when you trim a clip's head. The result is confusing because Premiere does several things at once behind the scenes, but you see only the final result. The following section breaks the process down into the steps that go "under the hood."

Trimming the head to the left (adding frames)

Note **Trimming the Head to the Left:** This shifts the clip's in point so that it's further away from its out point—so that the distance between the in and out points is wider than it was before the trim—resulting in a longer clip with new frames at the *beginning*. The ending of the clip (the tail) will not gain any new frames.

Figure 5.26 shows how your **Timeline** looks before the trim. If clip B, the clip you're about to trim, was magically removed from the sequence, you could visualize it the way it looks in the top row of Figure 5.26, but the actual **Timeline** looks like the bottom row. The process goes:

1. You drag to the left, shrinking the handle, as shown in Figure 5.27.

2. Premiere moves all the following clips to the right to make room for your now-longer clip (see Figure 5.28).

3. Premiere moves your trimmed clip to the right, so that its new in point ends up where its old in point used to be (see Figure 5.29). Its out point touches its nearest neighbor to the right.

   The result is that the sequence gets longer (because you've added frames), and the new clips are at the beginning of your trimmed clip (see Figure 5.30). All subsequent clips are moved to the left.

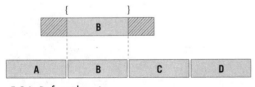

5.26 Before the trim.

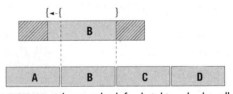

5.27 You drag to the left, shrinking the handle.

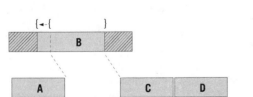

5.28 Premiere moves the following clips to the right.

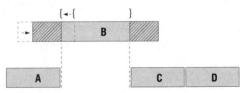

5.29 Premiere moves the trimmed clip to the right.

When you actually trim a head to the left, you don't experience all these steps. Instead, you start with something like Figure 5.31 and end with something similar to Figure 5.32. It looks like you've added new frames at the end of the clip, but that's an illusion. Your trim unrolled the head of

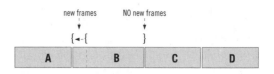

new frames   NO new frames

5.30 The sequence grows longer and new frames are added to the head of the trimmed clip.

the clip, so the new frames are at the start. (Think of that carpet again: when you unroll the left edge, the newly revealed parts appear where you're unrolling—at the left; they don't magically pop to the other side.)

5.31 Before the trim.

5.32 After the trim.

Also note that you dragged to the left (see Figure 5.33)—but the sequence grew longer at the right (see Figure 5.34). This is the source of most of the confusion. And a similar confusion occurs when you drag a head to the right, trimming in (removing frames/rolling up the carpet). We think of rightward movement as

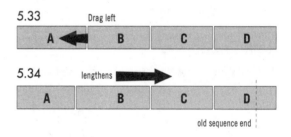

5.33   Drag left

5.34   lengthens

old sequence end

lengthening. But, in fact, dragging a head to the right with the **Ripple Edit** tool will shorten both the clip and the entire sequence. Figure 5.35 shows the breakdown.

Note that you dragged the head to the right (see Figure 5.36), but everything shifted to the left (see Figure 5.37). And though it may look like you've removed frames from the end of the clip, you've actually removed frames from the beginning of the clip.

If head trimming seems simple to you, you probably don't understand it. Even if you *do* understand it as a concept, it can be confusing when you actually try it. So try it out for yourself and reread this section as many times as you need to, until you get it. And once you *do* get it, you've mastered one of the most Premiere's most difficult concepts. Good for you!

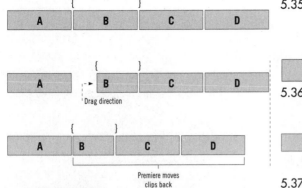

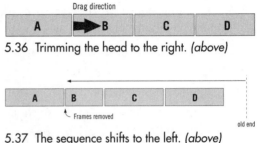

5.35 Breakdown of what happens when you trim a head to the right. *(left)*

5.36 Trimming the head to the right. *(above)*

5.37 The sequence shifts to the left. *(above)*

As you're working, remember that if you try to trim and Premiere won't let you drag a clip out any longer, it's because you've extended it all the way. There's no more carpet to unroll. Look out for those little triangle indicators.

If you truly feel you understand the **Ripple Edit** tool, it's time to move onto the next section, where you'll learn about the **Rolling Edit** tool, which is much more easy to work with and understand, thank you *very* much!

Rolling Edit tool

The **Rolling Edit** tool giveth; the **Rolling Edit** tool taketh away (see Figure 5.38). That is, it trims two clips at once, making one longer and the other shorter, so the net result is that the sequence stays the same length as it was before the edit. This is similar to what happens when you pour water between two glasses (see Figure 5.39). If you pour some water from glass A into glass B, you have less water in glass A and more water in glass B. But the total amount of water stays the same as it was before you poured.

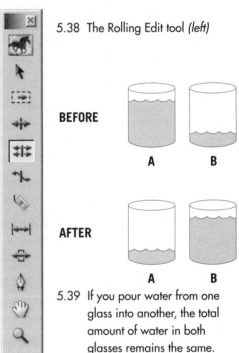

5.38 The Rolling Edit tool *(left)*

5.39 If you pour water from one glass into another, the total amount of water in both glasses remains the same.

Or imagine you have two notebooks, each containing a 50-page short story you'd written. You decide to write 10 more pages and staple them into the back of notebook A, but your editor has told you that the total number of pages in both notebooks can never exceed 100. So you rip 10 pages out of the front of notebook B. Your second story may start in the middle, but you've maintained the appropriate page count.

The **Rolling Edit** tool works with clips, not books or glasses of water, but the effect is much the same. To use it, click its icon in the **Tools** palette and then position your cursor on the crack between any two clips. You'll see the **Rolling Edit** icon appear, which looks a little bit like the top of a guitar, but is supposed to be arrows pointing in two directions, left and right, indicating that the clips on both sides of the crack will be trimmed (see Figure 5.40).

5.40 Clips on both sides of the crack will be trimmed.

Now drag to the left or to the right. If you drag to the left, clip A (the clip on the left) will get shorter, because you're trimming frames off its end (trimming in). Meanwhile, clip B (the clip on the right) will get longer, because you're adding frames to its beginning (trimming out). The number of frames you're adding to clip B is exactly the same number you're subtracting from clip A, so that the total number of frames remain the same (see Figure 5.41).

If you drag to the right, you'll make the same sort of double trim, only this time you'll lengthen A and, by an equal amount, shorten B (see Figure 5.42).

As with the **Ripple Edit** tool, the **Program Monitor** splits into two views, showing you the last frame of clip A on the left and the first frame of clip B on the right. The timecode at the bottom left indicates how many frames you're trimming.

Suppose you have a two-clip sequence in which clip A shows a man staring at something. Clip B is a delicious chocolate cake. You like the length of the entire sequence, but you feel like you're watching the man stare for too long. You start getting impatient, wondering what the dickens he's staring at. And when the sequence finally cuts to the cake, it's not on screen

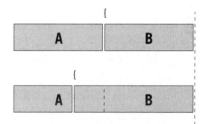

5.41 Trimming to left shortens clip A and lengthens clip B. The sequence's duration does not change.

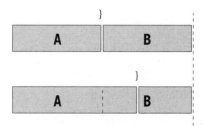

5.42 Trimming to the right lengthens clip A and shortens clip B. The sequence's duration does not change.

> ### Plus Means Right, Minus Means Left
>
> While trimming, you'll see some odd-looking timecode showing up in the **Program Monitor**. For instance, you might see +00;00;00;15 or –00;00;00;23. The numbers indicate how many frames you've trimmed (15 and 23 in the two examples given here). You might think that the plus and minus signs indicate adding and deleting frames, but, in fact, they don't mean that at all. A plus sign indicates a trim to the right; a minus sign indicates a trim to the left. So +00;00;00;15 means you've trimmed 15 frames to the right. This *does* mean you've added frames if you've trimmed the tail of a clip. But trimming the head of a clip to the right removes frames (think rolling up a carpet from its left edge—as you roll to the right, you roll up the carpet). Along the same lines, if you trim –00;00;00;23 frames from the head, you're adding 23 frames; if you trim the same amount from the tail, you're subtracting 23 frames.

long enough for you to get a really good look at it. In short: too much man, not enough cake. (How many women have ever thought this?) In rolls the **Rolling Edit** tool to the rescue (see Figure 5.43).

Note that while the **Ripple Edit** tool always changes the duration of your entire sequence, the **Rolling Edit** tool never does (unless you use it to trim the head of the first clip in the sequence or the tail of the last clip in the sequence. Generally, for each frame you add or remove, Premiere counters that by removing or adding frames from the adjacent clip, but at the ends there are no adjacent clips.) This is useful when you know you've already laid down a sequence that is

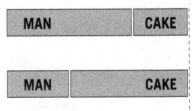

5.43 A common editing problem solved with the Rolling Edit tool.

exactly the length you need it to be. You can't add or remove any frames to the total number of frames in your sequence, so the **Ripple Edit** tool is out. But you alter each of your cuts with the **Rolling Edit** tool without affecting the total sequence duration.

The most difficult thing about the two tools is remembering which is which, especially when they have such similar names. If it helps, remember that the **Rolling Edit** tool is the one that looks like the top of a guitar. Just think of The Rolling Stones' lead guitarist, Keith Richards. The Rolling Stones have been around for four decades without changing. Similarly, the **Rolling Edit** tool doesn't change the duration of a sequence. And neither do the next two tools, the **Slide** tool (see Figure 5.44) and the **Slip** tool (see Figure 5.56).

Slide tool

It's party time at the zoo. Three hippos are sitting next to each other on the sofa. Next to them, on the same sofa, sit four lions. (It's a big sofa!) Three giraffes sit next to the lions (see Figure 5.45).

The rightmost hippo has to go to the bathroom, so he gets up, leaving a gap between the two remaining hippos and the lions (see Figure 5.46).

5.45 Three hippos, four lions, and three giraffes.

5.46 One hippo leaves.

The lions move down to close up the gap. They like being close to the hippos, but we're not sure how the hippos feel about it (see Figure 5.47).

This leaves a gap between the lions and the giraffes, but it's quickly filled by a fourth giraffe who has been longing to sit with his friends on the sofa (see Figure 5.48).

The total number of animals on the sofa is the same as it was before the hippo left. True, there's one less hippo, but to counter that, there's one more giraffe. The number of lions has stayed the same, but they've shifted to the left.

The **Slide** tool creates a similar shift, but with clips instead of animals. You generally use it to adjust three clips: A, B, and C. As with the lions, the middle clip—clip B—doesn't grow or shrink. It just slides to the left, as the clip before it—clip A—gets shorter. The clip after it—clip C—gets longer to fill up the gap clip B left behind when it shifted. (This is assuming you trim to the left. If you trim to the right, clip A would get longer, clip C would get shorter, and clip B would stay the same length, but shift to the right). The total duration of the sequence remains unchanged.

5.44 The Slide tool.

5.47 The lions shift to the left, closing up the gap next to the hippos but creating a gap next to the giraffes.

5.48 A new giraffe fills the gap.

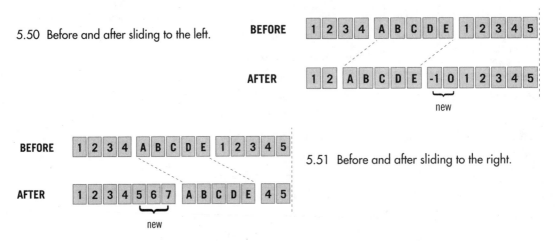

5.49 When using the slide tool, point to the center of a clip.

When you use the **Slide** tool, you point to the center of clip B, not to the crack between two clips, as you do with the **Rolling** and **Ripple Edit** tools (see Figure 5.49).

You then drag to the left or to the right. If you drag to the left, Premiere will trim frames away from A and add them to C, much like the **Rolling Edit**, which adds to one clip and subtracts from another, only in this case there's another clip in between, clip B. Since clip A is losing frames, that would leave a gap between clip A and clip B. So clip B slides to the right to fill up the gap. Which leaves space between clips B and C. Premiere adds new frames at the head of clip C to fill up the gap (see Figure 5.50).

You can also drag from the center of clip B to the right, adding frames the tail of clip A and subtracting them from the head of clip C (see Figure 5.51).

Note that you're dragging clip B, but it's really clips A and C that are being trimmed—even though you're not touching them. Clip B is just sliding over, to the left or the right, depending on which way you drag.

When you slide, the **Program Monitor** displays two smaller images at the top and two larger images at the bottom. The smaller images represent the first and last frames of clip B (its in and out points). Notice that no matter how much you slide, these images never change. That should prove to you that sliding doesn't change clip B. On the other hand, the two larger images do change as you slide. The left changing image represents the last frame of clip A; the right changing image represents the first frame of clip C. If you let your eyes roam from the bottom left image, to the top left image, to the top right image, and finally to the bottom right image, you can say to yourself, "Okay, we're going

5.50 Before and after sliding to the left.

5.51 Before and after sliding to the right.

5.52 While sliding, the Program Monitor displays four images: on the top row, the head and tail of clip B; on the bottom row, the tail of clip A and the head of clip C.

to see *this,* then we're going to cut to *that,* and when that ends, we're going to cut to *this new thing."* The timecodes along the bottom display the same information as when you're performing a rolling or ripple edit: trim amount on the left and duration on the right, both of which are specific to the clip that lies in the direction you're dragging (see Figure 5.52).

Imagine your sequence displays a stadium crowd watching a baseball game, a cut to the batter knocking the ball into the stratosphere, and then a cut back to the cheering crowd (see Figure 5.53).

You feel like the first crowd shot is too long and boring. Its only purpose is to establish that the crowd is watching something. The sequence would be better if there was a quicker cut to *what* they were watching. The batter clip is perfect: not too long, not too short. But the second crowd shot (the reaction) goes by too quickly. You don't really have time to see the excitement in the stands. So, using the **Slide** tool, you grab the batter clip by its center and drag to the left (all the while, watching the **Program Monitor** to see how one clip transitions into the next). This shortens crowd clip 1 and lengthens crowd clip 2. The batter clip stays the same length, but moves left in the sequence, so that it begins playing at an earlier time.

Figures 5.53–5.55 show other ways of visualizing the role of the **Slide** tool.

Slip tool

The **Slip** tool perplexes most beginners, because when they use it, nothing seems to change—at least not in the **Timeline** (see Figure 5.56).

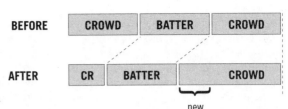

CROWD	BATTER	CROWD

5.53 Baseball sequence before trimming with the Slide tool. *(above)*

BEFORE

CROWD	BATTER	CROWD

AFTER

CR	BATTER	CROWD

new

5.54 Baseball sequence before and after a trim with the Slide tool. *(above)*

5.55 Another way of visualizing the role of the Slide tool. *(left)*

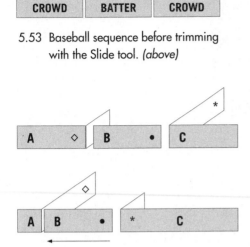

Before using the **Slip** tool:

After using the **Slip** tool:

But it actually causes a very profound change, and many editors would list it as one of the top 10 tools they'd take with them to a desert island.

To get a grasp on how it works, imagine a room in which a window is sandwiched between an armchair and a table. The view through the window is of an ugly factory (see Figure 5.57). If only we could move the window a little to the left or a little to the right, we'd be able to peer out at the serene landscape to either side of the factory! But we can't move a window.

Wouldn't it be great if we could reach through the window and magically move the landscape a little to the left or to the right, as in Figure 5.58?

This is one of the many situations in which real life fails us but editing lets us create magic. Using the **Slip** tool, you can, in a sense, reach through a window and move the landscape outside.

5.56 Slip tool.

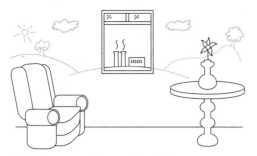

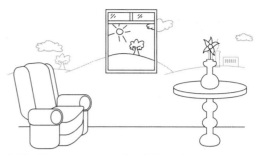

5.57 A room with an ugly view.

5.58 The same room after shifting the view.

5.59 When using the Slide tool, drag a clip from its center.

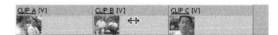

You use the **Slip** tool the same way you use the **Slide** tool, by dragging a clip from its center (not from its edge, as you would with the **Rolling** or **Ripple Edit** tools) (see Figure 5.59).

The **Slip** tool doesn't alter durations—the clip, and all neighboring clips, stay exactly the same length after a slip as they were before.

So if it doesn't change duration, what *does* the **Slip** tool change? It changes *which* frames (from the original source in the **Project** window) display between the head and the tail of the clip you're slipping. This is similar to the window example, in which you can't move the window or make it wider or narrower, but you can alter which part of the total landscape shows through the it. Think of a clip on the **Timeline** as being a window through which you can see a little bit of its total source footage. With the Slip tool, you can stick your hand through that window and drag the original footage to the left or to the right, revealing formerly hidden frames. Nothing happens to the clips to either side or the one you're slipping, just as nothing happens to the chair and table to either side of the window.

Another way to imagine slipping is to visualize the handles extending beyond either side of a clip (see Figure 5.60).

You can think of a slip as shifting the in and out points by equal amounts (see Figure 5.61).

Finally, you can imagine a clip as a scroll (like a Torah), and slip trimming as rolling one end of the scroll up as you unroll the other end by an equal amount (see Figure 5.62).

As with sliding, the **Program Monitor** shows you four images. This time, though, the top two images—the smaller ones—represent frames from the clips to either side of the clip you're slipping: the left image is the final frame of the clip to the left; the right image

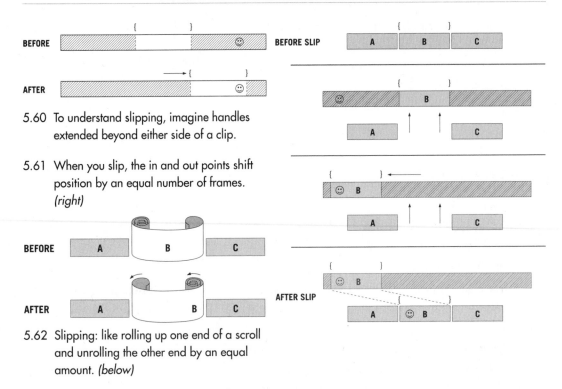

5.60 To understand slipping, imagine handles extended beyond either side of a clip.

5.61 When you slip, the in and out points shift position by an equal number of frames. *(right)*

BEFORE

AFTER

5.62 Slipping: like rolling up one end of a scroll and unrolling the other end by an equal amount. *(below)*

is the first frame of the clip on the right. Because slipping doesn't affect the clips to the left or the right, these images don't change. On the other hand, because the two larger images at the bottom represent the start and end frames of the clip you're slipping, naturally they change as you drag (see Figure 5.63).

Use these images to gauge the relationship between clips as you slip. As always, you can see how many frames you're trimming by reading the timecode in the lower-left corner of the **Program Monitor.** Plus (+) and minus (–) merely indicate the direction you're

5.63 While slipping, the Program Monitor displays four images: on the top row, the tail of clip A and the head of clip C; on the bottom row, the head and tail of clip B.

dragging: minus = left and plus = right. You can't say that you're just adding or just removing frames, because when you slip, you're doing both. So the total number of frames remains the same.

Suppose you shot 20 minutes of a crowd in the bleachers at a baseball game. You load the entire 20 minutes into the **Source Monitor**, but you only cut three seconds of it into the sequence. As you view your sequence, you realize that though you like the crowd shot being three seconds long, you don't like the specific three seconds of it that you're seeing. Perhaps there's a guy in the front row tying his shoe, and you need everyone to look excited and focused on the game. No problem. Just slip the shot until you've moved to frames before or after the shoe-tying, and you'll see the guy sitting up straight, watching the game.

TRIM WINDOW

If you have a to do a major amount of trimming, you may want to bypass all of the tools on the **Tools** palette and go directly to the **Trim** window, which is a special interface made just for trimming. To call up the **Trim** window, select the track you want to trim, and park the **Cur-**

5.64   Trim window button.

rent Time Indicator near an edit (near the crack between two clips—you don't need to park exactly on it). Then click the **Trim** button near the bottom of the **Program Monitor** (see Figure 5.64).

A new window will appear, which usually covers the **Source** and **Program Monitors**. If it does, you may think that you're still looking at the **Source** and **Program Monitors**, because the **Trim** window looks quite similar, but drag the window by its title bar and you'll see the **Source** and **Program Monitors** hiding beneath it. When you're done using the **Trim** window, you can close it by clicking the standard Windows close icon: the **X** in the upper right corner (see Figure 5.65).

If you look at the **Timeline**, you'll notice that the time marker has snapped to the edit you were parked closest to before you called up the **Trim** window. Now take a look at the **Trim** window's monitors. The left monitor, which is *not* a source monitor in the **Trim** window, shows you the final frame (the out point) of the clip to the **Current Time Indica-tor's** left, whereas the monitor on the right shows you the first frame (the in point) of the clip to the **Current Time Indicator's** right. These are just larger versions of the two frames you see in the **Program Monitor** when you're performing a rolling edit or a ripple edit.

5.65 Trim window.

In the **Trim** window, you can ripple edit the left clip by pointing to it in the left monitor and dragging left or right to trim its head in or out, respectively (see Figure 5.66).

You can ripple edit the right clip by pointing to its monitor and dragging left or right. Notice that your cursor changes to the trim bracket as you drag in the monitor (see Figure 5.67).

You can perform a rolling edit in the **Trim** window by pointing to the gray area in the center—between the two monitors—and dragging left or right. As you drag, you'll notice that your cursor changes to the guitar icon, well-known to rolling edit fans all over the world (see Figure 5.68).

After completing a trim, you can check out the results by clicking the **Play Edit** button in the **Trim** window (see Figure 5.69).

Premiere will play a little bit of your sequence, from just before the trim to just after it, so you can see the results of your actions. If you click the **Loop** button before clicking the **Play Edit** button, the results of your trim will play back over and over again, until you click the **Play Edit** button a second time to stop playback (see Figure 5.70).

When you finish dragging, you can press the **Page Down** button on your keyboard (located between the main keyboard and the numeric keypad) to move to the next edit. **Page Down** will keep moving you forward; **Page Up** will move you backward. If you make a mistake, press **Control+Z** to undo. By the way, **Page Up** and **Page Down** are not the same as the **Up** and **Down Arrow** keys. Look directly above the **Up** and **Down Arrows** and you'll see the **Page Up** and **Page Down** keys, right next to **Home** and **End**.

Instead of pressing **Page Up** and **Page Down**, you can click the **Go To Next Edit Point** and **Go To Previous Edit Point** buttons at the bottom left of the monitors, but **Page Up** and **Page Down** are quicker.

While working in the **Trim** window there are many ways you can trim besides dragging in one of the monitors or dragging between them. For instance, you can spin any of the jog wheels along the bottom of the window: the left one will ripple edit the left clip; the right one will ripple edit the right clip; the center one will rolling edit both clips at once. Or you can scrub the timecode displays.

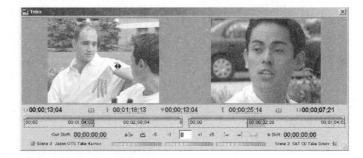

5.66 Ripple trim the left clip by dragging in its image.

5.67 Ripple trim the right clip by dragging in its image.

5.68 Perform a rolling edit by dragging in the gray area between the two clips.

5.69 Play Edit button.

5.70 Loop button.

The fastest way to trim in the **Trim** window is to use—you guessed it—keyboard shortcuts. Click one of the monitors or the line between them to tell Premiere whether you want to edit the left clip (ripple edit), the right clip (ripple edit) or both clips (rolling edit). Then press the **Left Arrow** key to trim to the left or the **Right Arrow** key to trim to the right. Each time you press a key, you'll trim left or right one frame. **Shift**+click the **Right** or **Left Arrow** keys to trim right or left by five frames at a time. You can change the number of frames **Shift+Arrow** clicking trims by choosing E**dit>Preference>Trim** from the menu. In the **Preferences** dialog window, you'll see that **Large Trim Offset** is set to **5**. If you change it to **10**, pressing **Shift+Left Arrow** will trim 10 frames to the left, and **Shift+Right Arrow** will trim 10 frames to the right (see Figure 5.71).

5.71 In the Trim Preferences you can change the amount Shift+Arrow keys trim.

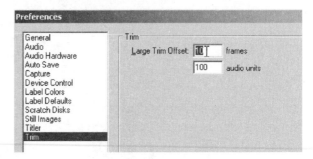

Remember that trimming left does not necessarily mean removing frames and trimming right doesn't necessarily mean adding frames. Both right and left trims can add or remove frames, depending on which side of the crack you're ripple editing. When you perform a rolling edit, you're both adding and removing frames whether you trim right or left. If you're confused about whether you're adding or removing frames (or doing both at the same time), reread the previous sections on ripple edits and rolling edits starting on page 105.

Also remember to close the **Trim** window when you're finished trimming. It's only for trimming, and many other Premiere tools won't work while you still have the **Trim** window activated.

TRACKS

So far, we've been exploring trimming as if the only movement in the **Timeline** was horizontal. But most sequences contain multiple tracks, stacked vertically on top of one another. The tracks are the rows in the **Timeline** that are labeled with names like Video 1, Audio 1, and Audio 2 along their left edges.

In even the simplest sequence, if there's sound, there will be at least one video track and one audio track. And if you add more sound—maybe some music playing under the dialog or some sound effects—you'll need to use additional audio tracks. You'll need extra video tracks when you want to superimpose one image over another, as with titles that display on top of images.

Generally, when you trim, you only affect one track at a time. For instance, if you trim an audio clip on the Audio 1 track, *nothing* will happen to an audio clip directly below it on Audio 2 track. The exception to this is linked audio and video. When you bring both audio and video in from a single source (like audio and video recorded at the same time, in the same camera), they are linked together. The video may be in the **Video 1** track and the audio may be in the **Audio 1** track, but if you try to trim just one of these tracks, Premiere will trim the other one too.

We'll delve deeper into linked audio and video in Chapter 10, but if you want to play with fire now, you can try unlinking linked video and audio by right-clicking either clip (video or audio) and choosing **Unlink Audio And Video** from the pop-up menu. You will then be able to trim each clip separately, delete just the audio or just the video (Use the **Selection** tool and the **Delete** key on the keyboard.), or even move just the audio or just the video to a new location. (Use **Selection** tool and drag.) To relink the clips, right-click again and choose the **Link Audio And Video** option from the pop-up menu.

Remember that every editing action—whether it's three-point editing or trimming—affects a specific track (or tracks, in the case of linked clips). So make sure you remember to select a track before you make an edit.

Unlinking video and audio is dangerous because you risk losing sync, which will make your video look and sound like a badly dubbed Spaghetti Western. Yet unlinking allows you to make one of the most creative editing choices, namely a split edit. To learn how to split without losing sync, see Chapter 10, which begins on page 235.

ADDITIONAL EDITING TOOLS

Rate Stretch tool

Sometimes a clip is too long or too short, and you can't insert it where you want it to go—for instance, in a gap between two other clips. Or you might just have clip that you need to speed up or slow down. Maybe it's a shot of slow moving traffic, and you need it to seem like a race.

You can alter clip timing with the **Rate Stretch** tool, which lengthens clips (slowing them down) or shortens clips (speeding them up) (see Figure 5.72). But note that Premiere can only affect duration by cutting out frames, in the case of speeding up, or duplicating frames, in the case of slowing down. This means that you'll never be able to achieve true slow motion. If you use **Rate Stretch** on a clip so that it's longer, Premiere will duplicate each frame however many times it needs to stretch the clip to the duration you want. The resulting motion will be choppy and staggered: move, pause, move, pause, move, pause.

5.72 Rate Stretch tool.

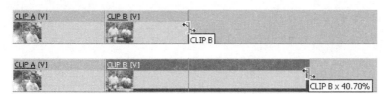

5.73 Before and after dragging a clip's tail with the Rate Stretch tool.

The only way to achieve real slow motion, in which an object travels smoothly (like a bullet flying slowly through the air), is in the camera.

Keeping that in mind, you can use the **Rate Stretch** tool by pointing a clip's tail and then dragging to the right or to the left: left drags will speed the clip up (and make it take up less space on the **Timeline**); right drags will slow the clip down (and make it take up more space on the **Timeline**) (see Figure 5.73).

Note the tooltip that tells you by how much you've altered the duration of the clip.

As with the **Selection** tool, you can't use the **Rate Stretch** tool to drag to the right if there's another clip in the way. You'll have to first move, delete, or trim the blocking clip.

You can alter duration with more precision by selecting a clip (clicking it with the **Selection** tool) and then choosing **Clip > Speed/Duration** from the menu, to show the dialog window in Figure 5.74.

5.74 Clip Speed/Duration dialog window.

In this window, you can scrub the speed value (larger numbers speed up, smaller numbers slow down) or type in a new duration. You can also make the clip run backwards by checking the **Reverse Speed** option. The **Maintain Audio Pitch** option will stop the sound from getting higher when you speed up or lower when you slow down, so if you want your actors to sound like The Chipmunks, leave this option unchecked.

Notice the little chain-link symbol between **Speed** and **Duration**. If you click this, the link will be broken. Click it again to relink. Changing speed will *not* alter duration (and vice versa).

Razor tool

This useful tool will split a **Timeline** clip into two clips, making an invisible edit—invisible because to the viewer, the transition between the two clips won't seem like a transition at all. After slicing a clip with the **Razor** tool, you can select one half of the clip and delete it or move it somewhere else. The **Razor** tool is also useful when you want to apply an effect to just half of a clip. Slice the clip in half and then just apply the effect to one of the two halves. (For more about effects, see Chapter 6.)

Figure 5.75 shows before slicing with the **Razor** tool. Figure 5.76 shows after slicing, and Figure 5.77 shows half of clip C moved to a new location.

5.75 Before slicing with the Razor tool.

5.76 After slicing with the Razor tool.

5.77 After using the Razor tool, you can relocate a slice.

If you hold down the **Shift** key while you use the **Razor** tool, you can slide through multiple tracks at once. The **Razor** tool is shown in Figure 5.78.

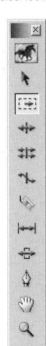

5.78 Razor tool.

5.79 Track Select tool.

Track Select tool

Sometimes you need to move all of the clips in a track at once, maybe shifting them to the right to make room at the beginning for some new clips. You can easily select a whole track by clicking a clip in that track with the **Track Select** tool, shown in Figure 5.79. Premiere will select that clip and all of the clips to its right, in that track. Then, still using the **Track Select** tool (don't switch to the Selection tool), drag the clip you clicked to a new location. It and all of its neighbors to the right will move with it. Or you can press the **Delete** key on your keyboard to delete all of the selected clips.

If you hold down the **Shift** key while clicking with the **Track Select** tool, all clips in tracks below (and to the right) of the clip you click will also be included in the selection.

Snap tool

As you trim clips and drag clips, it's often helpful to first mark your destination with the **Current Time Indicator**. For instance, if you want to trim a clip's tail out, so that it's three seconds longer than its current duration, you could first move the **Current Time Indicator** to three seconds later in the **Timeline**. Then you could use one of the trim tools to drag out the end of the clip until it kisses the **Current Time Indicator**. As you drag, Premiere will snap your trim tool to the **Current Time Indicator** (and to other important points, like the beginning and end of clips on other tracks). This is the default behavior, and it's generally useful.

5.80 Snap button.

But if snapping irritates you, you can turn it off by clicking the **Snap** button near the upper-left corner of the **Timeline** (see Figure 5.80). Clicking this same button again will turn snapping back on.

The **Snap** button snaps clips to the **Current Time Indicator**, but it doesn't snap the **Current Time Indicator** to clips. However, if you hold down the **Shift** key as you drag the **Current Time Indicator**, it will snap to clip edges, clip markers and sequence markers. (Markers are described later in this chapter on page 128.)

Viewing clips in the Timeline

You can easily change the way clips appear in the **Timeline**. For instance, you can collapse tracks so that the clips take up less space (see Figure 5.81), or you can expand tracks so that the clips take up more space but also show more information. To expand or collapse a track, click the triangle to the left of the track's name (see Figure 5.82).

If a track is expanded, you can change the height of the track by dragging the line that separates that track from the track below or above it (see Figure 5.83).

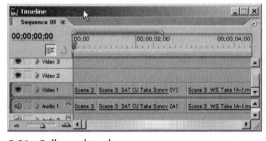

5.81 Collapsed tracks.

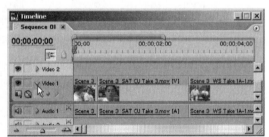

5.82 Expanded tracks.

5.83 You can change the height of a track by dragging the line that separates that track from the one below or above it.

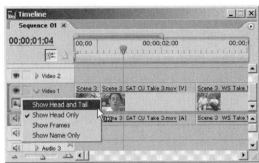

5.84 You can choose to display track thumbnails on clips' heads, heads and tails, on every frame, or not at all.

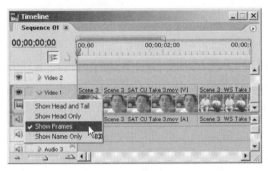

5.85 Thumbnails on every frame.

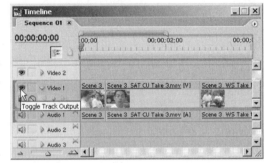

5.86 Click the eyeball to hide a track.

If you click the **Set Display Style** button (located just below the little eye or speaker icon), you can choose to display or not to display frame thumbnails in the track. Options include **Head and Tail, Head Only, Frames** (which will show you a thumbnail for every frame, if you're zoomed in enough), or **Names Only,** if you don't want to see any thumbnails. Regardless of your choice, you will only see thumbnails if the track is expanded (see Figures 5.84 and 5.85).

If you want to turn off a video track so that it doesn't display in the **Program Monitor** or output when you export your final sequence, click the little eyeball icon until it vanishes (see Figure 5.86). Click the empty box (where the eyeball used to be) to bring the eyeball back and to redisplay the clip in the **Program Monitor.** Similarly, the little speaker icon toggles audio clips on and off.

To the right of the eyeball or speaker, there's a small empty box. Click it, and a lock symbol will appear. Locked tracks can't be edited, so toggling this option on is a great way to stop accidents from trimming or changing tracks that you're happy with. Click the lock icon to make it vanish and to unlock the associated track (see Figure 5.87).

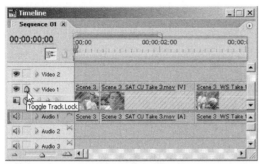

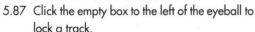

5.87 Click the empty box to the left of the eyeball to lock a track.

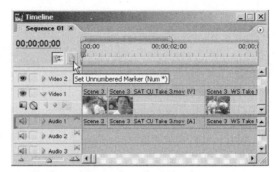

5.88 The Set Unnumbered Marker button.

Opening Timeline clips in the Source Monitor

If you double-click any clip in the **Timeline**, Premiere will load that clip into the **Source Monitor**, where you can choose new in and out points. However, those new points will not affect the in and out points in the **Timeline**. To change those points, use trimming tools and techniques. Change in and out points in the **Source Monitor** when you want to reuse the clip (with a new marked segment) later or earlier in the sequence.

Markers

Since editing involves timing, it's often helpful to be able to mark certain key points in the sequence. For instance, suppose you're making a documentary and you lay some voice narration down in the Audio 1 track. At some point, the narrator says, "…the planet Mars has two moons, one named Phobos and the other named Deimos…" You know you're going to want to cut to images of Phobos and Deimos when the narrator says their names. So you park the **Current Time Indicator** right at the point when the narrator says "Phobos" and add a marker. Then you do the same at the "Deimos" point in the narration.

Markers are like bookmarks. They tag a point in time that's important to you. To add one, move the **Current Time Indicator** to a specific point in time that you'd like to mark, and then click the **Set Unnumbered Marker** button near the upper-left corner of the **Timeline** (see Figures 5.88 and 5.89). You can add as many of these markers as you want. If you've enabled the **Snap** button, Premiere will snap your trims and drags to these markers.

To delete a marker, move the **Current Time Indicator** on top of it, then right-click it and choose **Clear Sequence Marker>Current Marker** from the pop-up menu (see Figure 5.90).

5.89 Markers in the Timeline.

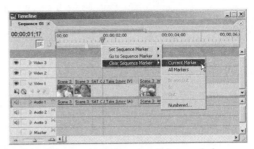

5.90 To delete a marker, right-click it and choose Clear Sequence Marker>Current Marker from the pop-up menu.

To move a marker to a new location on the **Timeline**, drag it there with the mouse.

If you double-click a marker, a dialog window will appear in which you can write a comment that will be associated with that marker, like "add image of Phobos here." The other options in the dialog allow you to add hyperlink and chapter commands for movies running on the web or in the Windows Media Player (or QuickTime player). See the online help for more information about these features.

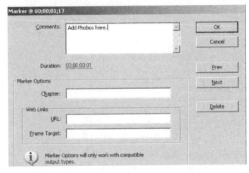

5.91 Double-click a marker to add a comment.

Comments and Options: To add a comment or set options as you insert a new marker, double-click the **Set Unnumbered Marker** button (see Figure 5.91).

To quickly add markers, press the asterisk (*) key on the *numeric* keypad. Each time you press this key, a marker will appear at the location of the **Current Time Indicator.** You can add markers this way while a sequence is playing. This is really useful when you want to listen to a soundtrack and add markers when you hear the narrator say important words or phrases. Each time one of these moments occurs, just press the asterisk key to add a marker.

You can also set up to 100 numbered markers. Numbered markers are just like regular (unnumbered) markers, except they have little numbers on them. These are useful if you want to associate a number with a note in MS Word file or on a sheet of paper.

To add a numbered marker, park the **Current Time Indicator** where you want the marker to go, and then right-click the time ruler at the top of the **Timeline**. From the pop-up menu, choose **Set Sequence Marker>Next Available Numbered.** The first time you

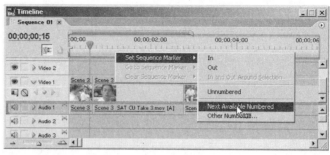

5.92 To add a numbered marker, right-click the time ruler and choose Set Sequence Marker > Next Available Numbered from the pop-up menu.

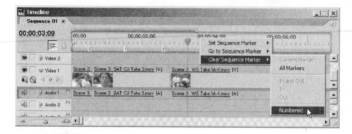

5.93 To delete a numbered marker, right-click the time ruler and choose Clear Sequence Marker > Numbered... from the pop-up menu.

choose this command, you'll see marker 0 appear. Then the next time, you'll see marker 1 and so on. If you want marker 1 to be followed by marker 10 (instead of marker 2), right-click on the time ruler and choose **Set Sequence Marker>Other Numbered** from the pop-up menu. Then type *10* (or any other number, up to 99) in the dialog that appears. You can send the **Timeline** to a numbered marker by right-clicking the time ruler and choosing **Go to Sequence Marker>Numbered...** from the pop-up menu (see Figure 5.92).

You can delete a numbered marker by right-clicking the time ruler and choosing **Clear Sequence Marker>Numbered...** from the pop-up menu. In the dialog window that appears, type the number of the marker you want to delete (see Figure 5.93).

In addition to sequence markers, you can also set markers on specific clips. These look just like sequence markers, only they appear on the clips themselves instead of on at the top of the **Timeline**. To set a clip maker, load the clip into the **Source Monitor**, park the **Source Monitor's Current Time Indicator** at the point where you want the marker to go, and click the **Source Monitor's Set Unnumbered Marker** button.

A small marker will appear on the **Source Monitor's** time ruler. When you add the clip to the **Timeline**, the marker will appear there too, on the clip.

You can't edit a clip marker in the **Timeline**. You can't delete it, drag it, etc. To edit it, double-click the clip in the **Timeline** to load it in the **Source Monitor**, and then right-click the clip in the **Source Monitor's** time ruler to access options to edit the marker. Or you can drag the marker to a new location in the **Source Monitor's** time ruler.

5.94 While the sequence is playing, tap the asterisk key on the numeric keypad to add markers.

Using markers to make a music video

Here's a cool trick you can do with markers.

1. Load an audio clip into the **Audio 1** track of an otherwise empty sequence.

2. Play the sequence, tapping the asterisk (*) key on the numeric keypad in time with the music, one tap for each beat.
   Premiere will add an unnumbered marker for each tap of the asterisk (see Figure 5.94).

3. When you're finished adding markers, press the **Home** key to return the **Current Time Indicator** to the beginning of the **Timeline**.

4. Select a group of images or videos in the **Project** window.

5. **Control**+click each image in the order that you'd like them to appear in the sequence.

6. Then press the **Automate to Sequence** button at the bottom of the **Project** window. (For more information, see "Automating to the sequence" on page 93.)

7. In the **Automate to Sequence** dialog window, set the **Placement** option to **At Unnumbered Markers** and click **OK** (see Figure 5.95).
   Premiere will add a clip at each unnumbered marker (see Figure 5.96).

Go to

If you need to jump the **Current Time Indicator** to a specific frame, type that frame's timecode using the numeric keypad, pressing the numeric keypad's **Enter** key when you're finished typing. For instance, the timecode for 3 seconds into the sequence is 00;00;03;00.

5.95 Set the placement option to At Unnumbered Markers in the Automate to Sequence dialog window. *(left)*

5.96 Premiere will add clips at each unnumbered marker. *(below)*

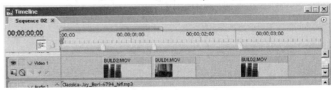

To go to this frame, simply type *300* on the numeric keypad and press **Enter**. Note that you only need to type the significant digits from right to left, and you don't need to type the semicolons.

If you type a two-digit number, Premiere will interpret it as frames. When you type *15*, it means just 15 frames into your sequence. If you intend to jump to 15 seconds into your sequence, type *1500* (15 seconds, 0 frames). If you intend to jump to 15 minutes into your sequence, type *150000*. You can also instruct Premiere to move the **Current Time Indicator** forward or backward a specific number of frames by typing the plus (**+**) or minus (**−**) key on the numeric keypad before typing a number. So if you're parked on 00;00;02;20 and you type *−10*, Premiere will jump you back 10 frames to 00;00;02;10.

If you click the **Source Monitor** before typing timecode, Premiere will move the **Source Current Time Indicator**. If you click the **Timeline** or the **Program Monitor** before typing timecode, Premiere will move the sequence's **Current Time Indicator**.

Info palette

Choosing **Window>Info** from the menu brings up a palette that displays useful information when you're trimming in the **Timeline**. If no clips are selected, the **Info** palette displays the location of the mouse cursor in the **Timeline**, *not* the location of the **Current Time Indicator**.

If you select a clip, the **Info** palette displays all sorts of useful information about that clip. If you select multiple clips, the **Info** palette displays the their total duration. You can even select a gap to see its duration in the **Info** palette.

 Tooltips: As you point to, select, and trim clips in the **Timeline**, useful information displays in tooltip pop-ups near your mouse cursor.

WRAPPING UP

Congratulations! You now understand 90% of an editor's job, which is three-point editing (discussed in the last chapter) and trimming. Those tasks are the meat and potatoes of editing—the rest is all gravy. If you like gravy, you'll enjoy the next few chapters, in which we'll discuss effects and transitions. As you read them, remember that Premiere is first and foremost an editing program. If you find that effects are your favorite part of the work, you might eventually want to move onto a dedicated effects package, like Adobe After Effects. Your effects experience in Premiere will shorten your After Effects learning curve.

Chapter 6

Effects and Transitions

If you think special effects are only for science fiction movies, read on! Premiere Pro lets you use effects to animate titles moving on or off the screen, to remove backgrounds so you can composite your actors into scenes, to create transitions between clips in the **Time-line,** to correct colors so that they look good on television, and even to alter or fade sounds.

You can also use them for science fiction movies.

This chapter will lead you through the general steps of applying effects. Subsequent chapters will delve into specific types of effects, such as motion (Chapter 9 on page 211), transparency (Chapter 7 on page 171), color correction (Chapter 8 on page 193) and audio (Chapter 10 on page 235).

There are two useful windows that you might want to bring up before you start working with effects: the **Effects** window, which allows you to pick an effect to apply, and the **Effect Controls** window, which allows you to adjust effects after you've applied them.

You can display either of these windows by choosing them from the **Windows** menu. Or, you can choose **Window>Workspace>Effects** from the menu. Doing so will redraw Premiere's interface, docking the **Effects** window with the **Project** window and the **Effect Controls** window with the **Source Monitor.** You can then switch back and forth between the **Project** window and the **Effects** window by clicking their tabs. You can switch between the **Effect Controls** window and the **Source** monitor the same way. When you're

6.1   The Effects Workspace.

done working with effects, choose **Window>Workspace>Editing** to switch back to a more standard interface (see Figure 6.1).

APPLYING AN EFFECT

You apply most effects to individual clips in the **Timeline** (see Figure 6.2). Transition effects, such as crossfades, are the exceptions, because you apply them to the cut between two clips (see Figure 6.3). If you want to apply an effect to multiple clips, you'll have to add it to each clip separately. The downside to this method is that when you later want to adjust the effect, you'll have to redo the adjustment on each clip. A better alternative involves nesting, in which you essentially turn an entire track (or several tracks) into a single clip, to which you can apply an effect. Nesting is covered later in this chapter on page 156.

Whether you're applying an effect to a single clip, a cut between two clips, or to a nested sequence, you'll follow the same steps, the first of which is bringing up the **Effects** window.

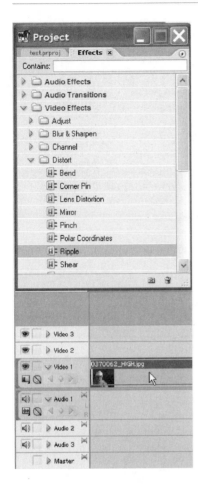

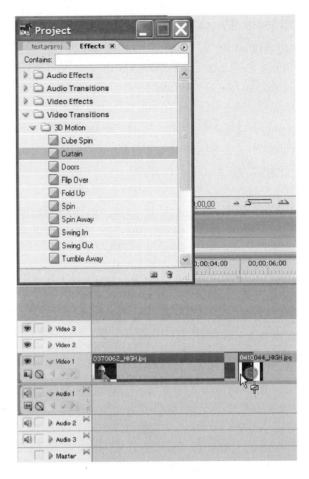

6.2   Dropping an effect on a clip in the Timeline.

6.3   Dropping a transition effect on the "crack" between two clips.

Using After Effects Plug-ins in Premiere

If Adobe After Effects is installed on your system, you'll have access to many of its effects within Premiere. These effects won't appear in a special place; they'll be mixed in with the other effects in various bin in the Effects window. Note that Premiere can only access After Effects plug-ins that are installed in After Effects' default plug-ins folder. You do *not* need to copy After Effect plug-ins to Premiere's folder in order to use these effects.

Effects window

If you choose **Window>Effects** from the menu, Premiere will open the **Effects** window, which contains multiple bins (a.k.a folders) in which effects are organized by type: **Audio Effects, Audio Transitions, Video Effect,** and **Video Transitions.** You can open a bin to view its contents by clicking the small triangle to its left. (Double-clicking the bin doesn't work.) Once a bin is open, you can close it by clicking the triangle again. Because the triangle twirls down when you open and up when you close, many people refer to clicking the triangle as "twirling open" or "twirling closed" a bin.

If you twirl open the **Video Effects** bin, you'll find a group of sub-bins inside (see Figure 6.4). Twirl open one of those—say, the **Distort** sub-bin—and you'll find a group of effects, each of which distorts a clip's image in some way.

To apply one of these effects to a clip in the Timeline, drag it from the **Effects** window and drop in onto the clip in the **Timeline.** For instance, if you drag the Ripple effect (**Window>Effects Window>Video Effects>Distort>Ripple**) onto a clip in the **Timeline** and then park the **Current Time Indicator** on that clip, you'll see by looking in the **Program Monitor** that Premiere has distorted the image as though it were under water.

You can add multiple effects to a single clip. For instance, if you twirl open **Video Effects>Pixelate,** you'll find an effect called **Crystallize.** Drag that effect and drop it onto the same clip that you added the **Ripple** effect to earlier. Before Premiere

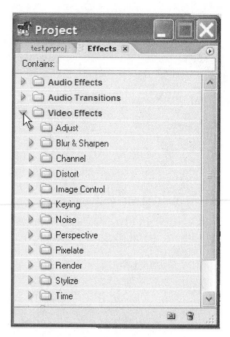

6.4   Twirling open a bin in the Effects window.

6.5   Some effects, like Crystallize, display options when you apply them.

adds this effect, it needs some information from you: a dialog window appears. Some effects will bring these up and others won't. It depends on how the effect designer programmed the specific effect. **Crystallize** breaks your image into colored shapes (see Figure 6.5). Drag the **Cell Size** slider (the triangle) to tell Premiere how big you'd like those shapes to be. Then click **OK.** Note in the **Program Monitor** that both the **Ripple** effect and the **Crystallize** effect are now applied to the clip.

When applying any effect in the **Video Effects** bin, you must drag the effect to the center area of a clip in the **Timeline**. You can't drag it between two clips, as though it was a transition effect. You can't drag it onto an audio clip either. If you want to drag effects onto cuts between clips to use them as transitions, use the effects in the **Video Transition** and **Audio Transition** bins. Drag the effects within onto the appropriate kind of clip, video or audio. You can also drag the effects in the **Audio Effects** bin directly onto audio clips in the **Timeline**. Adding audio effects and audio transitions will be covered in Chapter 10. We'll discuss transition effects later in this chapter.

Removing effects

To remove an effect or to adjust it in any way, you must select the clip to which the effect is applied and then choose **Window>Effect Controls** from the menu. Premiere will bring up the **Effect Controls** window. Don't confuse this with the **Effects** window. The **Effects** window (discussed on page 136) allows you to pick effects from bins and apply them to clips in the **Timeline**. The **Effect Controls** window allows you to adjust (or delete) effects that you've already added to clips.

If you select the clip to which you previously added the **Crystallize** and **Ripple** effects, you'll see a list of either four or five effects in the **Effect Controls** window: **Motion, Opacity, Ripple, Crystallize,** and (possibly) **Volume.** You added **Ripple** and **Crystallize,** but where did the others come from? **Motion** and **Opacity** are called fixed effects, because they are always added to every clip by Premiere. You can't delete them. **Motion** allows you to add movement animation to a clip, as in a title that flies in from the left. **Opacity** allows you to fade a clip in or out. **Opacity** and **Motion** and are covered in Chapters 7 and 9, respectively.

6.6   Before you can delete an effect, you must select its name in the Effect Controls window.

The **Volume** effect will only appear if the clip you selected before bringing up the **Effect Controls** window is either an audio clip or a video clip with a linked audio clip. As you probably can guess, this effect allows you to change or animate the audio level of a clip, making it fade in or fade out. Audio effects are covered in Chapter 10.

To delete the **Crystallize Effect,** click its name (the word "Crystallize") in the **Effect Controls** window and then press the **Delete** key on your keyboard (see Figure 6.6).

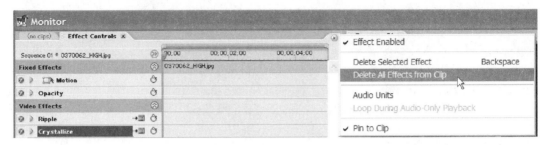

6.7   To remove all effects from the selected clip, choose the Delete All Effects from Clip option from the Effect Controls window's wing menu.

If you want to delete or alter effects on multiple clips, bring up the **Effect Controls** window and then select each clip, one by one. When you select a clip in the **Timeline**, whatever effects are applied to that clip will be revealed in the **Effect Controls** window. Once you see the effect name, you can click it and press **Delete** to remove it.

If you want to remove all of the effects from a clip, select the clip and then click the wing menu (the little triangle) in the upper-right corner of the **Effect Controls** window. Choose the **Delete All Effects from Clip** option. Of course, this command will only remove effects you've added (see Figure 6.7). It will not remove the fixed effects: **Motion**, **Opacity**, and **Volume**.

Instead of removing an effect, you might consider simply disabling it. That way, if you later change your mind and want the effect back, you can re-enable it. To disable an effect, select the effect's clip in the **Timeline** and bring up the **Effect Controls** window. Notice that to the left of every effect in the **Effect Controls** window, there's a small *f* in a black circle. Click this icon to disable the effect. To re-enable the effect, click the empty square where the *f* icon used to be (see Figure 6.8).

6.8   Click the *f* checkbox to disable an effect.

Copy/pasting

You can copy effects from one clip and paste them onto another. To do so, select a clip in the **Timeline** that has effects applied to it. Bring up the **Effect Controls** window and select any effects you want to copy by holding down the **Shift** key and clicking their names. If you only want to copy one effect, you don't need to hold down the **Shift** key—just click the effect's name. Use the keyboard shortcut **Control+C** to copy the effects. Or, if you want to do it the slow way, choose **Edit>Copy** from the menu. Select another clip in the **Timeline** and click somewhere inside the **Effect Controls** window to make it the active

6.9 To copy all of the effects from one clip to another, use the Paste Attributes command (Control+Alt+V). *(left)*

6.10 Adjusting an effect property of the selected clip the Effect Controls window. *(below)*

window. Press **Control+V** to paste the effects on the currently selected clip (slow version: Edit>Paste).

Or you can paste all effects from one clip to another by selecting the clip in the **Timeline,** pressing **Control+C,** selecting another clip, and choosing **Edit>Paste Attributes (Control+Alt+V)** from the menu. You don't need to have the **Effect Controls** window open when using this method (see Figure 6.9).

ADJUSTING PROPERTIES GLOBALLY

After you drag an effect onto a clip, you may want to adjust the effects properties. For instance, if you add a blur effect, you may want to make it more blurry or less blurry than it is by default. You can make a single adjustment that carries through for the entire duration of the clip. Or you can make adjustments that change the effect over time, maybe making the clip gradually change from very blurry to totally clear. Animating effects will be covered in the next section. In this section, we'll look at making global changes— changes that remain the same throughout the duration of the clip.

You make global changes in the **Effect Controls** window after adding an effect (see Figure 6.10).

1. For an example, add the **Gaussian Blur** effect (**Effects window>Video Effects>Blur and Sharpen>Gaussian Blur**) to a clip in the **Timeline**.

2. Then bring up the **Effect Controls** window (if necessary) and select the clip in the **Timeline**, if it isn't already selected. You should see the **Gaussian Blur** effect listed in the **Effect Controls** window. To the left of the effect, there's one of those little twirly triangles.

3. Click the triangle and the **Gaussian Blur** effect will expand to display its properties. (Click the triangle again to hide the effect's properties.)

An effect's properties are those aspects of the effect that you can alter. Different effects have different numbers and types of properties. **Gaussian Blur** has just two alterable properties: **Blurriness** and **Blur Dimensions**. **Blurriness** controls how blurry the clip will appear. Blurring a clip is sort of like smudging wet paint with your hand. **Blur Dimensions** controls the direction of the smudge.

Depending on the layout of the **Effect Controls** window, you may not be able to read the entire names of the properties. For instance, **Blur Dimensions** might show up as **Blur Dim...** If you want to be able to read full property names, point your mouse at the dividing line between the list of effects and the timeline area of the **Effect Controls** window. (The timeline area is used for animating properties, as discussed in the next section). When you've correctly positioned your mouse, the cursor will change to a double-headed arrow (see Figure 6.11). Hold down the mouse button and

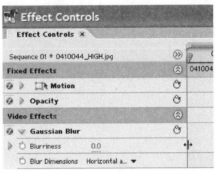

6.11 Widening the effects list in the Effect Controls window.

drag to the right to resize the effects list area, making it wider so that you can read full property names. You can also make the entire **Effect Controls** window wider (or taller) the same way you'd resize any window, by pointing to its edge and dragging away from the edge when you see a double-headed arrow.

To make the **Gaussian Blur** effect stronger (more blurry), scrub the **Blurriness** property value (the number, which is 0.0 by default) to the right. To make the effect weaker (less blurry), scrub the property value to the left. Or you can click the value (0.0) and type in a new value. Press the **Enter** key when you're done typing. As you adjust **Blurriness**, watch the **Program Monitor** to see the effect change. Of course, you won't see any changes if your **Current Time Indicator** is parked off the clip with the effect. Selecting a clip to make changes to the effect and viewing those changes are two separate operations. For best results, make sure that the clip is selected and that the **Current Time Indicator** is parked on a frame of that clip.

Sometimes after messing with effect properties, you may change your mind and want to return them all to their defaults. To do so, click the **Reset** button to the right of the effect's name (it looks like an arrow pointing to its own tail) (see Figure 6.12). In the case of the **Gaussian Blur** effect, this will return the **Blurriness** property to its default of 0.0, or not blurry at all.

Remember that some effects, like **Crystallize**, pop up a dialog when you first apply them. If you want to make adjustments later, you can bring up that dialog again. To test this out, add the Crystallize effect (**Effects window>Video Effects>Pixelate>Crystallize**), choose a cell size and then click **OK** to close the dialog. Then, in the **Effect Controls** window, click the **Setup** button (to the left of the reset button; see Figure 6.13) to bring up the dialog again. Note that the **Crystallize** effect has a **Setup** button but the **Gaussian Blur** effect doesn't. Some effects do; some don't. You have to check for the button. Certainly, any effect that pops up a dialog when you first apply it will have a **Setup** button to allow you to gain access to that dialog again at a later time. In the case of the **Crystallize** effect, you don't really need to click the **Setup** button, because the **Cell Size** property is also available on the **Effect**

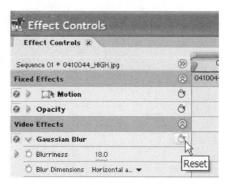

6.12 Click the Reset button to return all effect properties to default values.

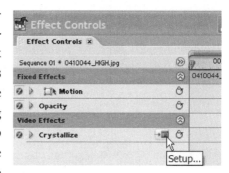

6.13 Some effects display a Setup button in the Effect Controls window. Click this button to reveal a window in which you can adjust additional effect properties.

Controls window. You can see it if you twirl open the **Crystallize** effect. But for some effects, you can only adjust certain properties in the **Setup** dialog. So if you can't find a property you're looking for in the **Effect Controls** window, check for a **Setup** button.

Program Monitor controls

Some effects can be adjusted directly in the **Program Monitor**. Premiere indicates if an effect can be controlled this way by marking it in the **Effect Controls** window with an icon that looks like an arrow pointing to a little square. The **Motion** effect, which is always in the **Effect Controls** window, has one of these icons next to it. So do some other effects, such as **Corner Pin** (**Effects window>Video Effects>Distort>Corner Pin**). After applying this effect, bring its properties up in the **Effect Controls** window. In the **Effect**

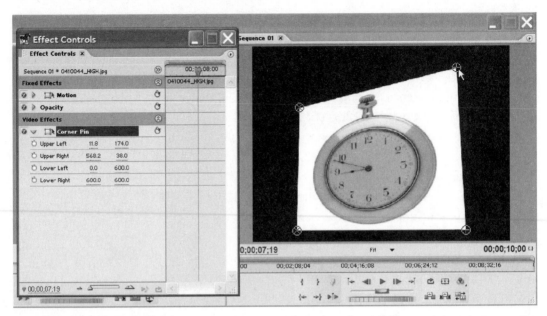

6.14 After selecting an effect's name in the Effect Controls window, draggable controls may appear in the Program Monitor.

Controls window, click the name of effect to select it. Since there may be multiple effects listed in the window, Premiere needs to know which one you want to adjust in the **Program Monitor**, which you can indicate by clicking the effect's name. Now that you've selected the **Corner Pin** effect, you should see four crosshair icons in the **Program** monitors, one at each corner of the image (see Figure 6.14). Try dragging these crosshairs to distort the image, creating odd perspective effects.

If you twirl down the **Corner Pin** effect to view its properties, you'll see four properties that correspond to the four crosshairs. Notice that as you drag the crosshairs, the property values change. Alternately, you can scrub the numbers and watch the crosshairs move.

Note

Accessing Control: In general, you have to click an effects' name in the **Effect Controls** window to access its controls in the **Program Monitor**. The exception to this is the **Motion** fixed effect. To move the clip to a new position, rotate it or scale it to a new size, click the clip in the **Program Monitor** (even if the **Motion** effect isn't selected). Premiere will display **Motion** controls and allow you to manipulate the clip by dragging it in the **Program Monitor**. For specifics about the **Motion** effect, see Chapter 9 on page 211.

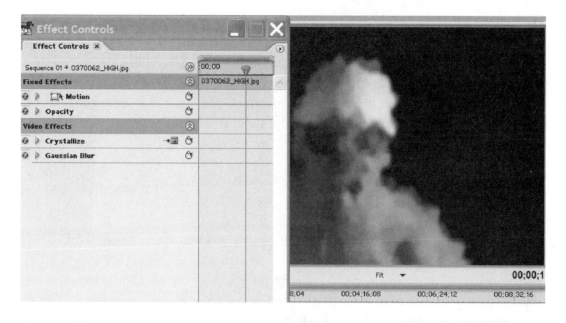

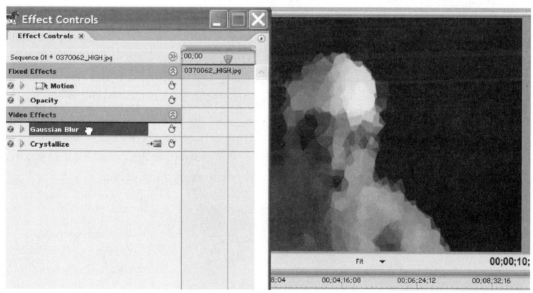

6.15 By changing the stacking order of the effects in the Effect Controls window, you can alter the image in the Program Monitor.

Effect stacking order

If you have multiple effects listed in the **Effect Controls** window, you can drag their names up and down in the list to change their stacking order (see Figure 6.15). You can't do this with the fixed effects. Premiere renders the effect at the top of the list first, then the next one down, then the next, and so on until it gets to the bottom. Often changing the stacking order can dramatically change the final result. For instance, if you apply Crystallize and the **Gaussian Blur**, you'll blur the cells created by the **Crystallize** effect, and as a result, the cells will no longer be recognizable. On the other hand, if you reorder the effects so that **Gaussian Blur** comes before **Crystallize**, you'll just blur the original image. Then the **Crystallize** cells will appear on top of that. You'll see a series of cells, each one with a blurred image inside it.

ANIMATING PROPERTIES

Keyframing

Animation in Premiere (and its many other programs, such as After Effects and Flash) is created by a process called *keyframing* (see Figure 6.16). When you keyframe, you set up the main poses of an animation, and Premiere takes care of the rest. For instance, if you want to make text fly in from the right and stop in the center of the screen, you will set up two keyframes, one in which the text is off right and another in which the text is centered. Premiere will analyze the two keyframes and automatically create an animation in which the text flies from its position in keyframe one to its position in keyframe 2. If you want to make a clip gradually get less and less blurry, you'll set up the **Gaussian Blur** effect with two keyframes, one in which the image is very blurry and another in which its not blurry at all. Premiere will take care of the animating process in between the two keyframes. If you want to make a clip crystallize into tiny cells, make the cells get bigger, and then make the cells get small again, you'll need three keyframes: **Crystallize** with a small cell size, **Crystallize** with a large cell size, and **Crystallize** with a small cell size again. As usually, you will provide the keyframes and Premiere will create everything in between them. That

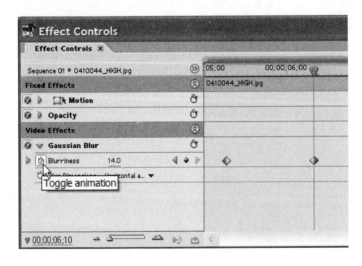

6.16 The Gaussian Blur effect's Blurriness property animated with two keyframes.

process—creating the animation frames between the keyframes—is called *tweening* (as in in-betweening). It's also sometimes known as *interpolation*. (You create keyframes; the computer analyzes them and then interpolates in between states from its analysis.) It's a very old process, one that has been used without computers for years by companies like Disney when they make long animated films. These companies hire lead animators who just draw the keyframes. Then they employ lower paid workers who draw all the in-between frames by examining the keyframes and filling in the blanks. The revolution of computer animation allows you to be the lead animator while a program, such as Premiere, acts as your tweener.

When setting up keyframes you always have to keep three things in mind: your starting state, your ending state, and the length of time you want the animation to take. In other words, if you position text to the right in keyframe one and center it in keyframe two, Premiere will understand that you want the text to fly in from the right and wind up centered, but how *long* should it take to do so? A second? A minute? An hour? You set the duration of the animation by spacing your keyframes closer together or further apart in time (see Figure 6.17). For instance, if you're animating a title flying in from the left, and the keyframe 1 is at 10 seconds into your sequence and keyframe 2 is at 25 seconds

6.17 Drag keyframes farther apart to make the animation slower.

into your sequence, it will take the text 15 seconds to fly in from the left. If you've set up an animation like this and you like the effect but not the timing, you can easily change it by moving the keyframes closer together or farther apart. For instance, if you move keyframe 2 to 45 seconds into your sequence (leaving keyframe 1 at 10 seconds), the animation will now take 35 seconds to complete. But otherwise it will be the same: the text will still fly in from the right, just slower.

Because timing is so important to animation, there's a timeline in the **Effect Controls** window. You can also animate in the main **Timeline** window, but it's convenient to have another timeline next to the effect properties. By default, the **Timeline** in the **Effect Controls** window only displays the selected clip.

Adding keyframes

In order to keyframe an effect property, you first need to move the **Current Time Indicator** to the location at which you'd like to set your first keyframe. You can drag the Indicator in the **Timeline** or the **Program Monitor**, but there's another Indicator that's specially made for the task, and it's right there in the **Effect Controls** window, to the right of the effects list. Notice that when you move this indicator, the indicators in the **Timeline** and the **Program Monitor** move along with it and vice versa. But in the **Effect Controls** window, you see only the portion of the timeline where the selected clip is located. This makes it easier to make sure you're placing keyframes within the boundaries of the selected clip's duration. If you deselect the **Pin to Clip** option in the **Effect Control**'s wing menu, the **Effect Control**'s timeline will reveal the entire length of the sequence, even parts of it where the selected clip isn't located.

Assuming you're animating the **Blurriness** property of the **Gaussian Blur** effect, let's say you want the clip to be really blurry at the beginning and sharp at the end. You'll begin this animation by placing the **Current Time Indicator** at the beginning of the clip, which is where you want to place your first keyframe (see Figure 6.18).

To add the keyframe, click the little stopwatch to the left of the **Blurriness** property. Premiere will add a small diamond icon to the **Effect Controls** window's timeline, at the location of the **Current Time Indicator** and in the same row as the **Blurriness** property. The diamond represents a keyframe.

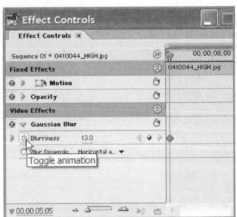

6.18 Click the stopwatch to animate a property and add the first keyframe at the location of the Current Time Indicator.

Leaving the **Current Time Indicator** parked on this keyframe, adjust the **Blurriness** property until the clip is so blurry you can't tell what it's supposed to be. This amount of blurriness will now be locked into the keyframe at the location of the **Current Time Indicator.** Premiere may mess with the amount of blurriness at other times—it may have to in order to animate blurriness—but you're guaranteed that at the keyframe, the blurriness will always be the amount you set.

Now move the **Current Time Indicator** to the end of the clip and adjust the **Blurriness** property down to zero, so that the clip is in sharp focus. Premiere will add another diamond keyframe symbol at the new location of the **Current Time Indicator.**

Note that you clicked the stopwatch only to add the first keyframe. Generally, you click the stopwatch once and then never touch it again. Clicking the stopwatch once tells Premiere that you want to animate a property (as opposed to just using it to set global values that stay the same for the entire duration of the clip). To add new keyframes, you just move the **Current Time Indicator** to where you want the new keyframe to be placed and then adjust the property value. If the stopwatch is on, Premiere will automatically add keyframes whenever you adjust the property. This is assuming your **Current Time Indicator** is parked somewhere where there isn't already a keyframe. If you're parked on a keyframe, any adjustments you make to the property will change the value at that keyframe rather than adding a new keyframe.

Clicking the stopwatch a second time will remove all the keyframes (see Figure 6.19). It's a way of telling Premiere, "I've changed my mind. I don't want to animate this property any more." And from then on, any property changes you make will be global, acting on the clip for its entire duration. Clicking the stopwatch a third time won't bring your keyframes back. It will just start all over again by setting a new keyframe at the location of the **Current Time Indicator.** If you accidentally click the stopwatch a second time and lose all your keyframes, use the undo shortcut, **Control+Z,** to get them back.

6.19 Clicking the stopwatch a second time will remove all the keyframes.

If you scrub the **Current Time Indicator** back and forth or play the part of the sequence where the selected clip is located, you'll see that Premiere has animated the clip from very blurry to very sharp. Let's say that you like the animation, but it's too slow. You'd like the clip to get sharp sooner and then stay that way for a while. Try selecting the second keyframe by clicking its diamond in the **Effect Control** window's timeline. Now drag the keyframe to the left until it's closer to the first keyframe. If you play the sequence now, you'll see the same animation as before, but it will run quicker and end sooner.

In general, don't select keyframes

If you want to get rid of a keyframe, click it to select it and the press the **Delete** key on your keyboard. In general, you only select keyframes when you want to move them (to speed up or slow down animation) or to delete them. You don't select them when you want to alter them. For instance, if you feel that the clip is too blurry at the first keyframe, don't select the first keyframe and then adjust the **Blurriness** property. That seems like a logical thing to do, but remember that as long as the stopwatch is turned on, you will create a new keyframe at the location of the **Current Time Indicator** whenever you adjust a property. Premiere doesn't care which keyframe is selected. It cares where the **Current Time Indicator** is. So if your **Current Time Indicator** is parked at 15 seconds and you select a keyframe at 11 seconds, any adjustments you make to the property will be stored in a keyframe at 15 seconds. Nothing will happen to the keyframe at 11 seconds, even though you have it selected. If there's already a keyframe at 15 seconds, your adjustments will alter its value. If there isn't a keyframe at 15 seconds, Premiere will create one there to store the adjustments you're making (see Figure 6.20). So to make the first keyframe less blurry, move the **Current Time Indicator** until it's parked on that keyframe. Then adjust the **Blurriness** property down a bit.

Navigating to a specific keyframe

When you're adjusting a keyframe, you must make sure that the **Current Time Indicator** is parked exactly on that keyframe. If it's even one frame before or one frame after that keyframe, you risk creating a new keyframe instead of adjusting the one you already have. At the bottom of the **Effect Controls** window, there's a slider that will allow you to zoom into the window's timeline (see Figure 6.21). Zooming in really close may help you accurately place the **Current Time Indicator**, but you still might miss by a frame or two.

A more exact method is to use the keyframe navigator buttons to the right of the property names. The buttons look like small triangles, facing left and right. Each time you click the right-facing triangle, Premiere will jump the **Current Time Indicator** to the next

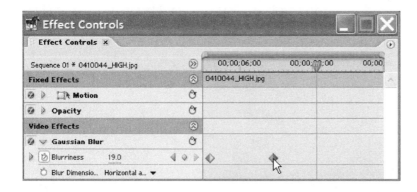

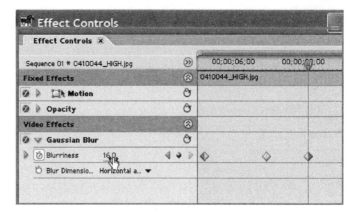

6.20   If you select a keyframe and then adjust an effect property, Premiere will ignore the selected keyframe and add a new keyframe at the position of the Current Time Indicator.

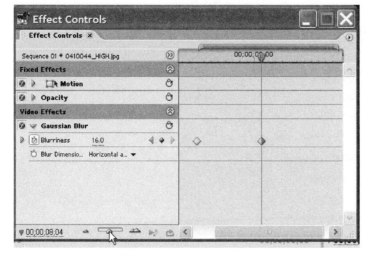

6.21   You can use the slider at the bottom of the Effect Controls window to zoom in on the window's timeline.

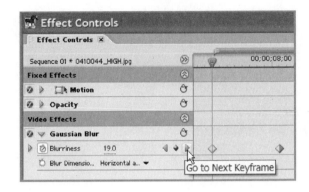

6.22 You can jump from keyframe to keyframe by clicking the navigator buttons.

keyframe; each time you press the left-facing triangle, Premiere will jump the **Current Time Indicator** to the previous keyframe. When you click either of these buttons, you're guaranteed that the **Current Time Indicator** will be parked exactly on a keyframe. Then any property adjustments you make will adjust that keyframe.

Note

No Navigator? If you don't see the navigator, it's because you haven't yet turned on animation for that property. The **Navigator** doesn't appear until you click the stopwatch. If you see a **Navigator**, but the triangle buttons are grayed out, that's because you only have one keyframe. You don't have access to both buttons until you have at least two keyframes in the **Timeline**. Then it makes sense to navigate there and back between two keyframes (see Figure 6.22). If you have only one keyframe and you drag the **Current Time Indicator** away from it, you will have access to a single triangle button, which will return the **Current Time Indicator** to the exact location of the keyframe.

Adding a keyframe without animating

In between the two triangles is a small circle. If you move the Current Time Indicator to a location where there isn't a keyframe and then click this circle, Premiere will add a new keyframe to that location—even though you haven't adjusted the property (see Figure 6.23). Since you haven't adjusted the property, Premiere just records the property's current setting to the new keyframe, which means that this keyframe will have the same value as

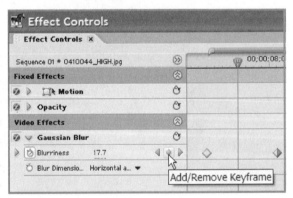

6.23 Click the circular button between the two navigators to add a new keyframe or remove an old one.

the keyframe before it. When two adjacent keyframes have the same value, there is no animation between them. Premiere can't animate from very blurry to very blurry. So this gives you a method of holding a property at a specific value for any length of time.

 Circle Button: If the Current Time Indicator is parked on a keyframe and you click the circle button, Premiere will remove that keyframe, just as if you'd selected it and pressed the **Delete** key on your keyboard. So the circle button will add a keyframe if there isn't one at the Current Time Indicator's location, but if one's already there, clicking the circle will delete it.

Suppose you've added the **Crystallize** effect and you want the cells to start small and then grow bigger and bigger between one second and two seconds. Then, between two seconds and three second, you want the cells to hold at their larger size. Finally, between three seconds and four seconds, you want the cells to return to their original small size. To create this animation, try the following:

1. Move the **Current Time Indicator** to one second and turn on the stopwatch.

2. Still at one second, adjust the **Cell Size** property way down so that the cells are really small (see Figure 6.24).

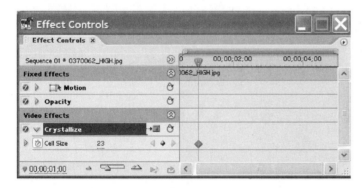

6.24 At one second, turn on the stopwatch and adjust the Cell Size property to a small value.

3. Move the **Current Time Indicator** to two seconds and adjust the **Cell Size** property way up, so that the cells are huge. As soon as you make the adjustment, Premiere will automatically add a new keyframe at the location of the **Current Time Indicator,** which is at two seconds (see Figure 6.25).

4. Move the **Current Time Indicator** to three seconds and click the small circle between the two navigator buttons (see Figure 6.26).

   Premiere will add a keyframe at three seconds (the location of the **Current Time Indicator**) that's exactly the same as the keyframe at two seconds, so there will be no animation between them.

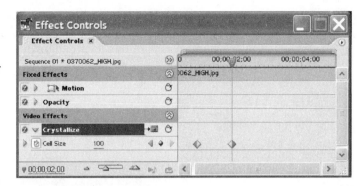

6.25 At two seconds, increase the Cell Size property to a larger value.

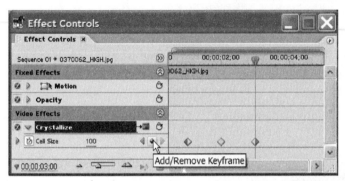

6.26 At three seconds, click the small circle button between the navigators to add a copy of the keyframe at two seconds.

6.27 At four seconds, decrease the Cell Size property back to a small value.

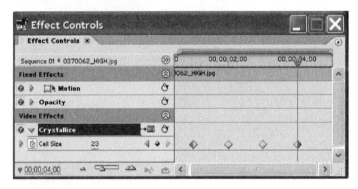

5. Finally, move the **Current Time Indicator** to four seconds and adjust the **Cell Size** property back down to a small size (see Figure 6.27).

If you play back the animation, you'll see that the cells grow in size between keyframes 1 and 2, stay the same size between keyframes 2 and 3, and then shrink in size between keyframes 3 and 4. To adjust any of the timing, drag keyframes closer together or further apart.

Copying and pasting keyframes

In the previous example, the goal was to start and end the **Cell Size** at the same, small value. If you want start and end keyframes to be exactly the same, it can be tricky to get them this way by simply adjusting the property. Of course, you can click the circle to add a new keyframe, but that will set the end keyframe's value to the same as the keyframe right before it, which might not be the same as the first keyframe. The easiest way to ensure that two nonadjacent keyframes have the same value is to copy the first one and paste it at the location of the second one. For example:

1. Start a new **Crystallize** animation by moving the **Current Time Indicator** back to the start of the clip and clicking the stopwatch twice. (The first click will remove all of the keyframes from the last example; the second click will set a new keyframe at the location of the **Current Time Indicator.**)

2. Adjust the **Cell Size** property so that the cells are small.

3. Now move the **Current Time Indicator** to halfway through the clip's duration and adjust the **Cell Size** property so that the cells are huge. (Premiere will add a second keyframe.)

4. Finally, move the **Current Time Indicator** to the end of the clip's duration. Instead of adjusting the property, select the start keyframe by clicking it and copy it to the clipboard (**Control+C**).

5. Then paste (**Control+V**), and you'll get a new keyframe at the **Current Time Indicator**'s location that's an exact copy of the start keyframe.

Adjusting multiple keyframes at once

If you want to manipulate multiple keyframes at once, marquee select them (drag a rectangle around them with the **Selection** tool) or hold down the **Shift** key and click each keyframe you want to be part of the group. After you've **Shift**+clicked a group of keyframes, you can press the **Delete** key to remove all of them, copy them all to the clipboard and then paste them somewhere else, or you can move them all by dragging any one of them to a new point in time. Dragging one of the selected keyframes will move all of them.

Adjusting keyframes in the timeline

In addition to manipulating keyframes in the **Effect Controls** window, you can also adjust them in the main **Timeline**. To test this out, apply the **Crystallize** effect to a clip and add a couple of keyframes, creating an animation in which the cell size gets bigger over the duration of the clip. Then (in the **Timeline**) click the **Show Keyframes** button just below

Bezier Curves and Easing (the keys to pro-level animation)

It doesn't take long for beginning animators to master keyframes. But there's more to animating than moving from point A to point B. For instance, most real-world objects don't travel in straight lines. To animate objects moving along curved paths, you have to master Bezier curves. Nor do real-world objects travel at a constant rate. They start slow and then speed up. Or, if they're moving fast, they gradually slow down before coming to a stop. This acceleration and deceleration is called *easing*. In this book, Bezier curves and easing are covered in Chapter 9, which is about motion animation. This is because curves and speed changes are most noticeable when objects are moving around. In fact, curves can only be used with motion animation (How would you curve an animated blur?), but any animation can ease. You can imagine some blurred text very slowly becoming unblurred. As the animation continued, the rate of unblurring could gradually move faster and faster. So when you read about Easing in Chapter 9, think about how it might apply to all animation—not just motion.

and to the left of the track name, the track that contains the clip to which you applied **Crystallize** (see Figure 6.28).

By default, the **Show Keyframe** button looks like a "No" symbol (a circle with a slash through it), indicating that keyframes are not showing. When you click this button, Premiere displays a pop-up menu. Choose the **Show Keyframes** option from this menu.

Where's Show Keyframe? If you don't see the Show Keyframe button, the track may be collapsed. To expand the track, click the twirly triangle to the left of the track's name (see Figure 6.29).

Premiere will now display the keyframes in the clips along that track, but the limitation here is that you can only view keyframes for one property of one effect at a time. So if you've animated Blurriness of the **Gaussian Blur** effect and **Cell Size** of the **Crystallize** effect, you'll have to choose which one of those properties you want to view. In the **Effect Controls** window, you can view both properties at once.

To pick which property you want to view in the **Timeline**, select one from the dropdown menu to the right of each clip name on the **Timeline**. This dropdown menu only appears when you've pressed the **Show Keyframe** button and chosen **Show Keyframes** from the pop-up menu. To see your **Cell Size** keyframes, click the dropdown menu and then choose the **Crystallize>Cell Size** option (see Figure 6.30).

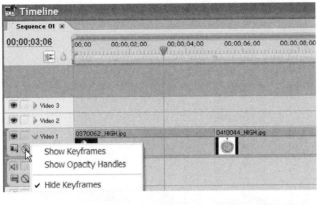

6.28 Click the Show Keyframes button in the Timeline window and select the Show Keyframes option in the pop-up menu to reveal keyframes in the Timeline.

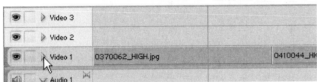

6.29 If tracks are collapsed, you won't be able to see keyframes. Click the twirly triangle to the left of the track name to expand the track.

You can also select an effect property by right-clicking a clip in the **Timeline** and then choosing the **Show Clip Keyframes** option from the pop-up menu. Premiere will then display a submenu, from which you can choose the specific property's keyframes you want to adjust.

After picking a property from the dropdown menu, Premiere will display that property's keyframes directly on the clip in the **Timeline**. You can drag these keyframes up and down to adjust their properties. Dragging a keyframe up will increase its property value; dragging it down will decrease its property value. So if you want to make **Cell Size** larger at one of the keyframes, drag the keyframe up (see Figure 6.31).

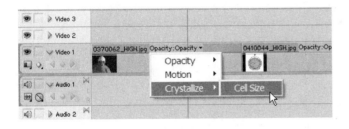

6.30 To reveal a specific property's keyframes in the Timeline, select it from the dropdown menu to the right of a clip's name.

6.31 To increase or decrease a keyframe's value, drag its keyframe up or down.

You can manipulate **Timeline** keyframes in most of the same ways you can manipulate **Effect Controls** keyframes. Try moving them closer together or farther apart (to speed up or slow down the animation), clicking them and deleting them by pressing **Delete** on your keyboard, copy/pasting them, etc. Notice the keyframe navigator next to the **Show Keyframes** button. This works the same way as its double on the **Effect Controls** window. When working with keyframes in the **Timeline**, the **Add/Remove** keyframes button (the little circle between the navigator buttons) is particularly useful: try moving the **Timeline's Current Time Indicator** to a location where there's no keyframe, click the **Add/Remove** keyframe button to add a new keyframe at that location, and then drag the keyframe up or down with your mouse to set that keyframe's value.

6.32 Control+click with the Pen tool on the orange line to add a new keyframe.

You can even add new keyframes directly inside the clip (without using the little circle button) by switching to the **Pen** tool (see Figure 6.32). If you hold down the **Control** key on your keyboard and click anywhere along the orange line that connects the keyframes (anywhere *except* on an existing keyframe), you'll create a new keyframe. You can then release the **Control** key and use the **Pen** tool to drag the keyframe up or down (strengthening or weakening that property's effect) or left and right (moving the keyframe to an earlier or later point in time). If you use the **Pen** (without the **Control** key) to drag the line between two keyframes, you'll adjust both keyframes at once. Even if there are no keyframes—if you've just applied the effect but haven't yet turned on any stopwatches—you can set keyframes with the **Pen** by **Control**+clicking along the orange line.

NESTING (APPLYING EFFECTS TO AN ENTIRE TRACK)

If you want to apply effects to an entire track (or to multiple tracks) at once, you'll have to preplan a little bit and assemble that track (or tracks) in a separate sequence. If you look in the **Project** window, you'll see your current sequence listed there as **Sequence 01**,

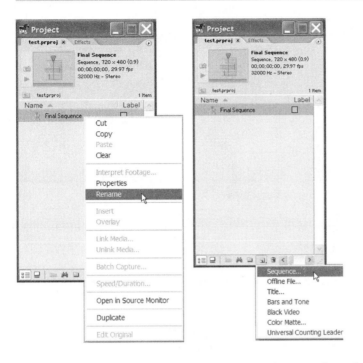

6.33 Right-click Sequence 01 in the Project window and choose the Rename option to rename it "Final Sequence."

6.34 Click the New button at the bottom of the Project window and select the Sequence option.

unless you've changed its name. When working with multiple sequences, it's a good idea to give them specific, meaningful names so that you can tell them apart. To rename *Sequence 01*, double-click its name in the **Project** window or right click its name in the **Project** window and choose **Rename** from the pop-up menu. Rename it *Final Sequence* and press **Enter** to finalize the name change (see Figure 6.33).

Now create a new sequence by clicking the **New** button at the bottom of the **Project** window. It looks like a pad of paper with the bottom of the first page slightly curled up (see Figure 6.34). From the menu that appears, pick **Sequence**.

Premiere will display a dialog in which you can choose settings for the new sequence. For sequence name, type *Blurry Background*. The name signifies what you're going to use this sequence for. In this case, you're going to assemble a bunch of clips that will be used in the *Final Sequence* as an interesting blurry flurry of colors that will play behind some titles. Click **OK** to accept the rest of the default settings (see Figure 6.35).

Premiere will open *Blurry Background's* **Timeline** and monitors (see Figure 6.36). Notice the tabs at the top of the **Timeline** with the two sequence names on them. The same tabs appear at the top of the **Program Monitor**. You can click the tabs to change the view from one sequence to another. Or you can drag a tab away from its window (**Timeline** or **Monitor**) to float it in a separate window. Clicking the little **X** icon in a tab's upper-right corner will close that sequence. To reopen the sequence, click its icon in the **Project** window.

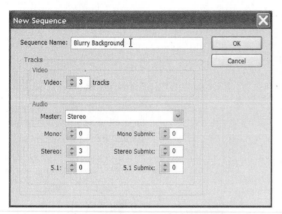

6.35 Using the New Sequence dialog window to
make the new sequence Blurry Background.

6.36 Premiere displays tabs in the Timeline and Project window for each sequence. *(above right)*

With the **Blurry Background** sequence open, import a bunch of footage into the **Project** and edit it into the sequence on the **Video 1** track. When you're done, close the sequence by clicking the **X** icon on its tab (see Figure 6.37).

It's not by accident that sequences appear in the **Project** window as if they are imported footage. For all intensive purposes, they *are* imported footage. To prove this to yourself, drag the *Blurry Background* sequence into the **Final Sequence** and place it on the **Video 1** track. (If you want, you can drag it into the **Source Monitor** first, mark in and out points, and insert or overlay it into the **Video 1**.) Notice that it comes into the sequence as if it's one clip. This means that you can apply an effect to it (see Figure 6.38).

Try this now: apply the **Gaussian Blur** effect to it and adjust the **Blurriness** property until it looks like indistinct colors and shapes. If you've read the chapter on titles (Chapter 11 on page 255), you can now add titles on top of this background. Place the titles in the **Video 2** track (see Figure 6.39).

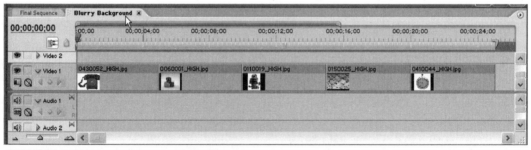

6.37 Arrange a series of image or video clips on Blurry Background's Timeline.

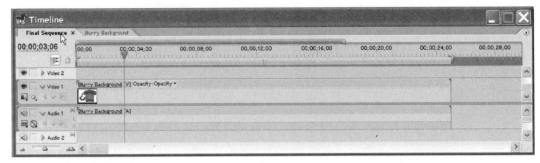

6.38 Drag the Blurry Background from the Project window into the Final Project sequence's Timeline.

If you want to add an effect to both the nested *Blurry Background* sequence *and* the titles in **Video 2**, you'll have to nest *this* sequence *(Final Sequence)* in yet another sequence. You can nest sequences within sequences within sequences up to any depth.

If you realize that you need to make a change to the *Blurry Background* sequence, just double-click it—either in the **Project** window or in the **Timeline** of *Final Sequence*. When you double-click it, the sequence will open for editing. Any changes you make to it will carry over into the nested version within *Final Sequence*.

You can also open a nested sequence by placing the **Current Time Indicator** within it, targeting its track (by clicking the track name, i.e., **Video 1**), and pressing the keyboard shortcut **Shift+T**.

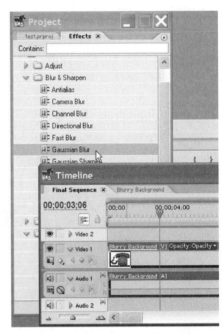

6.39 Apply the Gaussian Blur effect to the Blurry Background "clip" on Final Sequence's Timeline.

TRANSITION EFFECTS

Transition effects (which reside in the **Video Transition** and **Audio Transition** bins, in the **Effects** window), work differently from normal video and audio effects. Specifically, transitions affect the way one clip ends and the next clip begins. So when you add them, you must drag them to the crack between two clips (the cut) rather than to the middle of a single clip, as you would with a normal effect.

Transitions work best with trimmed clips. In other words, you should make sure that the end of the first clip (its tail) is not fully extended. Similarly, you should make sure that the beginning of the second clip (its head) is also not fully extended. Another way of saying this is that transitions require handles on both clips. Why? Because while transitions are animating, you see a little of both clips at the same time. Think about the most well-known transition effect: a crossfade. During a crossfade, as one clip is fading out and the other is fading in, you temporarily see both at once (superimposed over each other). But near the beginning of the transition, the second clip hasn't started yet. And near the end of the transition, the first clip is over. The clips don't overlap at any point; one doesn't start playing until the other is done. So how can Premiere show them both at the same time? It solves this problem by using extra footage from the clips' handles as overlap footage. In other words, when the first clip reaches its end, it keeps playing a little into its handle. And before the second clip is supposed to begin, it starts playing (a little early) using footage from one if its handles. This means that you must be okay with the audience seeing a little past the in and out points of your footage.

If you extend your clips all the way out, so that there are no handles, Premiere will still allow you to apply a transition, but it will have no choice but to repeat frames during the transition. Premiere draws a crosshatch pattern on the transition when it's using repeated frames. The effect will look as if time stands still while the transition is taking place. So unless you want this effect, make sure your clips have handles (see Figure 6.40).

6.40 Make sure the clips on either side of the transition have handles (extra hidden footage). Note that in this screenshot, the small triangle in the second clip's upper-right corner indicates that it's been retracted all the way to its final frame (no handle). This is okay, because the transition will go at this clip's start, where there is handle, not at its end.

After you've added a transition effect, you'll see it represented in the **Timeline** as if it's a small clip positioned between the two real clips. You can point to its edges and trim it in and out, just as you'd trim an actual clip. Trimming a transition in will make the transition run quicker. Trimming it out will make it run slower. If you change your mind and want to add a different transition, just drag another one from the **Effects** window and drop it on top of the original one. Premiere will replace the original transition with the new one.

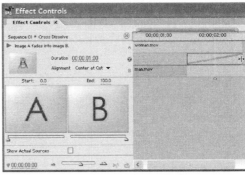

6.42 Trimming a transition in the Effect Controls window. *(above)*

6.41 You can trim a transition in the Timeline, just as if were a clip. *(above)*

 Number of Clips: In general, transition effects are applied to two clips at once, so that the first clip transitions into the second clip. However, there are times when you want to apply a transition to just one clip. This will allow you to create effect in which, say, one clip fades out but the next clip doesn't fade in.

To apply a transition to just one clip, you still need to drag the effect to the crack between two clips. But hold down the **Control** key as you drag. Premiere will then allow you to place the transition on the tail of the first clip or the head of the second clip (see Figure 6.41).

Adjusting a transition in the Effect Controls window

It's easier to adjust transitions in the **Effect Controls** window. To do so, make sure the transition is selected in the **Timeline** and then choose **Window>Effect Controls** from the menu. Or you can double-click a transition in the **Timeline** to bring up the **Effect Control** window (see Figure 6.42).

In the timeline part of the **Effect Controls** window, the transition and the two clips it affects are represented as if they are on three different tracks. The first clip is on the top track, **track A,** and the second clip is on the bottom track, **track B.** The transition is in

6.43 To see images from the clips in the Effect Controls window, click the Show Actual Sources option.

between them. You can point the edges of the transition or of either clips to trim them in or out. For instance, if you drag the end of **clip A** to the right and the start of **clip B** to the left, you'll overlap the handles more than their original amount. You can then trim out the transition so that it covers the whole overlap and runs longer.

On the left side of the **Effect Controls** window are the usual effect properties. Of course, these properties will be different for every transition effect. By default, the two clips are represented in the controls by a large letter **A** and a large letter **B**, but you can see the actual images from the clips in the **Effect Controls** window by checking the **Show Actual Sources** option (see Figure 6.43).

Note that you don't see stopwatches next to transition effect properties. That's because transitions are self-animating. You don't need to supply keyframes. And if you want to adjust the speed of a transition, you need to trim it, as described previously.

 Less Is More: Beginning filmmakers tend to overuse transition effects. As you watch professionally made films, you'll notice that most of the transitions are straightforward cuts, with occasionally dissolves, usually included to show the passage of time.

GRADIENT WIPE

Gradient Wipe (Effects window>Video Transitions>Wipe>Gradient Wipe) is more powerful than any of the other transition effects, but few people know how to use it. This is because **Gradient Wipe** uses a secret image to control the transition. You need to create this image in Photoshop or a similar paint program. Specifically, you need to create a full-screen image in which the only colors are blacks, whites, and grays. Generally, such images are called *gradients*.

Premiere will map each pixel in your gradient to a pixel in your transitioning clips. For instance if there's black pixel right in the center of the gradient, Premiere will think of the corresponding pixels, right in the middle of the transitioning clips, as black. It won't color these pixels black, but, during the transition, any pixel that Premiere thinks of as black will vanish first, followed by gray pixels, and then white ones, which always vanish last.

So if you control the effect with a gradient that is black on the left, gray in the middle and white on the right, the first clip will vanish (revealing the second clip, as with all transitions) from right to left—like a right-to-left wipe. If you control the effect with a gradient that's black in the center, then gray, then white, the first clip will vanish from the center on out.

When you make your gradients, make sure you save them at the correct width and height for video. In the U.S. and Japan, graphics created for video (non-widescreen) should be either 720×534 or 720×540. The second, slightly larger dimension are for higher-end (D1) video, but the difference is only six pixels, and for a gradient either set of dimensions show work. In European videos (non-widescreen) the gradient should be 768×576.

Once you've created your gradient, save it in a standard graphics format, such as JPEG, TIFF, or BMP. If you're working in Photoshop, you can save it as a PSD (a native Photoshop document), because Premiere and Photoshop are both Adobe products.

Don't bother importing the gradient into Premiere. Just save it somewhere on your hard drive where you'll know where to find it.

Now apply the **Gradient Wipe** effect. Premiere will display a dialog which shows the default gradient the effect will use if you don't supply one of your own. In the dialog, click the Select Image button. Premier will display an **Open** window. Navigate to the gradient file on your hard drive, select it, and click the **Open** button. Then click **OK** to close out of the dialog.

If you'd like to switch to a different gradient, click the transition in the **Timeline** and bring up the **Effect Controls** window. In the properties area, click the **Custom** button to redisplay the original dialog that allows you to pull a gradient into the effect (see Figure 6.44).

SAVING EFFECT PRESETS

You may want to apply the same effect—or group of effects—to many clips in many sequences (or even in many different project files). By saving effect presets, you can reapply effects, with their properties already adjusted to suit your liking.

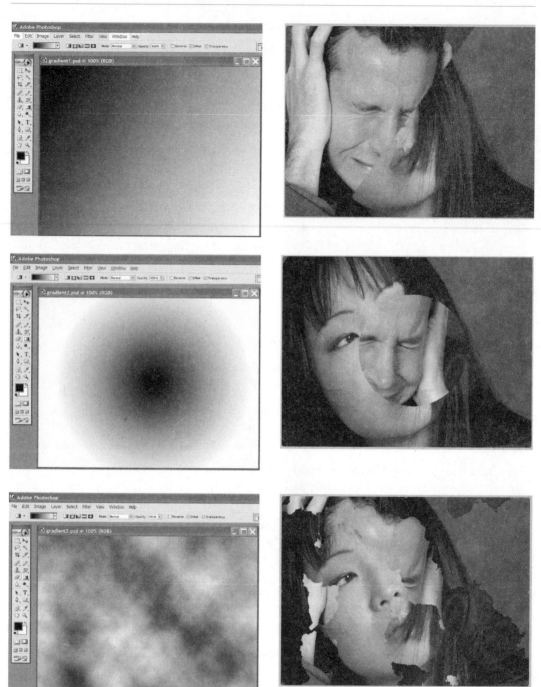

6.44 The Gradient Wipe transition effect, using three different gradients, designed in Photoshop.

Suppose you'd applied the **Corner Pin, Gaussian Blur,** and **Crystallize** effects to a clip and adjusted properties in all three effects, including animating some of those properties. To save these effects as a preset, try the following.

1. In the **Effect Controls** window, **Shift**+click the names of the effects you want to save in the preset.

2. Choose the **Save Preset** option from the **Effect Controls** wing menu. Premiere will display the **Save Preset** dialog window.

3. Type a name for your preset. Presets are saved as external files, and the name you type will be the file name for the preset you're currently saving.

4. Select a preset type: **Scale, Anchor** to **In Point,** or **Anchor to Out Point.**

    These options specify how you want to deal with keyframed effects that are later applied to shorter clips. For instance, if the original clip was two keyframes seconds long and contained three keyframes, the first one at 0 seconds, the middle one at 1 second and the final one at 2 seconds, Premiere needs to know what to do with these keyframes if you apply this preset to a 1-second-long clip.

    *   **Scale:** This option will squeeze or stretch the keyframe duration to match the duration of the clip you apply the preset to. So given the previous example, if you apply the preset to a 1-second clip, Premiere will place the first keyframe at 0 seconds, the second keyframe at a $1/2$ second, and the last keyframe at 1 second. If you apply the preset to a 4-second clip, the keyframes will appear at 0 seconds, 2 seconds, and 4 seconds.

    *   **Anchor to In Point:** The first keyframe of the preset is placed at the start of the clip you apply it to, and the subsequent keyframes appear at their original intervals. So using the previous example, if you apply the preset to a 5-second clip, the keyframes will appear at 0 seconds, 1 second, and 2 seconds. If you apply it to a one-second clip, the keyframes will appear at 0 seconds and 1 second. The final keyframe won't be able to fit on the clip, but Premiere will still apply it, past the clip's out point. So you will be able to reveal that keyframe if you trim the clip's tail out far enough.

    *   **Anchor to Out Point:** The same as **Anchor to In Point,** except the last preset keyframe is placed at the out point of the clip you apply the preset to and then the preceding keyframes appear at their original intervals. Keyframes that fall before the clip's in point are retained and can be revealed if you trim the clip's head out far enough.

5. Click the **OK** button.

Saved presets appear in the **Effect** window's **Presets** bin. You apply them the same way you apply any other effect. Drag a preset from the bin and drop it onto a clip in the **Timeline**. To reveal properties of the preset in the **Effect Controls** window, select the preset and choose **Preset Properties** option from the **Effect Control** window's wing menu.

LEARNING TO USE THE EFFECTS

Premiere comes with many effects, each of which have different properties that can be altered and animated. Where can you learn how to use them? One way to learn them is simply to apply them, mess with the settings and see what happens. For a more guided approach, you can use the online help. Many people avoid online help, but in the case of effects, it's the most straightforward way to learn them. In the help, Adobe has listed each effect, what it does and how each of its properties work.

To look up a specific effect, choose **Help>Contents** from the menu. Premiere will open the online help in your web browser, but you don't need to be connected to the internet to use **Help**. Along the left side of the screen, your browser will print the help contents (see Figure 6.45). Click **Applying Effects**. Your browser will then list all of the effects help pages in its right pane. For help with Video Effects, click the option called **Video effects included with Adobe Premiere Pro**. The browser will display a helpful list of all of the effects included with Premiere. Click any effect to learn how to use it.

To a list of all of the audio effects that come with Premiere, choose the option called **Audio effects included with Adobe Premiere Pro.**

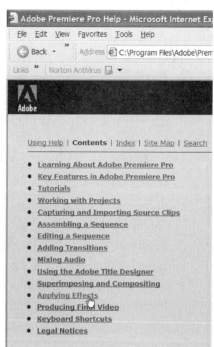

GENERATING PREVIEWS

n general, Premiere displays your sequence in real time when you play it. However, if you pile on too many effects and transitions, your sequence may playback more slowly than it's actual speed. This will not affect the final render out of the Premiere,

6.45 You can get help for all the effects that ship with Premiere by consulting online help.

which will always play at full speed. But it may affect the speed your sequence plays while you're editing.

Premiere warns you about **Timeline** segments that it can't play in real time by drawing a red bar in the time ruler that spans the duration of those segments. When you see one of these lines, you have three options:

- You can allow the segment to play back at a reduced speed (in which case you don't have to do anything.

- You can reduce the preview quality of the image (which may allow Premiere to play the segment back at full speed, because it doesn't have to worry about the quality of the image at the same time).

- You can render out a quick preview file.

To play back at reduced quality, click the **Program Monitor's** wing menu and select the **Draft Quality** option. This will change the monitor's display to one-half resolution. The **High Quality** option will force the monitor to always display images at

Wing: These options are also available from the **Source Monitor's** wing menu.

full resolution, which may mean Premiere has to play back at reduced speed, as discussed previously. **Automatic Quality** allows Premiere to switch back and forth between **High** and **Draft** quality as the need arises. If you choose this option, Premiere will choose whichever option allows it to come closest to play back at full speed.

If you select one of them there, it will only affect the display in the **Source Monitor**. Similarly, the options in the Program monitor only affect its display.

To generate a preview file, you must first tell Premiere which portion of your sequence you want to include in the preview. You rarely need to generate a preview for the entire sequence (this could be very time-consuming and might result in a huge file on your hard drive). You should only preview segments marked by a red line on the time ruler (and only the portion of those segments that you need to see in real time). To mark a segment for preview, drag the **Work Area** markers (which live just below the time ruler) to mark the start and end of the segment. In between the **Work Area** markers is the **Work Area** bar. You can drag this bar by the textured area in its center to move both **Work Area** markers at the same time (see Figure 6.46).

Once you've marked the segment you want to preview, press the **Enter** key on your keyboard (or choose **Sequence>Render Preview** from the menu). Premiere will create a new file on your hard drive, containing the preview. Premiere will display a **Render** dialog window with a progress bar and an estimate of how long it will take to render out a preview file (see Figure 6.47).

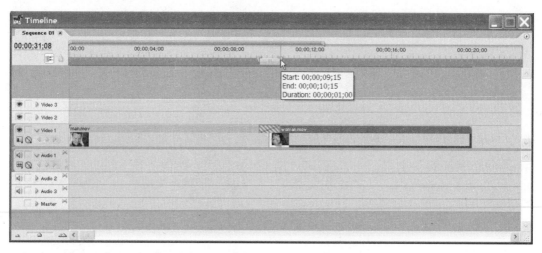

6.46 Drag the work area markers to surround the segment you want to preview.

6.47 After you press the Enter key, Premiere will display a progress bar.

Work Bar Shortcuts

Alt+[(left bracket) sets the starting **Work Area** marker to the location of the **Current Time Indicator**.

Alt+] (right bracket) sets the ending **Work Area** marker to the location of the **Current Time Indicator**.

Double-click the **Work Area** bar to set it to cover the entire sequence.

Alt+double-click the **Work Area** bar to set it to cover all clips contiguous to the clip at the **Current Time Indicator's** location (i.e., if there are gaps in the **Timeline**, the **Work Area** bar will not extend past them).

Other than this window, you won't have any sense of this new file being created. You won't see it open or import into Premiere. But you will see the red line disappear from the **Timeline** above the segment, and the preview will play back in the **Program Monitor**. The red line will be replaced by a green line. The **Timeline** segment under the green line will play back from the preview file, rather than from the **Timeline** (see Figure 6.48).

If you want to stop previews from automatically playing back in the **Program Monitor**, choose **Edit>Preferences>General** from the menu and deselect the **Play Work Areas After Rendering Previews** option. Once you've created a preview file, when you play the sequence, that portion of the **Timeline** will play at full speed (and high quality). This is because when Premiere gets to that part of the **Timeline**, it will display the preview file in

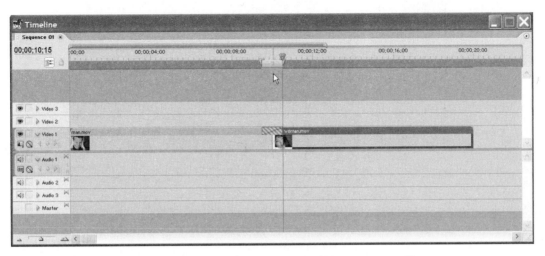

6.48 The green line (which the mouse cursor is pointing to) indicates a preview file.

the **Program Monitor** instead of the clips in the **Timeline**. When it gets to the end of that segment, it will start using the **Timeline** clips again. From your point of view the playback will be seamless. You won't be able to tell when Premiere is using **Timeline** clips and when it's using preview files.

Premiere will continue to use the preview file until you make even the smallest change to that part of your sequence (e.g., adjusting an effect property). At that point, it will revert back to displaying the clips in the **Timeline** and, most likely, you'll see another red line appear in the time ruler. You'll then have to create another preview to see the segment run at full speed again.

By default, Premiere saves preview files in the same folder as your project file. To change the location of preview files, choose **Edit>Preferences>Scratch Disks** from the menu. If the **Timeline** window is active, you can choose **Sequence>Delete Render Files** from the menu to remove that sequence's preview files from your hard drive.

WRAPPING UP

Premiere is just one of hundreds of programs in which you can apply and animate effects. The good news is that most of them work in similar ways. Once you understand Premiere's keyframes and tweening, you can easily transfer that knowledge to After Effects, Flash, Director, and 3D Studio Max. Or, if you're only working with Premiere, you can leverage your effects knowledge as you work with motion animation, compositing, color correction—and even audio processing. All of these topics will be discussed in the next few chapters.

Chapter 7

Compositing

The word "composite," as used by video and graphics professionals, is really a fancy word for collage. Compositing is the art of combining several different images into one single image. In Premiere, "images" can be still graphics or videos. When you combine them, you must stack them on top of each other, in different video tracks. By default, whatever is in the top track will cover everything below it. So you won't get to see the lower images. This is similar to the way a book's cover hides all of the pages inside it. You know there are pages in there, but when the book is closed, you can't see them. But, if you could cut a hole in the cover, you could see the pages—or at least the top page—through the hole. If you cut another hole through the top page, you could see part of the page beneath *it*. However, if you made the cover out of semitransparent plastic, you could see through it to the pages. You'd also be looking at the transparent cover at the same time; you'd see a mixture of both cover *and* pages.

In order to see through the top video track to the tracks underneath, you have to either cut a hole in it or make it partially or fully transparent. You don't necessarily have to make the whole track transparent, just part of it. After all, in a church, the walls are opaque, but the stained-glass windows are partially transparent. So when you look at a wall with a window in it, you can see through one part but not the other. When you look through the see-through part (the window), you see some of the outside and some of the glass at the same time.

There are three general ways of creating transparency in video tracks:

- You can create the transparency in your stills or videos before bringing them into Premiere, in programs like Photoshop or After Effects.

- You can create the transparency completely in Premiere.

- Or you can do both—start you transparency in Photoshop or After Effects, and finish or alter it in Premiere, adding more transparency or taking some away.

CREATING ALPHA CHANNELS

When you create transparency in Photoshop, Illustrator, or After Effects, you're creating an *alpha channel*. This sounds very scientific, but an alpha channel is just an invisible layer in which transparency data about each pixel is stored. In the alpha channel, it might say that the pixel in the upper-right corner of the image is completely transparent, whereas the pixel immediately below that is only 50% transparent. The pixel below *that* might not be transparent at all. Alpha channels can really be that detailed.

Typically, you create an alpha channel when you want to keep the foreground visible and make the background invisible. For instance, suppose someone gives you a company-logo graphic that is red and yellow against a black background. You may want to hide the black, so that you can composite the logo over other tracks in Premiere. If you don't hide the black, the logo will completely cover the tracks underneath. By hiding the black, only the actual logo will cover the layers, not the black background. So in Photoshop, you'll need to create an alpha channel that makes the black pixels completely invisible and the logo pixels completely opaque.

Photoshop alpha channels

Channels palette

To create an alpha channel in Photoshop, open an image and open the Channel palette by choosing Window>Show Channels from the menu. In the Channels palette, you should see a stack of four buttons, labeled (from the top down) RGB: red, green, and blue (see Figure 7.1).

If you see any other color channels, such as channels labeled cyan, magenta, yellow, or black, you've opened up an image intended for print, not for video. You can convert the image to an RGB image (R = red, G = green, and B = blue), by choosing Image>Mode>RGB from the menu (see Figure 7.2). Only RGB images are suitable for video.

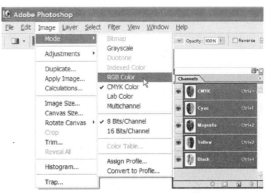

7.1 The red, green, blue, and composite (rgb) channel buttons in Photoshop's Channels palette. *(left)*

7.2 Only RGB images are suitable for video.

Red, green, and blue are the primary colors of all images intended for the screen (video images, web images, film images, CD-ROM images, etc.) Most of us were misled in elementary school, where we were taught that *the* primary colors were red, blue, and yellow. But there's no such thing as *the* primary colors. A "primary" color is just a color that can't be broken down into a mix of other colors. And which colors can't be broken down differs from color system to color system.

For instance, red, blue, and yellow might be the primary colors in a box of crayons. You can use your blue and red crayons together to make purple, so purple isn't a primary color; it's a secondary color, made from mixing together two primary colors. You can't "make" blue by mixing two other crayon colors, and you don't need to "make" blue. You already *have* a blue crayon. Blue is one of your primaries. But that's just within the color-system of your crayons. In the four-color printing system, blue is a secondary color. The primary colors of print are cyan, magenta, and yellow. And, as stated earlier, screen pri-

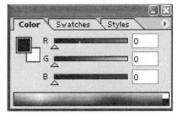

7.3 In RGB images, all colors are created by mixing together the three primary colors or the RGB system: red, green, and blue.

mary colors are red, green, and blue, which means all other colors are created my mixing combinations of red, green, and blue together (see Figure 7.3). Red, green, and blue are *not* created by mixing. They are the atomic units of screen color.

Because all colors in an RGB image are made out of a certain amount of red, a certain amount of green, and a certain amount of blue, it's possible to pull those colors apart and look at them separately. That's the job of the Channels palette, in which you can look at any pixel, and see just how much red, green, or blue is in it. There's nothing magic about the word "channel." It just means "information," as in "the red information, the green information, and the blue information" of each pixel.

To see all the red information in **your** image, click the **Red Channel** button in the **Channels** palette (see Figure 7.4). Click the **Green Channel** button to see the green information and the **Blue Channel** button to see the blue information. To see all the primary colors combined into the original mix, click the **RGB Channel** button. The RGB channel isn't really a channel at all, it's just the combination of the other three channels.

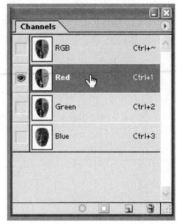

When you clicked the primary color channels, you may have noticed something odd: the red channel doesn't look red, the green channel doesn't look green, and the blue channel doesn't look blue. They all look gray. This is merely the way Photoshop displays them. Photoshop artists who spend hours mucking around in channels don't like working in a big sea of red (or green or blue) for long periods of time. It bugs their eyes out, and they start dreaming in primary colors. So to be gentle on the eyes, Photoshop displays the color channels as grayscale.

7.4   Click the red button in the Channels palette to view just the red information in an image.

But if you look at the red channel, anywhere you see a light shade of gray approaching white indicates that there's a lot of red in that part of the image (see Figure 7.5). Any dark patches have very little red in them. Completely black patches have no red in them at all. Similarly, in the green and blue channels, bright shades of gray indicate a lot of that channel's primary color is present, whereas dark shades of gray indicate that very little of that channel's primary color is present. If you look at a picture of a desert scene, with reddish sand under a blue sky, the red channel will contain a lot of light shades in the sand area (indicating a lot of red there) and very dark shades in the sky (indicating almost no red there), whereas the blue channel will contain a lot of light shades in the sky (a lot of blue there) and dark shades in the sand (very little blue there). If you're still confused about red, green, and blue channels, you can force the color channels to display in color by choosing **Edit>Preferences>Display & Cursors** and then checking the **Color Channels in Color** option (see Figure 7.6). But this may make your eyes fall out and roll across the floor.

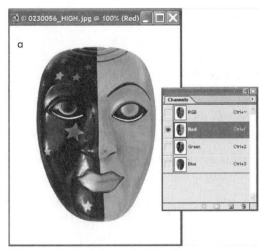

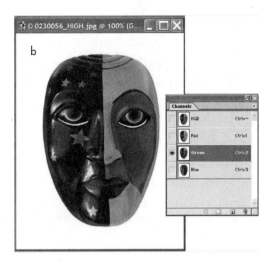

7.5   (a) The red channel. *(above)*
(b) The green channel. *(above right)*
(c) The blue channel. *(below)*

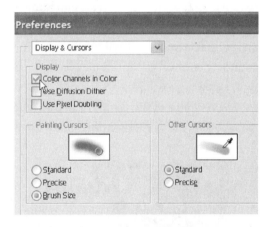

7.6   If you don't mind your eyes bugging out,
you can view color channels in color.

Adding an Alpha Channel

At the bottom of the Channels palette is an icon that looks like a little sheet of paper with the corner turned up. That's the New Channel button. Click it to create an all-black alpha channel (see Figure 7.7).

> **One Channel Read:** You can click this button multiple times to create many alpha channels, but Premiere will only read the top one. To delete unwanted alpha channels, drag their buttons to the trash can at the bottom of the **Channel** palette.

Remember, alpha channels set transparency levels for pixels in the image. Alpha "channel" just refers to the transparency "information" that's stored in an image. Black means completely transparent. Since every pixel on the new alpha channel is black, this means that Premiere will not display the image at all. It will be completely invisible if you import it as it is. Strangely, if you click back on the RGB Channel button to see it in color, it shows up. That's because, though Photoshop lets you store alpha channels in your images for use in other programs, it doesn't pay any attention to them itself. If it did, the **RGB Channel** button would be called the **RGBA** (red, green, blue, alpha) button.

7.7 Click the New Channel button to add an all-black (all-invisible) alpha channel.

White on alpha channels sets pixels to opaque (not transparent), so if you select the alpha channel by clicking its button and then paint on it with a white paintbrush, you'll create an image that partially displays in Premiere. The areas with corresponding white on the alpha channel will display; the areas with corresponding black won't (see Figure 7.8).

Gray alpha pixels set partial transparency. The closer the gray is to black, the more transparent the corresponding pixels will be in Premiere). You paint parts of the alpha

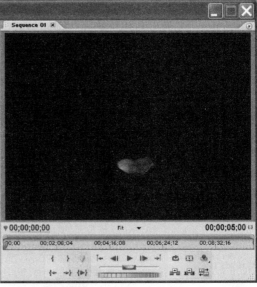

7.8 If you paint some white areas on a black alpha channel and then import the image into Premiere, the areas you painted white will display; the black areas will be hidden.

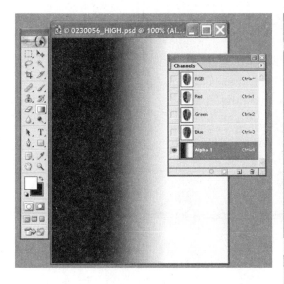

7.9   White reveals, black hides, and gray partially reveals.

channel with a gray paintbrush, those parts of the image will be see-through, but not invisible, in Premiere.

You can create an interesting effect by creating an alpha channel that is a black-to-white gradient. The black parts will cause complete invisibility, but the rest of the image will fade into view, as the gray pixels get lighter and lighter (see Figure 7.9).

Although it's fun to paint on the alpha channel, most people don't create transparency information this way, because it's too hard to get exact results. Typically, you'll want to make the image's background transparent and its foreground opaque. So you'll have to create an alpha channel in which all of the foreground pixels are white and the background pixels are black. Instead of painting, it's easier to create these alpha channels using selection tools. Before trying them, delete any alpha channels you've made and return to the full-color view by clicking the **RGB** button.

Using selection tools to make alpha channels

Selecting pixels is a huge topic—one way beyond the scope of this book—but it's important to learn about if you want to create accurate alpha channels. The following paragraphs will nudge into the subject slightly. For more information, read *Photoshop for Nonlinear Editors,* by Richard Harrington (CMP Books 2003).

Most of Photoshop's selection tools are at the top of its **Tools** palette, including the **Rectangular Marquee** tool, the **Lasso** tool and the **Magic Wand** tool.

To make a selection with the **Magic Wand** tool, you select it from the **Tools** palette and click the part of the image you want to keep visible. Anything selected will be visible in Premiere; anything not selected will be invisible. Try to click on a color that appears in many different parts of the image that you want to keep visible. The **Magic Wand** will select the pixel you clicked and all connected pixels that are of the same—or similar—colors. "Connected" means that the pixels must be touching each other. So selecting a person's red shirt will not also select his red tongue, because his tongue and shirt aren't touching each other (see Figure 7.10).

So the wand selects similar colors, but how similar is similar? That's up to you. Notice that at the top of the screen, on the **Options** bar, there's a setting called **Tolerance**. If you set this to a high number, the **Magic Wand** will be more tolerant of color differences. If you set it to a low number, Photoshop will be pretty literal and only select the exact color you clicked. The range for **Tolerance** runs from zero to 255. If you type zero, you'll only select the exact color you clicked. If you type 255, clicking anywhere will select the entire image (not very useful). Try midrange settings, such as 100 or 150, for best results (see Figure 7.11).

7.10   Clicking a pixel in the star selects it, because all the pixels within the star are the same color. Other stars are not selected—even though they are the same color—because they aren't touching the clicked star.

If you make a mistake and want to start over, choose **Select>Deselect** from the menu or press the keyboard shortcut **Control+D**. Photoshop will trash your selection, and then you can click again with the **Magic Wand**, this time with a different **Tolerance** setting. Note that you must set **Tolerance** before clicking with the **Magic Wand**. If you click and then try to raise or lower the **Tolerance**, nothing will happen.

Beginners often try to find a magic **Tolerance** number, that elusive number that will select all of the pixels in the part of the image they want to show and none of the pixels in the part of the image they want to hide. But this is generally impossible. The trick is to

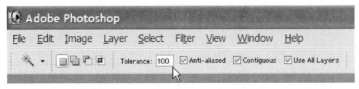

7.11   The Tolerance setting adjusts how many similar colors are included in the selection.

type a Tolerance setting that will select many of the pixels, click to select them, and then use other means to include the pixels that got left out.

Also, if the part of the image you want to show contains many colors, no possible setting of **Tolerance** will select them all, unless you set **Tolerance** so high that it selects all the colors in the entire image. So how do you proceed if you're trying to select, for instance, the American flag? Click on the blue, behind the stars, and you'll select the blue, but you won't select the stripes or stars, which are red and white—not blue.

The trick is to use the **Shift** key, which will add to a selection (see Figure 7.12). So in the example of the flag, you'd click first on the blue, then you'd hold down the **Shift** key and click the red, then you'd hold down the **Shift** again and click on the white. Each time you **Shift**+click with the **Magic Wand** tool, you'll add more areas to the selection. Actually, you'll have to **Shift**+click quite a few times to select the whole

7.12 Shift+click each star to select it with the Magic Wand tool.

flag, because the red stripes don't touch each other, and neither do the white stripes or the individual stars. If you're determined to only use the **Magic Wand** tool, you'll have to **Shift**+click each stripe and star separately to add it to the selection.

Here's a simpler technique: click the blue background behind the stars with the magic wand tool. This should select all the blue, because all the blue pixels are joined together. Then **Shift**+click one star, which will add that one star to the selection. From the menu, choose **Select>Similar**. Photoshop will select all the colors in the image that match those of the most recent selection (the white star). This should take care of all the other stars and white stripes. Now, **Shift**+click one of the red stripes, which will add it to the selection. Then once again choose **Select>Similar** from the menu. Photoshop will add all the other red stripes to the selection.

It's vital that each time you add to the selection by clicking with the **Magic Wand** tool, you remember to hold down the **Shift** key. If you don't, Photoshop will replace your previous selection with your new one instead of adding your new selection to the previous one. For instance, if you click the blue behind the stars to select it and then click one of the stars—forgetting to hold down the **Shift** key—Photoshop will deselect the blue and select only the one star.

If you accidentally click part of the image that you don't want to show, you can remove pixels from the selection by **Alt**+clicking them (see Figure 7.13). For instance, you can **Alt**+click the background (behind the flag) if you accidentally select it.

When you've finished selecting, you're not done working in Photoshop. What you currently have is just a selection, not an alpha channel. A selection looks like a dotted line around the selected pixels. Many Photoshop artists call this line the "marching ants." You need to convert the marching ants to an alpha channel—one in which everything inside the boundary is white and everything outside is black.

At the bottom of the **Channels** palette, there's a button that looks like a gray square with a white circle inside it. That's the **Save Selection As Channel** button. Click it, and Photoshop will make an alpha channel for you, in which selected pixels to mark are white (visible

7.13 If you accidentally select an area you don't want selected, Alt+click it with the Magic Wand tool.

in Premiere) and the deselect pixels are black (hidden in Premiere). Once you've converted the selection to an alpha channel, you don't need the selection anymore, so you can choose **Select>Deselect** (or **Control+D**) from the menu.

Note that with any image to which you want to add an alpha channel, there's always a part that you want selected and a part that you want deselected. You should always click the **Magic Wand** on the easier of the two parts—even if that's the part you want deselected. For instance, in this image you want to select the foreground, but it's filled with many different colors. So it will take a long time to grab it with the wand. You'll have to use many **Shift**+clicks and take many trips to the **Select>Similar** command on the menu. But the background is a solid color, so you can grab it all at once with a single click. But if you convert that selection to an alpha channel, you'll wind up showing the foreground and hiding the background, which is the opposite of what you want to do. Never fear! Just choose the **Select>Inverse** command from the menu (see Figure 7.14). Photoshop will flip the selection, selecting everything that's deselected and deselecting everything that's selected. Then you only need to click the **Save Selection As Channel** button and you're done (see Figure 7.16). Almost.

Blurring the edges

The trouble now is that your selection is perfect—too perfect. Everything you want to show is white. Everything you want to hide is black. Your image will look like a cardboard cutout in Premiere when you composite it over a new background. In real life, foregrounds and backgrounds blend together a little bit. You may not consciously perceive it, but when you place your hand over a book, your eyes blend a little bit of your hand color—just around the edges of your hand—with a little bit of the book color. So your alpha channel needs a few gray pixels where the black and white pixels meet. Remember that in an alpha channel, gray means semitransparent. And if you allow the pixels around the edge of the white area to be semitransparent, the showing part will blend in more realistically with their new background.

If you've already made an all black and white alpha channel, you can add some gray by blurring it a little.

1. Click the **Alpha1** button in the **Channels** palette to select the alpha channel,

2. Choose **Filter>Blur>Gaussian Blur** from the menu (see Figure 7.16).

3. Type in a very small number for the blur radius—maybe **2**—and click **OK**.

4. Photoshop will blur the black and white together, making a two-pixel wide blurred line where the black and white mix.

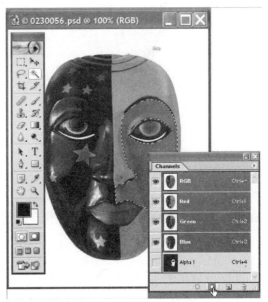

7.14 To make an alpha channel from a selection, click the Save Selection as Channel button in the Channels palette.

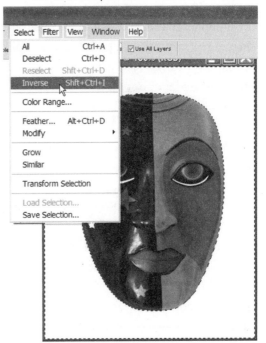

7.15 Sometimes it's easier to select the part you *don't* want selected and then invert the selection.

If you remember the need for gray pixels before saving the selection as an alpha channel, you can use the following technique instead of blurring. You can use either technique; it really doesn't matter.

1. Use the **Magic Wand** tool (or some other selection tool) to select the area you want to show.

2. Choose **Select>Feather** from the menu.

3. In the **Feather** dialog window, type a small number, the same small number that you use for blurring (see Figure 7.17). Click **OK**.

4. Save your selection as an alpha channel.

Photoshop will automatically make a black, white, and gray alpha channel, with a two-pixel gray line at the places black and white meet.

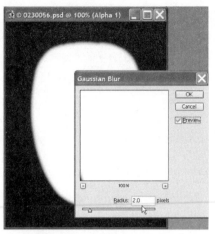

7.16 Soften the edges of a too "perfect" alpha channel with the Gaussian Blur filter.

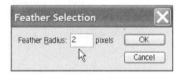

7.17 Feathering a selection before saving it as an alpha channel has the same effect as applying a Gaussian Blur after saving it as an alpha channel.

Lasso

For complex selections, it's hard to use the **Magic Wand**. You can try using the **Lasso** tool instead (see Figure 7.18), which will allow you to drag the mouse around and draw a selection boundary, just as if you were drawing it with a pencil. To use the **Lasso**, select it from the **Tools** palette. While holding down the mouse button, drag around the boundary of the area you want to select, as though you were drawing a line around it with a pencil. **Lasso** completely around the area, ending in the same place you started, and then release the mouse button.

The problem with the **Lasso** tool is that it takes a really long time—and a lot of precision—to make an accurate selection (one that doesn't include some of the background or leave out some of the foreground). What if you spend 10 minutes making the first half of a lassoed selection and then your hand gets tired or you get a phone call? If you release the mouse button half way through, Photoshop will finish the selection for you—leaving out the other half! You can solve this problem with liberal use of the **Shift** and **Alt** keys.

As with the **Magic Wand** tool, you can use the **Shift** key and the **Lasso** to add to a selection or the **Alt** key and the **Lasso** to subtract from a selection. In fact, the **Shift** and Alt keys work the same way (adding and subtracting) with all of the selection tools—even the ones not covered in this book.

To lasso effectively, start to draw a boundary with the **Lasso** tool. When you need a break, close up the boundary by returning to the starting point. Don't worry if you're not finished surrounding the whole area. When you're ready to resume, hold down the Shift key and start dragging again to lasso a little more of the area. Stop whenever you need a break (remembering to close up your current lasso drawing), and whenever you feel like continuing, start dragging again with the **Shift** key held down. If you accidentally lasso some background, you can remove it from the selection by **Alt**+dragging around it with the Lasso tool.

7.18 The Lasso tool.

You can even use both the **Magic Wand** tool and the **Lasso** tool on the same area, as long as you hold down the **Shift** key. For instance, if you click with the Magic Wand and it selects almost all of the pixels except for a few in the middle of the area, you can grab those quickly by switching to the **Lasso** tool, holding down the **Shift** key, and dragging to surround the remaining pixels.

When you finish selecting with the Lasso, save the selection as an alpha channel, and remember to either feather first or blur after.

Exporting files with alpha channels

After adding an alpha channel, you need to save your work in one of the file formats that support alpha channels. These include tifs, targas, picts, and psds (Photoshop's native format). You can't save your image a jpeg, because jpegs don't support alpha channels. Photoshop will let you save your image as a jpeg, but it will delete the alpha channel during the save.

It's fine if your starting image (before creating the alpha channel) is a jpeg. You can open a jpeg in Photoshop, add an alpha channel and then use the File>Save As command to save it out in one of the file formats that does support alpha channels (see Figure 7.19).

After Effects and Illustrator and Photoshop revisited

It's much easier to create alpha channels in After Effects and Illustrator. Basically, anywhere that you don't draw or place an image, you'll get an automatically alpha channel. In Illustrator, you literally don't have to do anything except create your image. When you're done, save it in Illustrator's native format—the ai format—and then import it into Premiere. Premiere never imports the "page" behind your illustrator artwork (that's just for print), so your images will always be on a transparent background.

Similarly, you don't have to do much in After Effects to get a transparent background. But you do have to make a small adjustment in the **Output Module** of After Effect's **Render Queue** before exporting. In the **Output Module**, make sure the **Channels** setting is set to **RGB+Alpha**. That way, the background of your composition will be transparent, rather than the background color of the **Composition** window (see Figure 7.20).

You don't always have to create an alpha channel, even in Photoshop. You generally have to do this when you're planning to import a Photograph or pre-made illustration. But if you're creating a graphic from scratch in Photoshop, just ignore the background layer and create everything in **Layer 1** (and higher layers, if you need them). You can create new layers by displaying the **Layers** palette (**Window>Show Layers**) and clicking the

7.19 Save the file in a format that supports alpha channels.

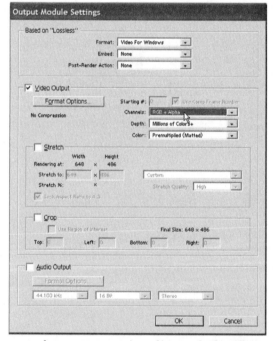

7.20 If you want to render a file out of After Effects with a transparent background, select RGB+Alpha for the Output Module's Channels setting.

New button (curled up piece of paper) at its bottom edge. To make sure you're drawing on **Layer 1** and not the background layer, click the **Layer 1** button in the **Layers** palette to make **Layer 1** the background layer. You can delete the background layer by dragging it into the trash.

Even easier, you can start a new Photoshop image with a transparent background layer. And if your background layer is transparent, you can draw directly on it. Wherever you don't draw, there will be transparency (see Figure 7.21). To create an image with a transparent background, choose **File>New** from Photoshop's menu, and then choose **Transparent** (under **Contents**) in the **New** dialog, before clicking **OK**. But if you forget to do this, and you have a white background color, you can use the Layer 1 method outlined previously.

7.21 If you create a Photoshop file with a transparent background, you don't need to make an alpha channel.

After using either of these methods, it's best to save your image as a psd, Photoshop's native format. Premiere has no problem importing psds, because both programs are made by Adobe.

Compositing the alpha channel image in Premiere

To composite your graphic into a Premiere sequence, import it into the project as you would any other file and load it into the source monitor. When you insert or overlay it into the sequence, move it to the **Video 2** track or a higher video track—any track but **Video 1**. All the parts of the image where the alpha channel was black will be invisible, and you'll be able to see through them to the image on **Video 1** (see Figure 7.22).

If you want to add a new video track, the easiest way to do so is to drag a clip from the **Source Monitor** (or the **Project** window) to the dark gray space above the highest video track, as though you wanted to drag the clip to an invisible track at the top of the **Timeline**. When you drop the clip, Premiere will create a new track for it (see Figure 7.23).

You can also create a new track (or several new tracks) by choosing **Sequence>Add Tracks...** from the menu. To delete a track, click its name and then choose Sequence>Delete tracks... from the menu. In the **Delete Tracks** dialog window, check the Delete **Video Tracks** option and choose **Target Track** from the dropdown menu. Then click **OK**. Naturally, if you delete a track, all of the clips on that track will be deleted, too. So if you make a mistake, remember to undo it (**Control+Z**).

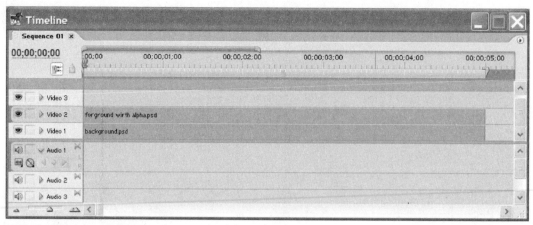

7.22 Arrange your Timeline so that your background image (or video) is on the Video 1 track and your foreground image (or video), the one with the transparency, is on a higher track.

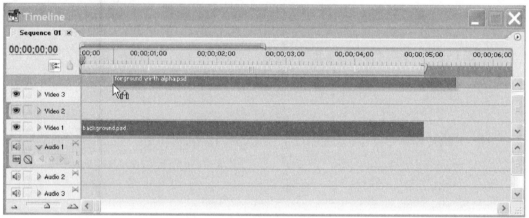

7.23 You can quickly add a track by dragging a clip to the gray area at the top of the Timeline.

You can also rename tracks, which is useful if you want to see at a glance what each track is being used for. If you're using the **Video 2** track for superimposed titles, you can change its name by right-clicking the name **Video 2** and choosing **Rename** from the pop-up menu (see Figure 7.24). Premiere will make the old name (**Video 2**) editable, and you can then type a new name, like "titles," and press **Enter**.

Still images that you import and place on tracks can last as long as you want them to. To make a title span 30 seconds of the sequence, use any of the trim tools to drag its tail out that long. For instance, you can use the **Selection** tool to point to the clip's tail. When you see the bracket icon, drag to the right to lengthen the clip. Drag to the left to shorten it.

ADJUSTING OPACITY IN PREMIERE

You can also place images or video without an alpha channel on **Video 2** or higher tracks. By default, they will completely cover the images in **Video 1**, but you can allow some of the **Video 1** image to show through by lowering the opacity of the images on the tracks above it. By lowering their opacity, you'll be making those images more transparent (less opaque), and as they get more transparent, you'll be able to see through them to whatever is below.

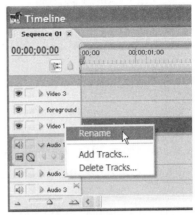

7.24 To rename a track, right-click its name and choose the Rename option from the pop-up menu.

You lower opacity by adjusting the Opacity property of the fixed **Opacity** effect. (Yes, it seems a little redundant, but the **Opacity** effect has only one property—called **Opacity**). As a fixed effect, **Opacity** is automatically applied to every clip in the **Timeline**, so if you want to mess with it, just select the clip and bring up the **Effect Controls** window (**Window>Effect Controls**). Then twirl open the **Opacity** setting and adjust the **Opacity** property. You can also animate the **Opacity** property, using regular keyframing techniques discussed in Chapter 5. Note that unlike the norm with most properties, the **Opacity** property is turned on by default. If you want to set global **Opacity** values (as opposed to keyframing), you'll need to click the stopwatch to turn it off (see Figure 7.25). Or you can adjust **Opacity** (and keyframe it) on the **Timeline**. See Chapter 5 for more information about adjusting effect properties on the **Timeline**.

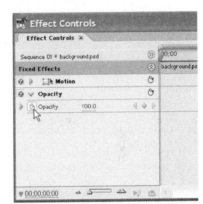

7.25 In the Effect Controls window, the Opacity property's stopwatch is on by default. Turn it off if you want to adjust opacity without animating it.

When you adjust **Opacity**, it makes the entire clip opaque, transparent, or semitransparent. This is different from alpha channels, which allow you to make part of an image opaque or part of an image transparent. And even the alpha channel techniques can fall apart when you want to knock out the background in a video. In Photoshop, you can only adjust still images. So what do you do if you've shot some video of the CEO and you want to remove the background and composite him over a video of a pig farm, so that it looks like he's standing in the sty? It would be pretty painful to remove the background in Photoshop, frame by frame.

Your best options are to either remove the background in an effects program, like After Effects, or to use one of the keying effects in Premiere.

CREATING OPACITY WITH A KEYING EFFECT

Keying effects are just effects, and you apply them to clips the same way you apply any other effects to any other clips (they're in the **Video Effects>Keying** folder) (see Figure 7.26). You can animate their properties (though it's rare you'll want to do this), and you can adjust them in the **Effect Controls** window. If this paragraph makes no sense to you (**Effect Controls** window? **Properties? Animate?**), then you should flip back to Chapter 6, read it through, and then return here. Don't worry: this chapter will still be here, waiting for you.

Keying effects only work well when the original footage was shot correctly. For best results, place the actors in front of a professionally made blue screen or green screen. Filmmakers use blue and green because there's very little blue and green in human skin, so if you film an actor in front of a blue screen, it's relatively easy to use a keying effect to "key out" the blue, making it transparent, and leave everything else opaque. If you film a human in front of a red screen and key out the red, you'll lose a lot of the actor's skin, too, because skin has a lot of red in it. But if you want to key out the background behind a frog, a red screen might work best.

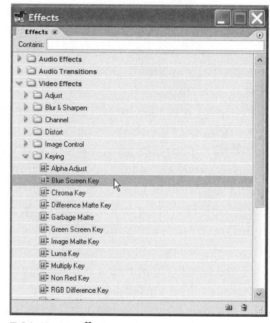

7.26 Keying effects.

When you light the scene, the blue/green screen should be lit separately from the actor in such a way that ensures that screen is evenly lit and the actor doesn't cast shadows on the screen. If there are shadows on the screen, its color won't be pure, which will make it much harder to key out.

It's a tall order—probably an impossible order—to key out a multicolored background in Premiere. So if someone gives you a video of the CEO in front of a tie-dye shirt stand and asks you to key out the background, you might want to politely request a reshoot. The only other option is to bring the footage into an effects program, like After

Effects, for a process called rotoscoping. Rotoscoping (which can't be done in Premiere), is a long and sometimes painful process, that often involves frame by frame work. So you should ask your collaborators what would be more cost-effective, reshooting in front of a blue screen or paying someone to spend three weeks rotoscoping.

Premiere ships with many keying effects, but the easiest ones to use, assuming you're keying green screen or blue screen footage, are the **Blue Screen Key** and **Green Screen Key**. Suppose your footage was shot against a well-lit, professionally made green screen (see Figure 7.27). Import the footage into Premiere, cut it into the **Video 2** track, apply the **Green Screen Key** effect (**Effects Window>Video Effects>Keying>Green Screen**), and there's a good change you won't have to do anything else. Whammo! The green background will just disappear. If there's some green left-over, you can adjust the effect's properties to get rid of it (see Figure 7.28).

7.27 A model shot against a green screen.

The **Green Screen Key** and the **Blue Screen Key** effects have four properties: **Threshold, Cutoff, Smoothing,** and **Mask Only**. The **Threshold** property is similar to Photoshop's **Magic Wand's Tolerance** adjuster. If you apply the effect and it doesn't key out all of the background, try raising **Threshold** until the background is completely gone. Or, if some of the foreground is keyed out, try lowering Threshold to bring it back (see Figure 7.29).

Cutoff controls how opaque nonkeyed areas are. If you start to lose the foreground, try adjusting **Cutoff** until it's completely opaque (see Figure 7.30).

Smoothing controls the appearance of the pixels around the border of the foreground, where the transparent and opaque areas meet. If the edge pixels look too sharp, try setting this property to low or high, similar to feathering in Photoshop. The **Mask Only** property allows you to see the alpha channel that is being created by the effect. It's similar to clicking the **Alpha Channel** button in Photoshop's **Channels** palette.

The **Chroma Key** effect is similar to the **Blue** and **Green Screen Key** effects. It's useful if you want to key out a color other than blue or green. To select the key color (the color you want to make transparent), click the effect's **Eyedropper** tool—twirl open the effect to

7.28 The Green Screen Key effect removes the green background, but you can see a little bit of the lower layer showing through the model's head.

see it. Hold the mouse button down, and roll your mouse out of the **Effect Controls** window and into the image in the **Program Monitor**. Release the mouse when the eyedropper icon is hovering over the key color. The **Similarity** property is similar to the **Green/Blue Screen Key**'s **Threshold** property or **Tolerance** in Photoshop. Raise **Similarity** to include more (similar) colors in the range of colors that will be keyed out. The better the shot was lit, the less you'll have to do this, because in a well-lit scene, all the colors in the blue/green/orange/whatever screen are the same color.

The **Blend** property adjusts the opacity of the foreground part of the image. So once you've keyed out the background, you can adjust this property to make what's left look partially transparent, like a ghost. Of course, you could do the same thing with the **Opacity** property of the fixed **Opacity** effect.

Just to be confusing, the **Chroma Key**'s **Threshold** property does something a little different than the Threshold property in the **Blue Screen Key** and **Green Screen Key** effects. In the **Chroma Key, Threshold** adjusts the transparency of the darker colors in the background. So if you accidentally have some shadows on your orange screen, you can try adjusting **Threshold** to key them out.

7.29 Going too far with the Threshold property.

7.30 Fixing the problem with the Cutoff property.

7.31 Make sure the Garbage Matte effect's name is selected in the Effect Control's window before you try dragging its controls in the Program Monitor.

Cutoff in this effect works differently than in the **Blue Screen Key** and **Green Screen Key** effects. It adjusts the lightness of the background color, making it darker or lighter. This is different from **Threshold,** which makes the darker colors more or less transparent. If the effect isn't recognizing the shadow colors as even being the color you're trying to key out, it might be because they are too dark or too light. Try adjusting **Cutoff** to bring them more into the key color's range. But don't drag the **Cutoff** slider beyond the **Threshold** slider, or you'll flip the colors into their opposites, and you'll wind up keying out the foreground and leaving the background opaque.

Smoothing and **Mask Only** act the same way as they do in the Blue Screen Key and Green Screen Key effects, described on page 189.

Sometimes a foreign object invades the shot, like a boom mic or a cable. It's not part of the foreground, so you don't want to keep it opaque (in fact, you wish it would go away!). On the other hand, it's not the same color as your blue or green screen, so the keying effect won't get rid of it. So before applying a keying effect, you might first want to apply the **Garbage Matte** effect (also in the *Keying* subfolder of the *Video Effects* folder) (see Figure 7.31). The **Garbage Matte** effect crops out part of the image.

After applying the effect, select its name in the **Effect Controls** window to display manipulators in the **Program Monitor.** Then drag the manipulators until you've cropped out the offending items. If the actor moves around, sometimes veering into the cropped area, you'll have to animate the crop so that it changes over time. To do this, twirl open the **Garbage Matte** effect and turn on the stopwatches for every property. Then move the **Current Time Indicator** through the clip and adjust the manipulators as necessary, making sure that the foreground actor is never cropped out. If you can't see the manipulators, it's because you've somehow deselected the **Garbage Matte** effect. Click its name in the **Effect Controls** window to select it and rereveal the manipulators in the **Program Monitor.**

Garbage Matte is not meant to be a complete solution. After using it, you'll have a crude key at best. So you'll want to add it one of the keying effects discussed earlier in this chapter.

If you want to learn how to use the other keying effects that ship with Premiere, you can look them up in the online help. Choose **Help>Contents** from the menu. And in the left browser pane, click **Superimposing** and **Composition**. On the right page, click **Using Keys, Using Matte Keys, Creating a Garbage Matte, Creating a Color Matte,** or **Removing a Black or White Matte.**

Note **Keying in After Effects:** If you happen to own the Professional Edition of After Effects 6.0, you might want to bypass keying in Premiere and do it in After Effects instead. AE 6.0 Pro ships with an effect called **Keylight**, which won an Academy Award for Technical Excellence. If you don't see **Keylight** listed under the **Keying Effects** (and you're sure you're using the Pro version of AE 6.0), you might have forgotten to install it. That's easy to do, because it doesn't automatically install with After Effects. There's a separate install program on the AE 6.0 install disk for **Keylight**. Also on the install disk, you'll find a clearly written **Keylight** manual in Adobe Acrobat (pdf) format, which will teach you how to use the effect. When keying, there are generally four issues you have to deal with: knocking out the background, getting rid of background color that's reflected in the foreground, dealing with the edge pixels where foreground meets background, color correcting the foreground so that it matches the new background you're compositing it over. **Keylight** deals with all four of these issues.

WRAPPING UP

As computers applications have spread throughout the graphic arts, compositing has become more and more pervasive. Viewers are now so sophisticated that they think nothing of seeing 10 images at once, all blending together in interesting ways. So to stay ahead of your audience, you'll have to blend together *11* images. I hope the techniques in this chapter will help you create stunning composites.

As you mix more and more images together, you will naturally want them to look good. Because images tend to come from all different sources—Photoshop, Illustrator, scanners, camcorders—there's a great risk that they won't appear to all be part of the same world, or they may contain colors unsuitable for video. In the next chapter, you'll solve these problems by learning the subtle art of color correction.

Chapter 8

Color Correction

Have you ever had to reject a shot because the color looked wrong? Or, even worse, have you ever had your entire video rejected because the colors strayed from within the "legal limits?" Premiere's **Color Corrector** effect is waiting patiently in the **Effects** window to help you solve these problems.

The **Color Corrector** effect is just like other effects. You'll find it in the **Video Effects>Image Control** bin, and you can drag it onto clips in the **Timeline**, and adjust properties in the **Effect Controls** window (see Color Plate 8.1). See Chapter 6 on page 133 to learn more about applying, adjusting, and animating effects.

But color correction is especially important in video, because what you see on your computer screen monitor is definitely not what you get on your TV. In fact, inappropriate colors (colors not chosen specifically for television) can cause all sorts of problems. They can create a buzz on your TV's speakers, add noise and static to the image, or just look bad. Many television stations and networks will reject videos that haven't been properly color corrected, because they don't want their viewers to complain when videos cause their TVs to buzz or flicker.

Luckily, Premiere has some special tools to help keep your videos are broadcast safe. In addition to the **Color Corrector** effect, Premiere includes special graphs called *vectorscopes*, *waveform*, and *parades* to help you evaluate and fix color problems. While adjusting **Color Corrector** properties, you can watch the graphs to make sure your adjustments aren't causing more problems than they are fixing (see Color Plate 8.2).

You can also use the **Color Match** effect to make an off-color clip look more like the other clips in your sequence.

193

But before adjusting colors, you should do what you can to adjust your workspace. The goal is to remove any hindrances that keep you from seeing true colors. Hindrances can include subpar equipment, poor lighting, and even confusing desktop colors.

COLOR CORRECTION ENVIRONMENT

In order to achieve the best possible color correction results, you should try to work in a neutral color environment with properly calibrated video equipment.

Broadcast Monitor: If you're working in a professional environment, then you'd better be using a broadcast video monitor to preview your work. The image on your computer screen is simply not the most accurate representation of how it will look on television. So you'll want to do your best to work with a good video monitor. Also, because you'll be making all of your color correction decisions based on what you see on the screen, you'd better make sure the monitor is properly calibrated. The next section will discuss some simple techniques to help you calibrate a video monitor.

 TV Tip: If you can't afford a broadcast monitor, a regular TV is better than nothing. Its colors will still be more accurate than those on your computer monitor (assuming the video you're making is intended for TV).

External Waveform Monitor and Vectorscope: As discussed previously, Premiere ships with special tools to help you color correct: waveform monitors and vectorscopes. These are software versions of hardware tools, just as computer chess or scrabble are software versions of physical games. Waveform monitors and vectorscopes are used to measure the video signals coming out of your computer to ensure that they will be properly broadcast and/or recorded onto videotape. While Adobe Premiere's built-in video scopes are useful for analyzing your images, they are not as accurate as dedicated external scopes. So, if possible—especially if you are working with uncompressed video—you should use the aid of an external waveform monitor and vectorscope to make color correction decisions.

Room Lighting: It is nearly impossible to ensure accurate color correction results if you are working in a room flooded with yellowish incandescent lights or greenish fluorescent lights. Do your best to work in a room with neutral lighting on dimmers with bulbs that are 6,500 Kelvin.

Room Color: Our eyes play tricks on us. For example, when we see a white shirt under a red light, our minds immediately tell us that it's supposed to be white even though it actually looks pink. Likewise, the same white shirt may appear slightly pinkish as it picks up the light reflected off of a red wall. So you'll want to do your best to work in a neutral gray environment. In fact, that's why most of Adobe Premiere's interface is beige and gray, and in a later section on page 200, we'll see how to prevent the colorful elements of Windows XP from interfering with the color correction process.

CALIBRATING BROADCAST MONITORS

A video signal consists of two parts: luminance and chrominance (lightness/darkness and color). A computer monitor should not be used to make color correction decisions because it cannot accurately represent luminance and chrominance signals. A broadcast-quality video monitor should be used and properly calibrated with a standard color bars test pattern. If you don't have a broadcast monitor, then any television or video monitor is usually better than nothing.

Note ***Warm up:*** Make sure the video (client) monitor has warmed up for about 10–15 minutes before you use it for color correction.

In order to see the results of your color correction on your video monitor, follow the setup instructions described in the Chapter 12 section "Recording to Videotape" on page 295. As soon as everything is connected and configured, you'll see your footage from the computer on your video screen.

Premiere will add a new item to your **Project** window: those bars you sometimes see on television, late at night, after a station has gone off the air (see Figure 8.1). (You used to see these, anyway. Are there stations that go off the air anymore?)

1. Drag the bars to your **Timeline** and trim them out so that they last a few seconds.

2. Now move the **Current Time Indicator** over that segment in the timeline. You should see the color bars on the client monitor (see Color Plate 8.3).

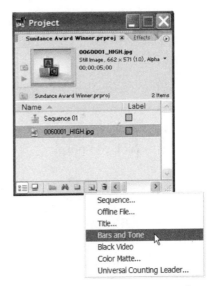

8.1 You can create Bars and Tone by clicking the New button at the bottom of the Project window

You will now need to adjust various controls on your client monitor. These specific controls may be located in different places on different monitors, and they may have different names or labels than the ones described here. Use the following instructions as a rough guide, checking your monitor's manual for specific information.

3. First, adjust the monitor for luminance, which deals with the brightness and contrast of the image. Turn the monitor's **Color** (or **Chroma**) setting all the way down so that the test pattern on the monitor is black and white.

4. Near the lower-right corner of the test pattern is an area that contains three black stripes. This is called the *pluge*. Adjust **Brightness** until the first two stripes of the pluge look the same.

5. Adjust Contrast (or Picture) until the third stripe of the pluge is barely visible.

6. Adjust the monitor for chrominance, which deals with the image's levels of hue and saturation. For best results, you should use a monitor with a **Blue-Only** button. With **Blue-Only** on, adjust **Hue** (or **Tint** or **Phase**) until the inner cyan and magenta areas look the same.

7. Adjust **Color** (or **Chroma**) until the outer white and blue areas look the same.

8. Turn off **Blue-Only**.

9. If your monitor doesn't have a Blue-Only feature, you can substitute by looking at the monitor through a Wratten 47B blue filter, available at professional photography stores.

   If you don't have a filter, then you have to trust your own judgment.

10. Turn up the **Color** to the level just before the red bar begins to look oversaturated. Then adjust **Hue** so that the yellow bar doesn't look too green and the magenta bar doesn't look too purple.

Since electronic parts age, monitor calibration is something that should be done on a regular basis. Also, because our eyes become tired after long work periods, colorists should take breaks every once in a while.

VIDEO SCOPES

1. From the **Program Monitor's** wing menu, select **New Reference Monitor** (see Figure 8.2 on page 197).

   The **Reference Monitor** is an additional window that you can use to view different characteristics of the video image.

2. From the wing menu in either the **Reference** or **Program Monitor,** you can choose the **Gang to Program Monitor** or **Gang to Reference Monitor** option so that the **Current**

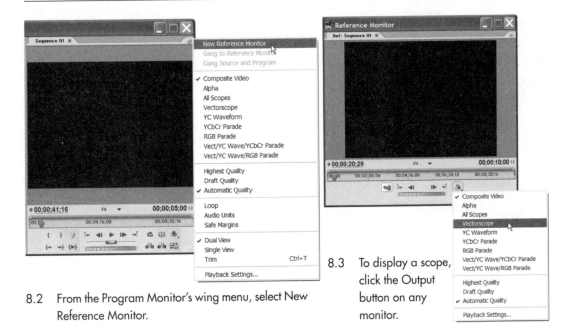

8.2 From the Program Monitor's wing menu, select New Reference Monitor.

8.3 To display a scope, click the Output button on any monitor.

Time Indicators of the two monitors stay in sync, ensuring that they will always display the same frame (see Color Plate 8.4).

3. From the **Reference Monitor's** wing menu, you can activate one the several video scopes that help you with the color correction process.

    You can also choose a scope by clicking the **Output** button on any monitor, which means that you can display a scope in the **Reference Monitor, Source Monitor,** or **Program Monitor.** Or you can display one scope in the **Reference Monitor** and another in the **Source Monitor.** For instance, it's often useful to display the **Vectorscope** and the **YC Waveform** monitor at the same time (see Figure 8.3).

    The scopes all share the common feature of being viewable but not adjustable. They don't have any controls; they are intended just to give you information. To color correct your video, you will generally apply the **Color Corrector** effect (described on page 202), which you'll find in the **Effects** window's **Video Effects>Image Control** bin. As you adjust the properties in this effect, judge the results by watching both the image on the your client monitor and the scopes in the **Reference Monitor.**

    The **Vectorscope** measures the chrominance (color) of a video image. Note the color-abbreviations around the circle: **R, Mg, B, Cy, G,** and **Yl.** These stand for red, magenta, blue, cyan, green, and yellow, respectively. Once you understand this, you can see that you're looking at a color wheel. The blob in the middle of the wheel represents the colors in the current frame, the frame where the **Current Time Indicator** is parked. The image shown in Color Plate 8.5 has a lot of red in it, which is why most parts of the blob are in the red area of the wheel. You should expect a more colorful image to create a blob that's spread out around more of the wheel.

The center of the wheel represents totally desaturated colors (grays). The parts of the blob closest to this center point represent the gray pixels in the image. The further out parts of the blob get towards the edge of the wheel, the more saturated (full of color) they are. As you can see in Color Plate 8.5, the blob represents a spectrum of reddish pixels. So there are lots of reds in the frame—some so desaturated that you can hardly detect that they are red, and some quite saturated (very red).

Pure red lives in the **X** by the capital **R**. If any parts of the blob reach this **X**, they show you have pure-red pixels in your image.

You need to watch out for blob parts that spike beyond the **X** or out of the wheel altogether. They would indicate that your frame contains supersaturated pixels—too hot for TV. If you see any spikes of this kind, you'll have to make **Color Corrector** adjustments to bring them down into the safe region inside the wheel. As you make adjustments in the **Color Corrector,** watch the **Vectorscope** until you see the spikes retreat to inside the wheel (see Color Plate 8.6).

For a more intuitive grasp of the **Vectorscope,** try displaying a Photoshop image of three gradients: white-to-red, white-to-blue, and white-to-green (see Color Plate 8.7). You will then have three color ranges: totally saturated red to totally desaturated red, totally saturated blue to totally desaturated blue, and totally saturated green to totally desaturated green. Because the only colors in the image are red, green and blue, you should only see blobs on the **Vectorscope** in these ranges (see Color Plate 8.8). In fact, the blobs will look like three lines, emanating from the center (desaturated) to right out of the wheel (oversaturated). It's easy to choose colors on a computer monitor that are too saturated for TV. That's why we need external monitors and **Vectorscope.**

The **YC Waveform** scope measures both luminance (lightness and darkness) and chrominance of a video image. Video signals contain two parts—sometimes called channels: the **Y** channel, which contains the luminance data and the C channel, which contains the color (or chrominance) data. Premiere's **YC Waveform** displays both, showing chrominance as a blue blob and luminance as a green blob (see Color Plate 8.9). Many people use **Waveform** scope to analyze luminance only. To do so, uncheck the **Chroma** option at the top of the monitor (see Color Plate 8.10).

High means light; low means dark. The blob on the graph represents the luminance range of the pixels in your image. If you're looking at a night scene, you should expect most of the blob to be down near the bottom of the graph. A shot of a glowing lightbulb should display a blob close to the top of the graph. The units on the left are IRE (Institute of Radio Engineers) values. They measure the luminance of pixels. When viewing color bars on a waveform monitor, the center stripe of the pluge should read at 7.5 IRE, and the bright, white area towards the lower left should read at 100 IRE.

Note *No Substitute for Hardware:* The Waveform in Adobe Premiere does not accurately give you this reading, however, and it should not be fully trusted when doing serious color correction work. The built-in scopes are useful as guides and will tell you immediately if your levels are too high or too low, but whenever possible, you should use properly calibrated external scopes.

You can also use the Waveform to look for luminance problems in frames. For instance, if parts of the blob spike too high or too low, you'll need to adjust whites and blacks (or shadows and highlights) in the **Color Corrector** (see Color Plate 8.11). There's much debate about what is too bright or too dark for TV (and legal luminance values are different if different countries), but you should try to keep your blob within the 120 to −20 range. If your video is going to be broadcast on a specific network or station, check with their technicians for appropriate IRE minimums and maximums.

If the blob flattens out at the top or the bottom, that could indicate clipping. Clipping means that many pixels that should be varying shades of white or black have all gone to pure white or pure black—so those parts of the image are lacking in detail. Clipping is sometimes the result of overzealous color corrections. Say your image is too dark: you color correct it to make it brighter. But you make it too bright, and some of the pixels become "whiter than white." Since nothing can really be whiter than white, those pixels all become white (they clip at white). If there are many, many white pixels, you should see flat areas on the top of the **Waveform** (see Color Plate 8.12). If the **Waveform's** bottom is flat, there may be clipping in the dark ranges.

Note that flat waveforms aren't always bad. Blue text on a white background should have a flat waveform, because there are so many white pixels. But a standard photograph or video should show variation along the top and bottom—like a mountain range (see Color Plate 8.13).

If you see a blob in the middle of the waveform that never touches the legal minimum or maximum, that means your image is lacking contrast (see Color Plate 8.14). If no part of the blob touches the top or the bottom, this means the image has no true whites or blacks.

Other scopes include the **YCbCr Parade**, which is similar to the **Waveform** but is used to compare levels of luminance against levels of chrominance, luminance on the left and chrominance on the right (see Color Plate 8.15).

And finally, the **RGB Parade,** which is also similar to the **Waveform** but is used to compare the different amounts of the red, green, and blue (see Color Plate 8.16). This scope and the **Vectorscope** are useful for recognizing undesirable color casts. For instance, if you see the green blob spiking up much higher than the red blob, this means your image has a green cast to it. If your image is spiking too bright (out of legal video limits), the spike might just be in one of the color channels (see Color Plate 8.17). Using the **Color Corrector,** you can bring that channel down within legal limits, without affecting the other channels.

Alternatively, the **Vect/YC Wave/YCbCr Parade** and **Vect/YC Wave/RGB Parade** views allow you to see three of the previous scopes simultaneously (see Color Plate 8.18).

Note   ***Measuring Signal:*** Video scopes measure the video signal by scanning the pixels in the image. Some external scopes have an option to use a single-line display, which allows the scope to analyze only one horizontal row of pixels, thus making it easier to calibrate and test for accuracy. The video scopes in Adobe Premiere do not have this feature, so they are always analyzing many scan lines to provide an overall reading. Also, without a real-time effects card, these scopes cannot provide readings while playing the sequence, but they will update when you are paused and when you move the **Current Time Indicator** from frame to frame.

NEUTRALIZING WINDOWS XP

To avoid possible distractions from the colored windows and buttons of Windows XP, you may want to bring up your system display properties by right-clicking your desktop and choosing the **Properties** option from the pop-up menu (see Figure 8.4).

In the **Appearance** tab, select **Windows XP** style from the **Windows and Buttons** menu and set the **Color Scheme** to **Silver** (see Figure 8.5 on page 201).

8.4   To open Windows display properties, right-click the desktop and choose the Properties option from the pop-up menu

COLOR CORRECTION GOALS

There are two main goals in the color correction process:

- Restore the original look of a scene.
  This usually means correcting for a technical problem, such as an improperly white-balanced image.

- Modify the look of a scene to achieve shot-to-shot consistency and/or to create a certain look or style.

8.5 In the Appearance tab, choose Windows XP style from the Windows and Buttons menu and Silver from the Color Scheme menu.

Even if all of your shots were properly white balanced, they still might not look right when viewed together in the context of your sequence. Or, you may want to intentionally create a colorcast to give your images a mood.

FOUR STAGES OF COLOR CORRECTION

1. Enhance tonal range by adjusting a scene's white, gray, and black levels.
    Images with poor contrast tend to look dull and flat.

2. Neutralize colorcasts; black should look black (not green), white should look white (not pink), etc.
    Images with an unintentional colorcast simply do not contain accurate colors.

3. Achieve shot-to-shot consistency.
    Do important objects appear to be the same color in your sequence?

4. Create a final look or style (e.g., change a day scene into a night or dusk scene). Once your images look proper, apply additional color correction to create a mood (e.g., joyful or sinister).

ANALYZE FOOTAGE BY ASKING THE FOLLOWING QUESTIONS

1. Are there luminance and color challenges? In other words, is the shot well lit and properly white balanced?

2. Were any special treatments created during the shoot? Is the scene supposed to have a colorcast?

3. Does the image look flat? Is there good contrast?

4. Are there details in the shadows (darkest parts of the image) and highlights (brightest parts of the image)?

5. Are flesh tones accurate? Do your subjects look sick or sunburned?

6. Are there objects in the image with inaccurate color? For example, does that delicious green apple look slightly brown?

COLOR CORRECTION WORKSPACES

Adobe has included with Premiere a workspace that is suitable for color correction. Choose **Window>Workspace>Color Correction (Shift+F12)**, and your windows will rearrange themselves. Your **Monitor** window will include the **Reference Monitor,** and your **Project** window will display your **Effect Controls** (see Figure 8.6 on page 203).

Gang up: Do your scopes seem out of whack? For instance, are you looking at a bright-red tomato but seeing green in the vectorscope? This may be because you've forgotten to gang the **Reference Monitor** to the **Program Monitor**. If they're unganged, they have their own independent **Current Time Indicators.** So the tomato on your **Program Monitor** is displaying because your **Timeline Current Time Indicator** is parked on a tomato frame. But the reference monitor might be parked on a green caterpillar frame. To ensure that the monitors keep in sync, click the **Gang** button in the **Reference Monitor.**

USING THE COLOR CORRECTOR EFFECT

Nesting and Presets: As with any effect, you can apply the Color Corrector to a single clip. But if you find yourself making the same adjustments over and over again to multiple clips in the Timeline, consider nesting the current sequence in a new sequence and then applying the Color Corrector to the whole nested sequence at once. To learn more about nesting, see Chapter 6. At times, you may be reusing the same clips in different sequences or even in different projects. Rather than reapplying the Color Corrector effect each time and readjusting all of its properties, save an effect preset that you can add to any clip you want. Effect presets are also explored in Chapter 6 in "Saving Effect Presets" on page 163.

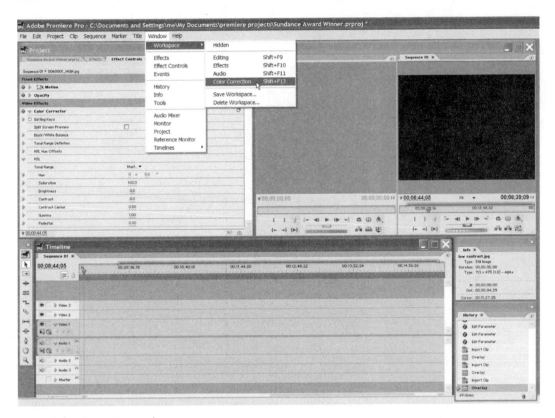

8.6   Color Correction workspace.

From the **Effects** tab, in **Video Effects>Image Control,** apply the **Color Corrector** effect to a clip or nested sequence.

In the **Effects Controls** window, click the **Split Screen Preview** to compare the look of the clip with and without the **Color Corrector.** When using **Split Screen Preview,** your color corrections will only show up on the right side of the **Program Monitor.** The left side will stay uncorrected, so that you can compare the results (see Color Plate 8.19). Of course, when you first apply the **Color Corrector,** you haven't adjusted any properties yet, so both sides of the split will look the same.

In the **Black/White Balance** controls, the **Color Corrector** includes **Black, White,** and **Gray Point** eyedroppers that are supposed to help you quickly set new black, white, and gray levels in your image. The idea is that you click with the black eyedropper on something that is supposed to be black in the image. If what you click on is actually dark-gray, Premiere will adjust the colors so that it becomes black. You then click something that's supposed to be white with the white eyedropper and something that's supposed to be neutral-gray with the gray eyedropper. (To use an eyedropper, click it but don't release the

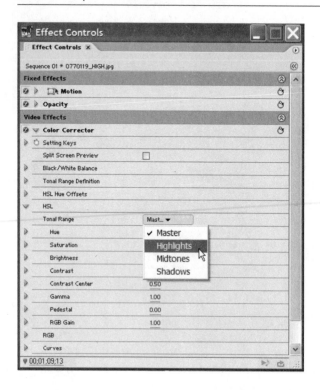

8.7   Most Color Corrector properties adjust highlights, midtones or shadows.

mouse button until you've rolled over the part of the image you want to sample.) Unfortunately, the eyedroppers don't work very well if your images contain a lot of noise, which makes sampling the correct pixel extremely difficult. For noisy (and more realistic) footage, you may want to disregard the eyedroppers and use some of the other controls instead (see Color Plate 8.20).

When color correcting, you often want to change colors in just parts of the image. For instance, if the night sky is a little greenish, you might want to remove the green cast from the sky without also removing green from an actor's shirt. You can't select just the sky, like you could in Photoshop, but you can select just the darker pixels, just the brighter pixels, or just the midrange pixels. So if the sky is very dark green and the shirt is very light green, you should be able to correct the sky without touching the shirt.

When adjusting most of the properties in the **Color Corrector** effect, you need to first tell Premiere whether you're adjusting shadows (dark pixels), highlights (light pixels) or midtones (pixels that are not to light or too dark). For instance, the **RGB** controls allow you to adjust the three primary colors separately. Suppose you're bringing red down a little bit: are you bringing it down in the shadows, midtones, or highlights? If you want to bring it down in both the shadows and highlights (but not the midtones), you can always apply the **Color Corrector** effect twice (see Figure 8.7 on page 204).

So how dark does a pixel have to be to qualify as a shadow? How light does it have to be to be a highlight? That's up to you. You can define ranges as shadows, midtones and highlights by adjusting the **Tonal Range** properties. If you check the **Preview** option, every color in the image becomes black, white and gray (see Color Plate 8.21). As probably guessed, black pixels are shadow pixels, white pixels are highlight pixels and gray pixels are midtones. You can scrub the **Shadow** and **Highlight** properties to add (or remove) more black and white. When you're finished setting the ranges, uncheck the **Preview** option (see Color Plate 8.22).

Now when you color correct using the **HSL** or **RGB** properties, you should first choose to operate on the highlight, midtone, or shadow range. If you twirl open either the **HSL** or **RGB** property group, you'll see that the first property is a **Tonal Range** drop-down. From the dropdown, you can choose highlight, midtone or shadow. Depending on which option you choose, the **HSL** or **RGB** controls will only effect the pixels in that range. You can also choose **Master,** in which case color adjustments will affect the entire image.

As an alternative, you can adjust the color wheels in the **HSL offset group**. These give you access to all the ranges at once.

In the **HSL Hue Offsets** controls, you can adjust hue, saturation, and lightness of shadows, midtones, highlights, and overall master levels by moving the corresponding center points to different spots on each color wheel. You may need to widen the effect properties area of the **Effect Controls** window to see all four wheels (see Color Plate 8.23).

For instance, if you want to move the midtones more towards a bluish tint, drag the center of the midtones wheel towards blue. If you drag towards the outer edge of the circle, you'll pick a saturated blue (a very blue blue); if you drag just a little bit away from the center, you'll tint the image with a very desaturated blue, a blue that's barely there at all (see Color Plate 8.24).

When correcting bad color casts, it's useful to remember that every pixel must have *some* color. For instance, you can't just remove red. Taking out red means adding some other color. So it's useful to know which colors are opposites of each other. For instance, red and cyan are opposites. So if there's too much red in the highlights, try dragging the center point of the highlights circle towards cyan.

For a quick guide to color opposites, take a look at the **Vectorscope**. The opposites lie directly across from each other on the wheel. As you can see, red and cyan are directly across from each other (see Color Plate 8.25).

You may also want to watch the vectorscope (or the **RGB Parade**) as you adjust colors. If you make the image more yellow, you should see the blob in the scope move into the yellow ranges. Keep an eye on any spikes that rise outside the wheel's boundaries. You may also want to check the waveform monitor to ensure no values fall above or below legal IRE limits.

In the HSL properties

Hue: Adjusts color without changing its brightness or amount of color.

Saturation: Adjusts the amount of color. At 100% the saturation is unchanged, while 0% saturation contains no color and looks black and white.

Brightness: Adjusts brightness of all pixels, including shadows.

Contrast and Contrast Center: In addition to adjusting the range between light and dark pixels, you can also adjust a bias so that darker pixels are modified more than lighter pixels, or vice versa.

Gamma: Adjust contrast within the midtones without affecting black and white levels.

Pedestal: Adjusts the black level, but at a larger range than the **Brightness** control.

RGB Gain: Adjust the white level of the image exponentially, so that lighter pixels are affected more than darker pixels (see Figure 8.8 on page 207).

In the RGB properties

Tonal Range: Specifies whether the **RGB** controls will affect master, black, white, or midtone levels.

Red/Green/Blue Gamma: Adjusts midtones of the color without affecting its dark and light levels (see Figure 8.9).

Red/Green/Blue Pedestal: Adjusts the darkness of the color within a large range.

Red/Green/Blue Gain: Adjusts the lightness of the color exponentially.

The **Curves** are perhaps the most powerful controls of the **Color Corrector** effect. In the **Curves**, you can adjust all aspects of hue, saturation, and brightness in each of the red, green, blue, and luminance components of the image. (You may need to widen the effects controls area to see all four curves.) The lower left of each graph represents its corresponding dark levels, the middle of each graph represents midtones, and the upper right represents the bright levels. Click on one of the diagonal lines to add a control point. For instance, if you want to adjust a midtone, click the middle of a line. Then drag the point to adjust its related component. Drag up to increase; drag down to decrease; Add more points in the curve to make finer adjustments. To delete a point, select it (by clicking it)

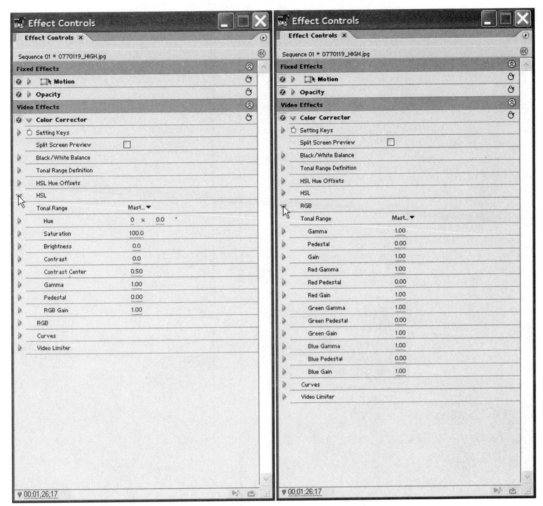

8.8   HSL properties.   8.9   RGB properties.

and press the **Delete** key on the keyboard. Each curve can have up to 16 points (see Figure 8.10 on page 208).

You can use the **Video Limiter** properties to make sure that your luminance and color ranges never exceed legal values.

In the Video Limiter properties

Enable Limiter: Toggle to enable the Video Limiter controls.

Luma Max: Specifies a maximum brightness of the image, measured in IRE broadcast units. A value of 100 IRE is standard in most broadcast environments.

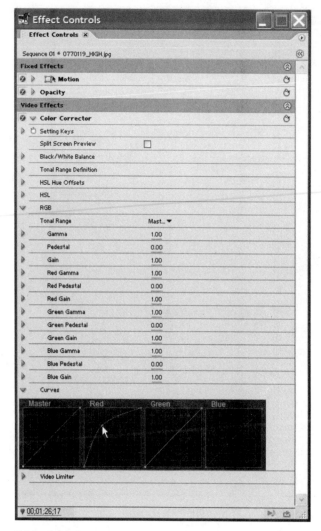

8.10 Adjusting curves.

8.11 Video Limiter properties.

Chroma Min and Chroma Max: Specifies the minimum and maximum levels of color in the image, measured in IRE. To conform to broadcast chrominance standards, you may want to make sure these values fall between –20 and 110 IRE.

Video System: Specifies NTSC or PAL.

Method: Specifies how to treat luminance and chrominance values that fall outside of your limiter settings. **Reduce Saturation** will change bright colors to white and dark colors to black. **Reduce Luma** will change bright pixels to gray. **Smart Limit** attempts to limit chrominance and luminance while maintaining the overall image. Try all three choices while watching your external monitor (see Figure 8.11).

USING THE COLOR MATCH EFFECT

This effect allows you to make the selected clip's colors match the colors of another clip. To test it, try the following steps:

1. Place two clips in the timeline—the clip you want to adjust and the clip you want to match.

2. If necessary, first correct the two clips with the **Color Corrector** effect.

3. Park the **Current Time Indicator** over the clip you want to adjust so that you can see it in the **Program Monitor**.

4. Disable ganging of the **Reference Monitor** (by clicking a second time on the **Gang** button), and from its wing menu, select the **Composite Video** option, which will essentially turn the **Reference Monitor** into a second **Program Monitor**.

5. Park the **Reference Monitor's Current Time Indicator** within the clip you want to match. You should now see the clip you want to adjust in the **Program Monitor** and the clip you want to match in the **Reference Monitor**.

6. From the **Effects** tab, in the **Video Effects>Image Control** bin, apply the **Color Match** effect to the clip you want to adjust.

   Because the **Color Match** controls rely on the same awkward eyedropper tools as the **Color Corrector**, the **Color Match** effect leaves a lot to be desired. However, if your images are free of noise, then it can work very well.

7. With the clip you want to adjust selected, bring up the **Effect Controls** window and twirl open the **Color Match** effect.

8. For best results, set the **Method** property to **Curves**.

9. Use the **Sample** eyedroppers to select colors from the clip in the **Reference Monitor**.

10. Use the **Target** eyedroppers to select the colors you'd like to change in the **Program Monitor**.

    For instance, if you'd like to change a red shirt in the **Program Monitor** to the color of a green leaf in the **Reference Monitor**, click the leaf with a **Sample** eyedropper and the shirt with the corresponding **Target** eyedropper. When using the eyedroppers, hold down on them and drag them onto the color you want to select. They won't work if you click them.

11. Finally, twirl open the **Match** property group and click the **Match** button. You may need to apply the **Color Corrector** effect to adjust the **Match** (see Color Plate 8.26).

WRAPPING UP

Some people love color correction. Others find that it veers too close to physics and too far from art for their liking. In truth, color correction is a mixture of art and science. But if you find yourself getting muddled with vectorscopes, IRE levels, and waveform monitors, remember that the best and simplest tool is an external monitor or TV. Checking your work on a monitor other than your computer monitor can give you a ton of useful info, painlessly and quickly.

Note ***About the Color Images in this Section:*** Color video is additive. As a result, some of the images in the color section—which is printed subtractively with color inks—may not reproduce accurately on the printed page. For a more complete explanation of this issue, see *Additive and Subtractive Color in Color Correction for Digital Video* by Steve Hullfish and Jaime Fowler, 2003, CMP Books.

If you're yearning to leap into a topic that's more accessible, check out Chapter 9 (after the color plates), where you'll explore the fun world of motion animation.

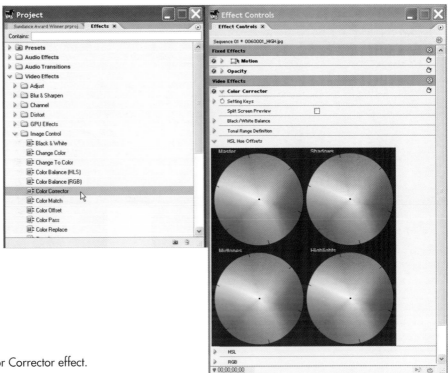

8.1   The Color Corrector effect.

8.2   Vectorscopes, Waveforms, and Parades. *(below)*

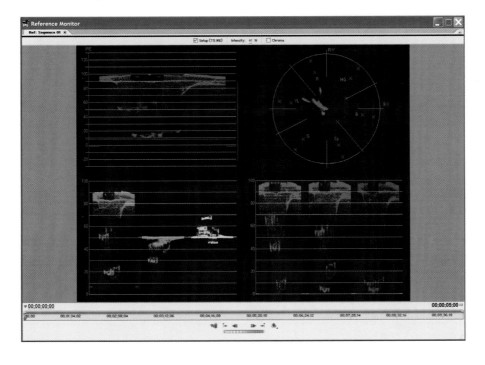

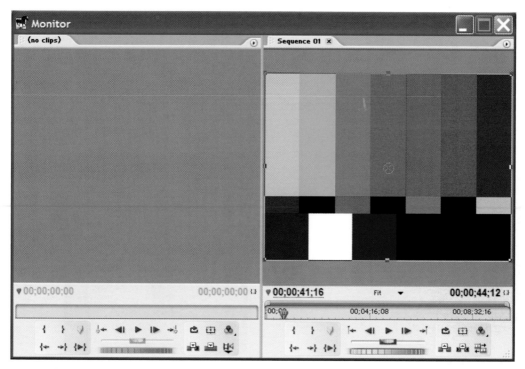

8.3   Color bars.

8.4   To keep the Reference Monitor in synch with the Program Monitor, click the Gang to Program Monitor button.

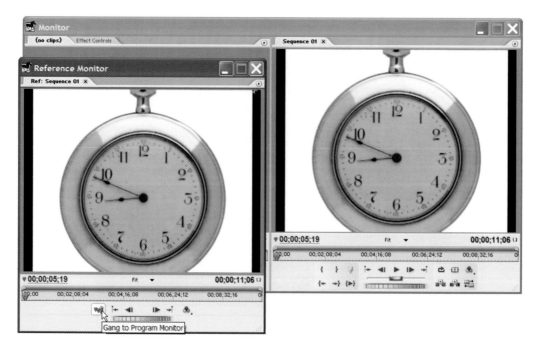

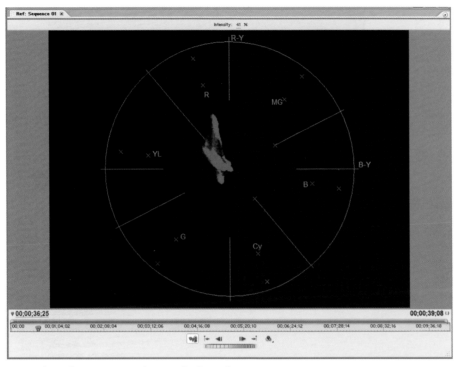

8.5   This is how a very red image looks in the vectorscope.

8.6   Beware of spikes that extend beyond the wheel's boundaries.

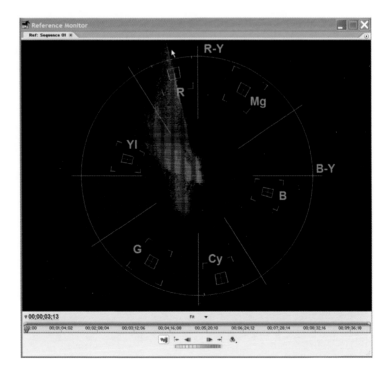

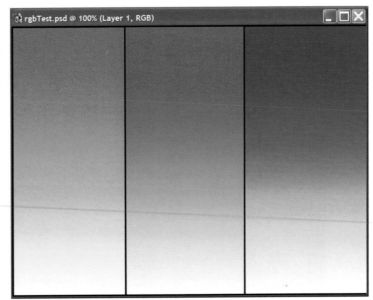

8.7 An image displaying three gradients: white to red, white to green, and white to blue.

8.8 The vectorscope analyzing the red, green, and blue gradient images. *(below)*

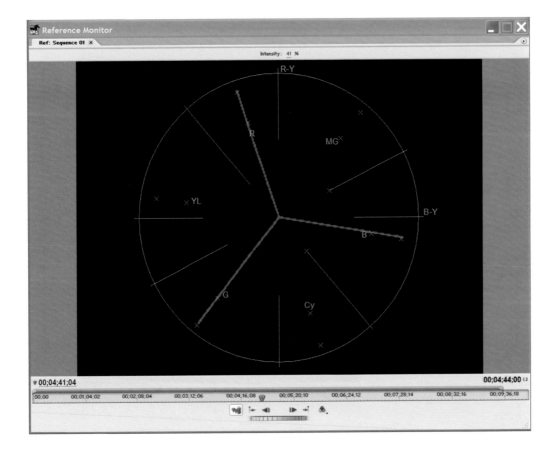

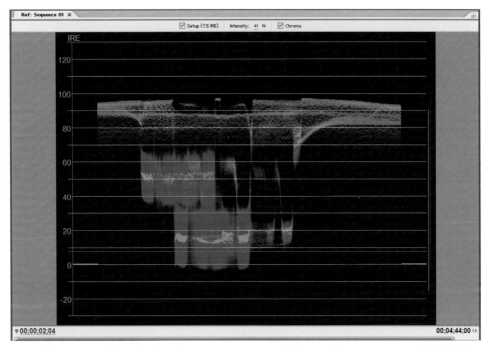

8.9   The YC Waveform displays luminance as a green blob and chrominance as a blue blob.

8.10 To see luminance only, uncheck the Chroma option at the top of the monitor.

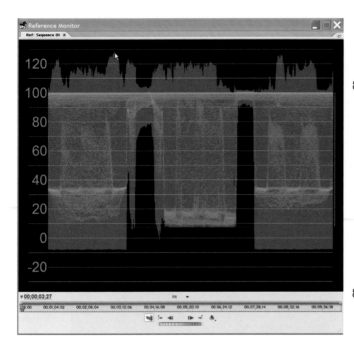

8.11 Look out for spikes in the Waveform.

8.12 Clipping at white creates flat areas at the top of the Waveform. *(below)*

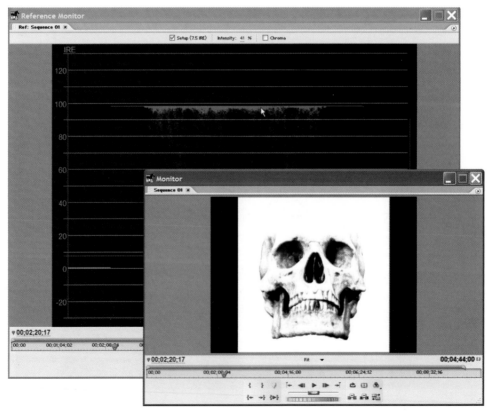

8.13 This image should clip at white. *(above)*

8.14 An image that lacks contrast. *(below)*

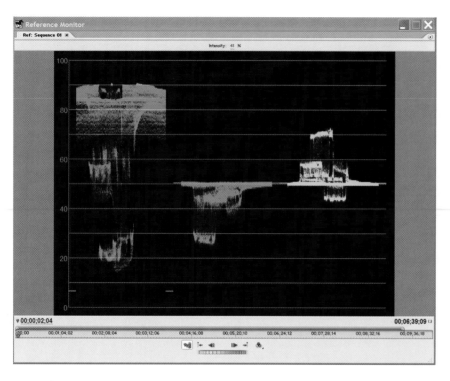

8.15 The YCbCr Parade. *(above)*

8.16 The RGB Parade. *(below)*

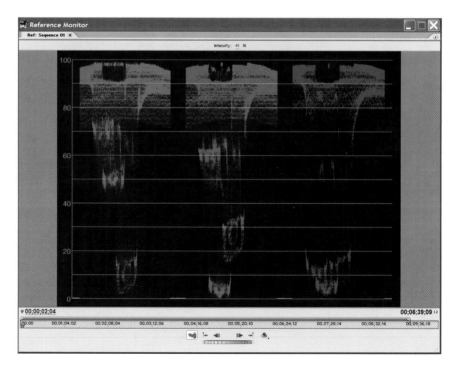

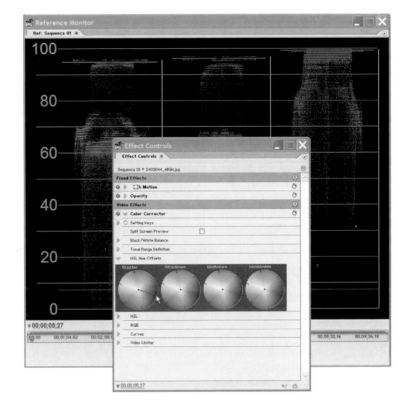

8.17 A spike in the blue channel, created by tinting in Color Corrector effect.

8.18 The Reference Monitor displaying several scopes at once. *(below)*

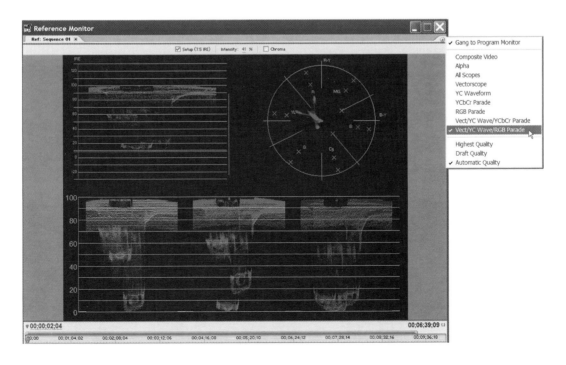

8.19 If you check the Split screen Preview option, the Program Monitor will display color correction on the right and an uncorrected image on the left.

8.20 You can tell Premiere what parts of the image are supposed to be black, white, and neutral gray by using the eyedroppers.

8.21 With the Preview option checked, every pixel turns black, white, or gray.

8.22 With the Preview option checked, scrub the Shadows and Highlights values.

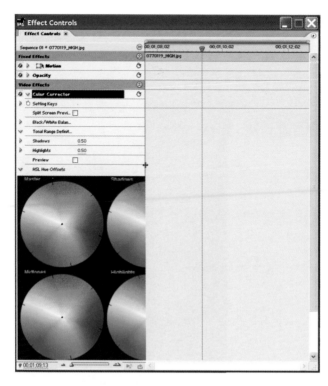

8.23 You may need to widen the effect properties area to see all the color wheels.

8.24 Tinting the midtone area with a saturated blue. *(below)*

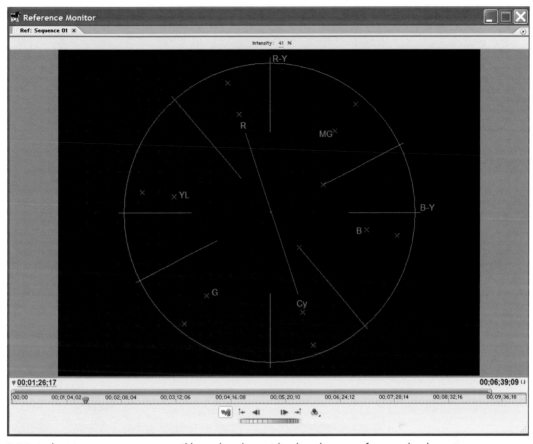

8.25 In the Vectorscope, opposites (like red and cyan) lie directly across from each other.

8.26 Before and after applying the Color Match effect.

Chapter 9

Motion

INTRODUCTION

Motion, a fixed effect that Premiere automatically applies to every clip in the **Timeline**, lets you animate images or videos moving around the screen. If you select a clip, bring up the **Effect Controls** window, and twirl open the **Motion** effect, you'll gain access to four animation properties: **Position, Scale, Rotation,** and **Anchor Point** (see Figure 9.1). You can adjust these properties in three places: the **Effect Controls** window, the **Timeline** and the **Program Monitor,** where you can animate movement by literally dragging images around the screen.

When animating **Motion**, as with any animation, it's important to remember to factor in time as well as position. After turning on a property stopwatch, the general procedure you should follow is:

1. Move the image into its starting position.

2. Move the **Current Time Indicator** to a new point in time.

3. Move the image to its ending position.

Premiere will tween the image so that it moves from the starting position you set to the ending position you set. The length of time the image takes to move from the starting position to the ending position is governed by how for you moved the **Current Time Indicator.** If you want to speed up the animation, you'll have to move the keyframes, which

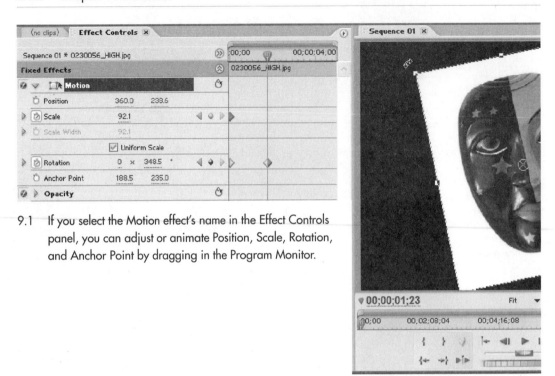

9.1 If you select the Motion effect's name in the Effect Controls panel, you can adjust or animate Position, Scale, Rotation, and Anchor Point by dragging in the Program Monitor.

Premiere creates at your starting and ending times, closer together. If you move the key-frames farther apart, the animation will run slower.

The biggest mistake beginners tend to make is forgetting the time element. Sometimes they forget to turn stopwatches on, and you can't animate any property unless its stop-watch is on. Or they will move an image into its starting position, turn on a **Position's** stopwatch, and then move the image to its ending position. The missing step here is mov-ing the **Current Time Indicator**. If you never move the **Current Time Indicator**, then you'll record the end position keyframe at the beginning of the movement. In other words, both the start and end positions will be at the same point in time, which is impossible, so Pre-miere will overwrite your initial starting position with your ending position—and the image won't move. It will just park itself at the ending position. So remember:

1. Select a clip in the **Timeline**.

2. Display the **Effect Controls** window.

3. Twirl open the **Motion** effect.

4. Click the stopwatch by the **Position** property.

5. In the **Program Monitor**, drag the clip into its starting position.

6. Move the **Current Time Indicator**.

7. Drag the image to its ending position (see Figure 9.2).

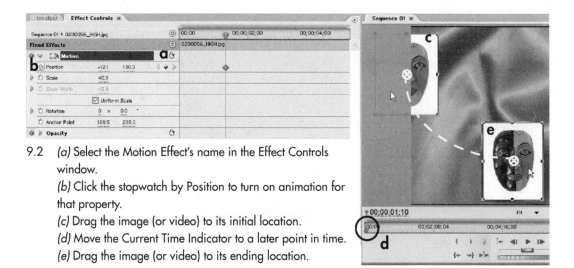

9.2   (a) Select the Motion Effect's name in the Effect Controls window.

(b) Click the stopwatch by Position to turn on animation for that property.

(c) Drag the image (or video) to its initial location.

(d) Move the Current Time Indicator to a later point in time.

(e) Drag the image (or video) to its ending location.

8.   To make the image move to another position, move the **Current Time Indicator** again, and then place the image in another position.

9.   Continue to move the **Current Time Indicator** and then the image for each new location you want the image to travel to.

You never need to click the stopwatch again. If you do, all your keyframes will be erased, because clicking the stopwatch a second time tells Premiere you don't want to animate that property any more.

Position

In Premiere, as in most other computer animation programs, a clip's spatial position is read by two points, called x and y. X is the clip's horizontal position. Y is the clip's vertical position. Zero for both x and y is in the upper-left corner of the screen: $0x$ is the left edge of the screen; $0y$ is the top edge of the screen. If you raise the value of x from zero, the image moves to the right (see Figure 9.3). If you raise the value of y, the image moves down (see Figure 9.4). X and y can also be set to negative values, which sends the image off the screen to the left and top, respectively. Or, if you set the x and y position values to really big numbers—bigger than the dimensions of the screen—the image will move off the right and bottom of the screen. It's perfectly acceptable to move the image off the screen. That's how you animate a graphic coming from off screen: set a keyframe in which the image is off the screen, move the **Current Time Indicator** to a later point in time, then move the image onto the screen. Premiere will fly the image from off screen to on screen.

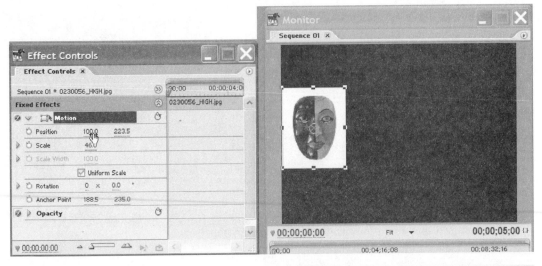

9.3 Adjusting the Position property's x value.

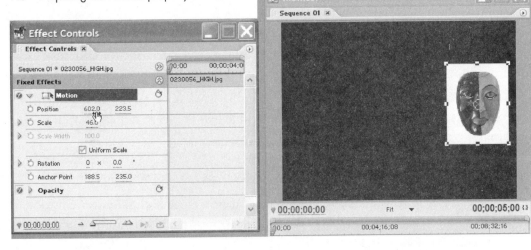

What's in a Name?

Just like many other effects, the **Motion Effect** places draggable controls in the **Program Monitor**. But with other effects, before you can access the controls, you have to select the effect's name in the **Effect Controls** window. This is not the case with the **Motion Effect**. Make sure that the **Current Time Indicator** is parked somewhere within the selected clip, so that one of its frames is clickable in the **Program Monitor**. Then click the image in the **Program Monitor** to reveal controls that let you move, resize, or rotate the currently selected clip. You don't even need to have the **Effect Controls** window open, though it's helpful if you want to animate the effect.

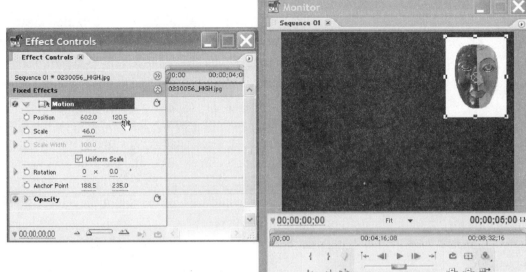

9.4   Adjusting the Position property's y value.

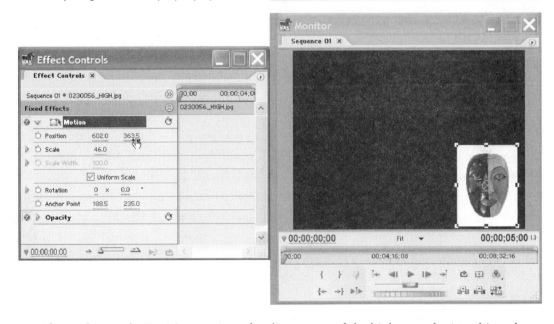

If you change the **Position** setting of a clip on one of the higher tracks (anything above **Video 1**) so that it doesn't fill up the whole screen, you'll be able to see through to the images on the tracks underneath. So if you have a picture of a horse on **Video 1** and a full-screen picture of a cow on **Video 2**, you won't be able to see the horse, because the cow will completely obscure it. But if you adjust the cow's position, moving it over a bit to the right, you'll be able to see at least some of the horse—wherever the cow isn't covering it up.

Anchor Point

X and y positions are pixel values. In other words, if a clip's x position is 150, that means it's 150 pixels to the right of the edge of the screen. But clips are large rectangles. What does it mean to say that a clip is positioned at 150 pixels from the left? Which *part* of the image is at 150 pixels left? The left edge of the image? The right edge of the image? The top? The center?

In fact, an image's position is read from its anchor point, which is one pixel of the image. By default, an image's anchor point is its center, which means that if an image is 100 pixels wide and 100 pixels high, its anchor point will be at 50x and 50y in the image's own internal coordinate system. That also means that if you position it at 0x,0y, the image will be half off the left edge of the screen and half off the top of the screen. This is because the image's anchor point, which is 50 pixels into the image from both its dimensions, will be positioned at 0x,0y. So only pixels 50–100x and 50–100y will be on screen.

Images have their own internal coordinate system that, like the screen's coordinate system, sets 0x,0y in the upper-left corner. Only in this case, it's the upper-left corner of the image instead of the screen. In other words, the image's anchor point might be at 10x,10y, which means that its anchor point is 10 pixels from the left edge of the image and 10 pixels from the right side of the image. Meanwhile, its position might be at 100x,100y, which would mean that the image's anchor point is 100 pixels from the left edge of the screen and 100 pixels from the top of the screen (see Figure 9.5).

The anchor point also acts as the image's rotation pivot. So if you leave the anchor point at its default location (the center of the image) and then animate **Rotation**, the image will rotate around its own center, like a wheel. If you'd like the image to swing like a pendulum instead, you'll need to move its anchor point way up—off the image itself. Then the image will be able to rotate around an invisible point above it. Moving the anchor point off the image itself is also the way to animate orbits. If your image is of the earth and you want to make it orbit around an image of the sun, move the earth's anchor point off itself and onto the sun, because an image will always rotate around its anchor point (see Figures 9.5 and 9.6).

If you scale an image, making it bigger or smaller, it will scale out from its anchor point. So if an image's anchor point is in its center and you the image to make it wider, it will get wider to the left and to the right of its anchor point, growing out from its center as though it's a piece of taffy and you're pulling on both ends (see Figures 9.7 and Figures 9.8).

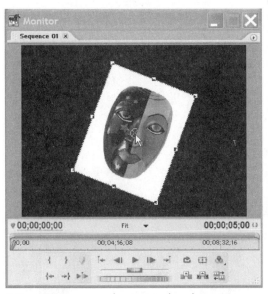

9.5 Rotating around a centered anchor point.

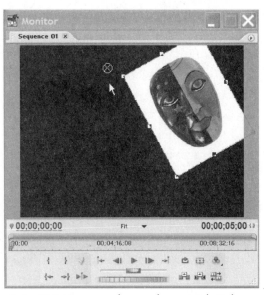

9.6 Rotating around an anchor point that's been moved off the image.

9.7 Scaling out from a centered anchor point.

9.8 Scaling out from an anchor point that's been moved to the image's left edge.

If, on the other hand, you want it to grow from its left edge, like a progress bar, you'll need to first move its anchor point to its left edge. If you want it to grow from the bottom up, like a blade of grass, you'll have to move its anchor point to its bottom edge.

Though the anchor point property has a stopwatch, it's somewhat rare for people to animate the anchor point. More often, people will simply adjust the anchor point globally (with the stopwatch turned off), setting it permanently in a new position. But you will need to animate an anchor point if you want to create Ken Burns–style motion photography. That technique is covered on page 233.

Rotation

Unlike **Position** and **Anchor Point**, which are read from *x* and *y* pixel positions, Rotation is set to a degree value from 0 to 360. If you look at the **Rotation** property in the **Effect Controls** window, by default it will read 0×0.0. The second number (after the ×) is the degree, so if you want to rotate the image halfway around its anchor point, you'd change this value to 180 (180° is half of 360°, which is a full circle). In this case, the **Rotation** property will read 0×180. The first number, the zero, indicates how many times the image has orbited its anchor point. So 3×0.0 means "three times around." 3×15 means three times around plus an additional 15°. Many people have remarked that this property would make more sense if the symbol between the two numbers was a plus sign instead of an ×, which we think of as meaning multiplication.

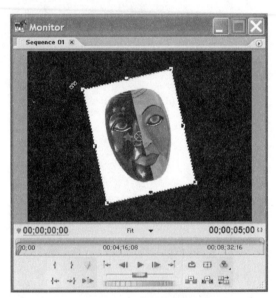

9.9 If you select the Motion effect in the Effect Controls window and move your mouse cursor just outside the boundaries of the image, you can freely rotate it in the Program Monitor.

It doesn't make any sense to adjust the first number unless you're animating. If you just want to permanently turn the image so that it's facing a different direction than it was originally, adjust the second number (after the ×). It doesn't make sense to say "three times around" unless the image is actually spinning.

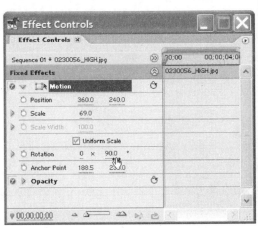 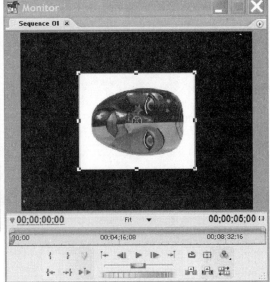

9.10 An image rotated 90° by scrubbing the Rotation value in the Effect Controls window.

On the other hand, if you want the image to spin five times around its anchor point, turn the stopwatch on for its **Rotation** property, move the **Current Time Indicator** to a new point in time, and then change the **Rotation** property value to 5×0. If you want it to spin five and a half times around its anchor point, turn the stopwatch on, move the **Current Time Indicator** to a new point in time, and then change the **Rotation** property value to 5×180 (see Figure 9.10).

Note **Mirror Opposite:** No matter how much you rotate an image, you'll never flip it to its mirror opposite. If you want to do that, try applying either **Video Effects>Transform>Horizontal Flip** or **Video Effects>Transform>Vertical Flip**.

Scale

Whereas **Position** and **Anchor Point** use pixel values, and **Rotation** uses degrees, **Scale** uses percentages. So if an image's scale is set to 100, it's 100% of its actual size, in other words not changed at all. If it's set at 50, it's half its original size. If it's set at 200, it's double its original size.

If you want to animate a full-screen image starting as a pinprick and growing to its full size, set its first keyframe to **Scale** 0 and its second keyframe to **Scale** 100. While you

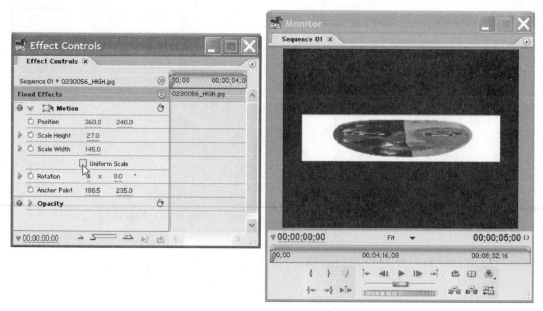

9.11 If you uncheck the Uniform Scale option, you can scale width and height separately, distorting the image so that it's out of proportion.

can scale an image to much larger than its original size, it will start looking blocky (pixi-lated) if you scale it up too large. If you want to "zoom in" on a photo of a person until his eye fills the entire screen, then you should import a really huge photo of a person to begin with. It should be so big that at 100%, the eye fills the entire screen. Then you can animate the "zoom in" by scaling the image *down* in its start keyframe so that you can see the whole face. In the end keyframe, the image should zoom up to its actual size.

Another way around the blocky-image problem is to scale vector images, the type of image you can create in Adobe Illustrator. Vector images can be scaled to any size—even thousands of times bigger than their original dimensions—and they will always look crisp and sharp.

By default, when you adjust **Scale** in the **Effect Controls** window, Premiere makes the image bigger (or smaller) in both dimensions at the same time, making it both wider and tall (or narrower and shorter). This guarantees that the image always stays in proportion. But if you want to change just an image's width, or just its height, uncheck the **Uniform Scale** option in the **Effect Controls** window. (You'll have to twirl open the **Motion** effect to find it.) Premiere will then give you access to separate controls for scaling width and scaling height (see Figure 9.11).

Picture-in-Picture: You can use **Scale** to create the ever popular picture-in-a-picture effect. Just place the main image in **Video 1** and the "picture-in-a-picture" image (or video) in **Video 2**. Then scale the clip in **Video 2** image down, so that you can see **Video 1** peeking out behind it. To place the **Video 2** clip in a particular region of the screen, use the **Position** property's *x* and *y* values, or select the **Motion** effect in the **Effect Controls** window and then drag the image directly in the **Program Monitor.**

EFFECT CONTROLS WINDOW

As with all effect properties, you can adjust or animate **Position, Scale, Rotation,** or **Anchor Point** in the **Effect Controls** window. First select a clip in the **Timeline,** then choose **Window>Effect Controls** from the menu and twirl open the **Motion** effect. **Motion** is a fixed effect, which means that it's always there—you don't have to apply it, like you do with the effects listed in the **Effects** window.

Some people are intimidated by the **Effect Controls** window, because they feel it forces them to adjust properties by the numbers. While it's true that dragging an image in the **Program Monitor** could be more intuitive, you should remember that you can scrub the numbers in the **Effect Controls** window, which is also a pretty intuitive (nonmathematical) way of working. To get a sense of this, point to the **Scale** property value. While holding down the mouse button (Don't click and release—hold down!), drag to the left or to the right. Of course, if you want to set a property value to an exact number, you can do that too. Just click the current value, type a new value, and press **Enter.**

If you want to animate changes to a property, remember to turn on that property's stopwatch, by clicking it. You can then create new keyframes by moving the **Current Time Indicator** and adjusting property values. When you move the **Current Time Indicator,** you can move it in the **Timeline,** the **Program Monitor,** or the **Effect Controls** window. The **Effect Controls** window's **Timeline** gives you the most complete view of keyframes on the currently selected clip. You can view keyframes in the **Timeline** too, but only for one property at a time.

To learn more about how to animate using keyframes, see "Animating Properties" on page 144 in Chapter 6.

TIMELINE

To view or animate a **Motion** property in the **Timeline,** expand the selected clip's track. You can expand a track by clicking the twirly triangle next to its name. In the bottom row

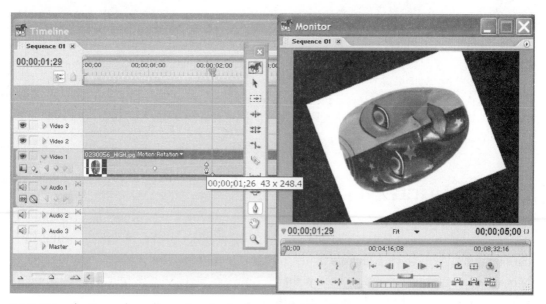

9.12 Using the Pen tool to adjust a Rotation keyframe in the Timeline.

of the expanded track, under the track name (e.g., **Video 1**), you'll find the **Show Keyframe** button, which looks (by default) like a "no" symbol (a circle with a slash-line through it), indicating that no keyframes are being displayed. Click this button and choose **Show Keyframes** from the pop-up menu. After choosing this option, you must then tell Premiere which keyframe you want to see. In the **Timeline**, you can only see keyframes for one property at a time. If you've added keyframes to **Position** and **Scale**, you'll have to view just the **Position** keyframes or just the **Scale** keyframes in the **Timeline**. If you want to view keyframes of multiple properties at the same time, you can do so in the **Effect Controls** window's **Timeline**.

To select a property, click the **Show Keyframes** button and choose the **Show Keyframes** option from the pop-up menu. Click the dropdown menu next to the clip's name, and pick a property. You can also select an **Motion Effect** property by right-clicking a clip in the **Timeline** and then choosing the **Show Clip Keyframes** option from the pop-up menu. Premiere will then display a submenu, from which you can choose the specific property's keyframes you want to adjust.

You can adjust keyframes by dragging them up and down (which increases or decreases their associated property's value) or left and right (which moves them to different points in time) with the arrow tool or the **Pen** tool (see Figure 9.12). To add new keyframes, click the orange line with the **Pen** tool.

To learn more about manipulating keyframes in the **Timeline**, see Chapter 6.

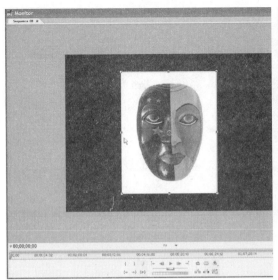

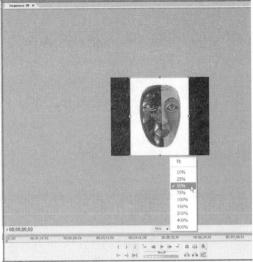

9.13 When you click on an image in the Program
      Monitor, manipulators appear.

9.14 To zoom in or out, select a percentage from
      the menu just below the Monitor.

PROGRAM MONITOR

You can adjust **Motion Effect** properties in the **Program Monitor,** which may be the most intuitive way to work. If you've ever used the **Free Transform** tool in Photoshop, you'll quickly feel at home in the **Program Monitor.**

The main thing you have to remember is that you must select the clip in the **Timeline** and the park the **Current Time Indicator** somewhere within that clip. Then click the clip's image in the **Program Monitor.** You'll see several manipulators appear (see Figure 9.13). For instance, you'll see small squares around the edges and corners of the image.

You also may not be able to see the manipulators if you're zoomed in too far into the image in the **Program Monitor,** if you're viewing it at a large level of magnification. To zoom out or in, click the dropdown menu just below the monitor in the center, and choose a magnification level (see Figure 9.14). If the image is scaled way up, you may have to choose a very small level of magnification, such as 10%, before you'll be able to see the handles around the image's edges.

To scale an image, drag any of the squares around its edges. If you drag the squares in towards the center of the image, you'll scale it smaller. If you drag them out, away from the image, you'll scale it larger. Dragging a corner square will scale the width and the height at the same time, while dragging a top, bottom, or side square will scale in one dimension only (i.e., just the width or just the height). Note that if you've left the **Uniform Scale** option checked in the **Effect Controls** window, dragging any square will scale both

9.15 To scale the image, drag a handle.

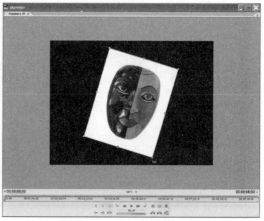

9.16 To rotate an image, move the mouse cursor just outside the image's bounding rectangle and drag.

width and height at the same time. If you uncheck this option, you can hold down the Shift key and drag one of the corner handles to temporarily scale width and height together (see Figure 9.15).

To rotate an image, roll the mouse just slightly away from one of the squares, outside the edge of the image. When the mouse cursor changes to a curved, double-headed arrow, you can hold down and drag to rotate. The image will rotate around its anchor point (see Figure 9.16).

To move the image to a new position, drag it from anywhere within its border, but make sure you don't drag it from one of the squares around its edge, or you'll scale it by mistake (see Figure 9.17).

You can see the clip's anchor point in the **Program Monitor**. It looks like an X inside a circle—⊗. However, you can't adjust it there. To adjust an anchor point, scrub the anchor point property values in the **Effect Controls** window (see Figure 9.18).

BEZIER CURVES AND EASING

In the real world, very few objects move in perfectly straight lines. Real objects curve. Luckily, you can create curved movement by dragging in the **Program Monitor**. You can also control acceleration and deceleration by creating curves in the **Timeline**.

Time curves? This may sound confusing, but it's actually a very powerful concept. An upward-sloping curve in the timeline creates animation that gradually speeds up over time. A downward-sloping curve gradually slows down. The animator's word for speeding up (accelerating) and slowing down (decelerating) is *easing*. Easing in means

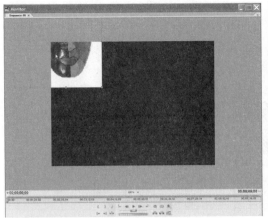

9.17 Drag the image to move it to a new position.

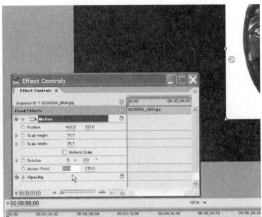

9.18 To move the anchor point, scrub the values in the Effect Controls window.

gradually speeding up, as is easing in to full speed; easing out means gradually slowing down, as in easing out of full speed.

You create both easing in the **Timeline** and curved motion in the **Program Monitor** by manipulating Bezier curves (pronounced BEZ-ee-ay). Bezier curves, the same sort of curves you can draw with the **Pen** tool, are based named after the French mathematician Pierre Bezier. Luckily, we don't have to use math to create Bezier curves in Premiere. Premiere does the math for us.

Curves that control movement in the **Program Monitor** are called **Spatial Curves**. Curves that control easing in the timeline are called **Temporal Curves**. In addition to manipulating **Spatial** and **Temporal** curves in the **Timeline** and **Program Monitor**, you can also manipulate them (to a lesser degree) in the **Effect Controls** window.

Spatial curves

If you set just two keyframes for an object's **Position** property, Premiere will animate that object moving in a straight line—the shortest distance between the positions at the two keyframes (see Figure 9.19). But if you add a third keyframe, moving the object to another position, Premiere will automatically move the object along a (Bezier) curved path (see Figure 9.20).

In the middle of the path, at the second keyframe, you should see a small square. This marks the location of the object at that keyframe. If you want, you can drag the square to a new location in the **Program Monitor** to change where the object moves to on keyframe 2 (see Figure 9.21). In Bezier curve terminology, this square is called a vertex point. The object is anchored to this point at keyframe 2.

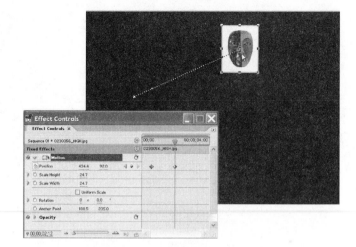

9.19 With just two keyframes, an object moves in a straight line.

9.20 A third keyframe causes Premiere to create a curved path.

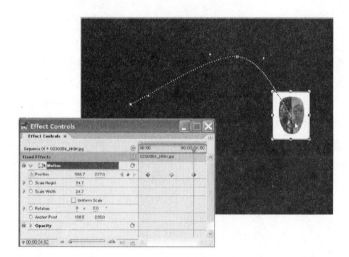

To either side of the anchor point, you should see tiny dots. These draggable controls are called *direction handles* (see Figure 9.22). Try dragging one of them to change the direction of the curve (see Figure 9.23). The direction handle on the left controls the direction of the curve as it approaches the vertex. The direction handle on the right controls the direction of the curve as it leaves the vertex. In Bezier curve terminology, the lines controlled by these direction handles are called direction lines. You don't see the direction lines appear until you drag one of the direction handles. Visible direction lines means you control the curve. Invisible direction lines (and two floating, detached direction handles) means Premiere controls the curve. When Premiere controls a curve for you, it's called an **Auto Bezier** curve.

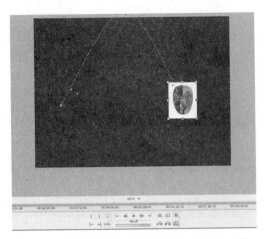

9.21 Drag the middle vertex point to change the object's location at its second keyframe.

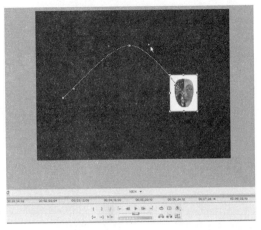

9.22 The draggable dots to either side of a vertex are called direction handles.

Long direction lines create curvy curves. If you drag a direction line closer in towards its vertex, the curve emanating from that vertex will grow straighter (see Figure 9.24). If you drag a direction line all the way into a vertex, the "curve" emanating from it will become a straight line. But as you try this, you may notice that the so-called straight line is not completely straight (see Figure 9.25). This is because each curve is controlled by two vertices. By dragging one vertex's direction line all the way in, you've eliminated its influence over the curve. But the vertex on the other side of the curve is also influencing it, so to make a perfectly straight line, you have to drag its direction line all the way in too.

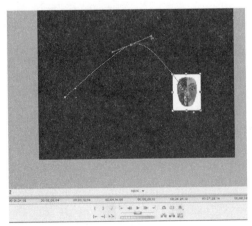

9.23 Drag a direction handle to see direction lines, which control the angle at which curves enter and leave a vertex point.

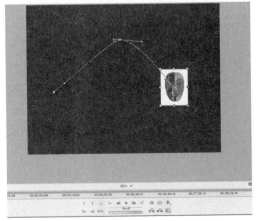

9.24 The closer you drag a direction line in toward its vertex, the straighter the line becomes.

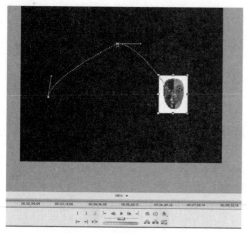

9.25 To create a straight line, drag a direction handle all the way into its vertex.

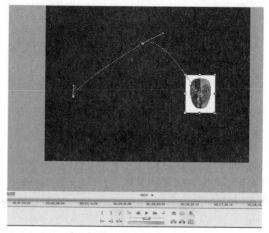

9.26 To make the line perfectly straight, you have to drag the direction handle of the opposite vertex all the way in.

With both direction lines shortened to nothing, neither vertex can influence the curve—so there's no curve (see Figure 9.26).

Collapsing direction lines teaches you something about how Bezier curves work, but it would be a pain if you had to drag them in every time you wanted to create a straight line. To instantly suck in its direction lines, **Control**+click a vertex. To turn the resulting straight line back into a curve, **Control**+click the same vertex again. **Control**+clicking vertices toggles them between straight and curved.

You can also change vertices from curved to straight by right-clicking them and choosing **Spatial Interpolation>Linear** from the pop-up menu. To change a straight vertex into a curved vertex, right-click it and choose **Spatial Interpolation>Auto Bezier** from the pop-up menu (see Figure 9.27). You can bring up the same pop-up menus and make the same changes by right-clicking keyframes in the **Effect Controls** window (see Figure 9.28). If you **Shift**+click or marquee select multiple keyframes, you can right-click on one of them and change choose an option from the **Spatial Interpolation** pop-up menu. Your choice will affect all selected keyframes.

You may have noticed that as you drag a direction handle, the opposite direction handle moves too. This is purposeful. Premiere assumes you want to keep your curves smooth, so while you adjust the incoming curve, Premiere adjusts the outgoing curve (or vice versa). But you might not want a smooth curve. To break the connection between the two direction handles, **Control**+drag one of them. To reconnect them, **Control**+drag the same handle a second time.

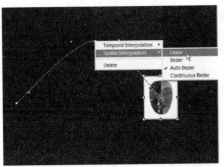

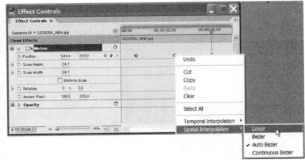

9.27 To change a line from straight to curved or vice versa, Control+click its vertices or right-click them and, from the pop-up menu, choose Spatial Interpolation>Auto Bezier (for curves) or Spatial Interpolation>Linear (for straight lines).

9.28 You can also choose a change curve types by right-clicking keyframes in the Effect Controls window.

Note ***Control Key:*** The **Control** key does two different things: **Control+dragging** a direction handle breaks the connection between it and the opposite direction handle. **Control+clicking** a vertex converts toggles it between a straight point and a curved vertex (see Figure 9.29).

You can also sever the connection between the lines by right-clicking a vertex (or its associated keyframe in the **Effect Controls** window) and choosing **Spatial Interpolation>Bezier** from the pop-up menu (see Figure 9.30). After choosing this option, you

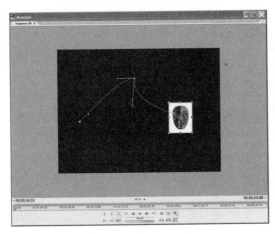

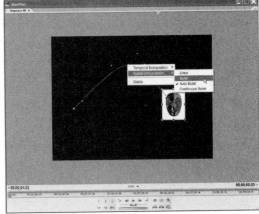

9.29 To sever the link between a vertex's two direction handles, Control+drag one of them.

9.30 To sever the link between two direction handles, right-click their vertex and choose Spatial Interpolation>Bezier from the pop-up menu.

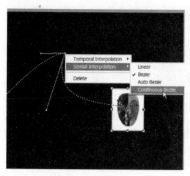

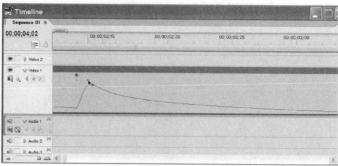

9.31 To reconnect the handles, right-
click their vertex and choose
Spatial
Interpolation>Continuous
Bezier from the pop-up menu.

9.32 Drag a Timeline direction handle up or down to alter a
Temporal curve. High means fast; low means slow. So this
animation is changing from fast to slow between the two
keyframes. In other words, it's easing out.

won't see a change in the **Program Monitor** until you drag one of the direction lines.
When you do, you'll notice the opposite line doesn't move with it. To reconnect the two
lines, right-click the anchor point or its keyframe and choose **Spatial Interpolation>Con-
tinuous Bezier** from the pop-up menu (see Figure 9.31).

Temporal curves

Though you can set make temporal adjustments in the **Effect Controls** window or the
Program Monitor (by right-clicking a keyframe or anchor point), you have much more
control in the **Timeline**. Though spatial curves only applies to the **Position** property of the
Motion effect, temporal curves can be adjusted for any effect property. A blur could speed
up or slow down. So before trying to adjust curves in the **Timeline**, you first need to display the keyframes for a specific property. To learn how to do this, see Chapter 6.

You can manipulate curves in the **Timeline** with either the **Selection** tool or the **Pen**
tool. To adjust the slope of a curve, making it leave or enter its keyframe from a higher or
lower angle, drag the little circle up or down. This circle represents a direction handle. In
the **Timeline**, high means fast and low means slow. So if the curve is high as it leaves
keyframe 1 and low as it approaches keyframe 2, the animation will start fast and then
gradually slow down, or ease out (see Figure 9.32).

You can adjust the influence a keyframe has over the curve by dragging a direction
handle to the left or the right. The further you drag it away from its keyframe, the more
influence that keyframe will have over the curve. The curve will be more curvy near that
keyframe. If you drag the handles all the way in towards their keyframes on both sides of

Bezier Curve Types

When you right-click a keyframe or vertex and select the **Spatial Interpolation** or **Temporal Interpolation** option, you can pick from several different Bezier types: **Linear**, **Bezier**, **Auto Bezier**, **Continuous Bezier**, and **Hold** (Temporal Interpolation only).

Linear: Straight lines in the **Program Monitor**. No easing (acceleration/deceleration) in the **Timeline** (see Figure 9.33).

Auto Bezier: Smooth curve in the **Program Monitor**, indicated by two dots floating a little ways away from their vertex with no lines connecting them to the anchor points. As soon as you drag one the dots, the type automatically changes from **Auto Bezier** to **Continuous Bezier**. In the **Timeline**, **Auto Bezier** describes animation that starts slow, speeds up and then slows down again, like a car driving from one driveway to another, across the street (see Figure 9.34).

Continuous Bezier: Just like **Auto Bezier**, except you can drag the direction handles. When you drag one handle, Premiere adjusts the opposite handle to keep the curve smooth (see Figure 9.35).

9.33 Linear curve.

9.34 Auto Bezier curve.

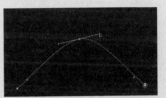
9.35 Continuous Bezier curve.

Bezier: Severs the connection between the two handles, allowing you to create sudden changes in direction in the **Program Monitor** or abrupt easing changes in the **Timeline** (see Figure 9.36).

Hold (Temporal only): Disables animation. So if an object is on the left in keyframe 1 and on the right in keyframe 2, it will not move from the left to the right. Instead, it will stay on the left until the **Current Time Indicator** reaches keyframe two, at which point it will pop to its new position on the right (see Figure 9.37).

In the **Timeline** and **Effect Controls** window, different keyframe shapes indicate the different types of **Temporal** curves.

In the **Program Monitor**, the different curve types are indicated by the relationship between anchor points and direction lines.

9.36 Bezier curve.

linear continuous Bezier hold
   auto Bezier   Bezier

9.37 Types of temporal curves indicated by the shapes of Timeline and Effect Controls window keyframes.

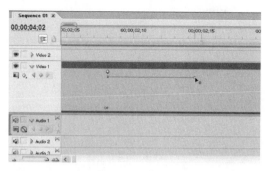

9.38 Drag a handle to the left or right to adjust influence.

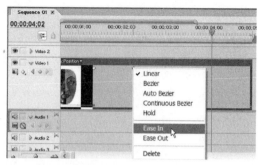

9.39 To quickly create common types of Temporal curves, right-click a keyframe and choose Temporal Interpolation>Ease In or Temporal Interpolation>Ease Out from the pop-up menu.

a curve, neither keyframe will exert any influence over the curve, so the curve will become a straight line (no easing) (see Figure 9.38).

As with anchor points in the **Program Monitor,** you can right-click on **Timeline** keyframes to change their temporal types. **Control+**clicking a **Continuous Bezier, Bezier,** or **Auto Bezier** keyframe in the **Timeline** will change it to a **Linear** keyframe. **Control+**dragging out from a **Linear** keyframe creates **Continuous Bezier** handles. **Control+**dragging a direction line circle severs the connection between it and its opposite handle, changing the keyframe's type to **Bezier.**

To create quick temporal curves, right-click a vertex or keyframe and choose **Temporal Interpolation>Ease in** or **Temporal Interpolation>Ease out** from the pop-up menu (see Figure 9.39).

One common misconception is that easing will make animations run faster. If an animation takes one second to complete, it will still take one second to complete after easing. But during that one second, the animation might start slow and then speed up. The only way to make the animation quicker or slower than one second is to drag its keyframes farther apart (slower) or closer together (quicker).

NESTING

Sometimes you may want a whole bunch of clips—either all on the same track or on multiple tracks—to move around together as a single unit. The best way to achieve this effect is through nesting sequences. Make sure that all of the clips you want to move together are in one sequence and no other clips are in that sequence. Then create a new sequence and drag the original sequence (from the **Project** window) onto the **Timeline** of the new sequence. To learn more about nesting, see "Nesting" on page 156 in Chapter 6.

KEN BURNS–STYLE ANIMATION

When you want to pan around in an image and then zoom into parts of that image to examine details, stay away from the **Position** property. Instead, animate anchor point and then **Scale**. When you want to zoom in on an image, you'll have to simulate it by scaling it up, but you always scale around the anchor point. So if your goal is to zoom in on a person's eye, you won't achieve it if the anchor point happens to be on his lips—even if you adjust position so that the eye is in the center of the screen.

Adjusting the anchor point will effectively change the image's position on screen, because **Position** is the position of the anchor point. In other words, if the anchor point is on the person's lips and the **Position** is $100x,100y$, that means his lips are at $100x$ and $100y$. If you adjust the anchor point so that it's on the person's nose, the image will move so that his nose is at **Position** $100x$ and $100y$.

Let's say that you want to pan up a person's head from his neck to his eyes and then zoom in on one eye.

1. Start by importing a really huge image of the person into Premiere so that when you scale it up, it will not look blocky.

   The image should be big enough so that at 100% scale, the eye fills up the entire screen.

2. Scale the image down a bit, so that you can see most of the face on the screen, then adjust the anchor point so that it's on the person's neck.

3. Adjust the position so that the anchor point (on the neck) is centered in the screen.

   This will place the person's neck in the center of the screen. It is the only time you'll touch **Position**.

4. Turn the stopwatch on for **Anchor Point** to set this position as the first keyframe.

5. Move forward in time by dragging the **Current Time Indicator** to the right a bit.

6. Set a new keyframe for **Anchor Point** by adjusting its values until one of the person's eyes it's on one of the person's eyes (instead of his neck).

   This will create the pan from neck to eye (see Figure 9.40).

7. Turn on the stopwatch for **Scale** and make sure the **Uniform Scale** option is checked.

8. Move the **Current Time Indicator** again, to a point further to the right.

9. Then scrub the **Scale** property value higher until the eye fills the entire screen, which should occur when the value is at about 100 (see Figure 9.41).

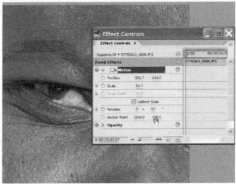
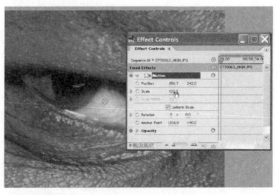

9.40 To pan around in a large image, animate the anchor point property.

9.41 To zoom in on a detail, make sure the anchor point is centered on that detail and animate an increase in Scale.

Note **Resolution:** A common misconception is that if you're going to zoom way into an image, the image must have a very high resolution. Resolution—the ppi of an image—only matters for print images. It's not true that all video images should be 72ppi. It doesn't matter what ppi an image is, unless it's intended for print. Changing it to 300ppi will not make it look better. What matters is how large the image is. So if you want to zoom way in on an image, make sure it's many pixels wide and many pixels high.

WRAPPING UP

This chapter and the next should remind you of the two equally important aspects of video. This chapter is about motion and the next is about sound. Both need to be strong, evocative and working together for the video to excite its audience.

Chapter 10

Audio

Audio work can seem quite complex in Premiere, so it's worthwhile remembering that it really consists of just three major steps:

- Importing audio

- Messing with audio

- Outputting audio

This chapter covers the first two of these steps. Audio output, which is just part of general output from Premiere, is covered in Chapter 12.

The simplest form of audio input is simply importing video that has audio tracks—in other words, video and audio that were filmed at the same time with the same camera. You can import such audio and its accompanying video using import and capture techniques covered in Chapter 3 on page 33. Or you can import an audio-only file, such as an MP3 or WAV. You can even record audio directly into Premiere, using a microphone hooked up to your computer's sound card.

The fun part is messing with audio after importing it. Various kinds of messing include changing the volume, adding audio effects, and mixing tracks of audio together to form a harmonious or contrasting result.

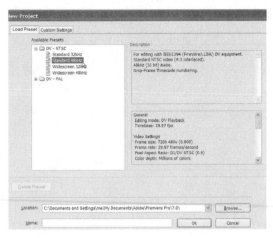

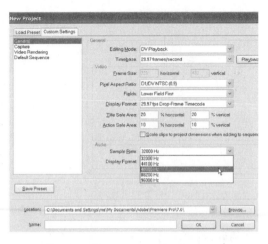

10.1 Selecting a project preset for 48kHz sampled sound.

10.2 Selecting a kHz option in the Custom Settings tab of the New Project window.

IMPORTING AUDIO

Setting up a sequence for audio

Before you can import anything into Premiere, you must create a project, unless you are updating an old project. You can do this immediately after starting up the program by clicking the **New Project** button on the **Welcome** screen. Or, if you've bypassed the **Welcome** screen, you can choose **File>New>Project** from the menu. The basic procedures for creating projects are covered in Chapter Two, but here we need to focus on the audio sample rate, which is the number you see listed after the video types in the **New Project** dialog window (see Figure 10.1).

KHz

Whether you're looking at NTSC (US and Japan) or PAL (Europe) projects, you see them listed as Standard or Widescreen. That choice determines the dimensions of your video image. But the numbers after those options tell Premiere what kind of audio you want to output when you're finished editing the project. The default choices are 32kHz and 48kHz. The kHz stands for kilohertz, a measure of how many sounds will play on your soundtrack per second. In the real world, sound is continuous. In a computer, sound starts and stops, like Morse code. The goal is the get the stops and starts so close together that the human ear is fooled into believing it's listening to continuous sound. The bigger the kHz number, the more continuous the sound. So usually 48kHz is the correct choice (see Figure 10.2). As it happens, DV sound (the sound recorded by your DV camera) is recorded at 48kHz, so this is also a good choice for DV projects.

The right kind of track for the right kind of sound

Once you've set up a project, you'll need to set up a sequence. You get one sequence by default when you create a project. The default sequence contains three audio tracks—**Audio 1**, **Audio 2**, and **Audio 3**—and one master track. Ultimately, the three audio tracks (or however many you use) are all mixed together into the master track, which, if you imagine your audio tracks as flour, sugar, and eggs, is the big mixing bowl where you make your cookie dough. It's the master track that is exported when you output your final project.

Premiere can work with three kinds of audio:

- Mono

- Stereo

- Surround sound (5.1 sound)

Premiere sequence tracks are set up to accept one of those three types of sounds. This means that you can't put stereo sound in a mono track and vice versa. So what kind of tracks are the three that you get automatically? They're stereo. This means that if you import mono or 5.1 sounds, you won't be able to place them into any of your existing tracks. And no, you can't change a track from a stereo track to a mono track. But you can add new tracks of whatever kinds you want. And if your old tracks get in the way, you can remove them.

To add a new track, choose **Sequence>New Tracks** from the menu. In the **Add Tracks** dialog, key in how

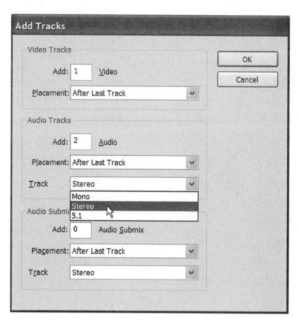

10.3 You can determine if a sound is mono, stereo, or 5.1 by selecting it in the Project window.

many new audio tracks you want and what type of audio they should contain (see Figure 10.3). To delete audio tracks, choose **Sequence>Delete Tracks** from the menu. In the **Delete Tracks** dialog, check the **Delete Audio Tracks** option and choose **All Empty Tracks** from the dropdown menu. Or, before choosing the **Delete Tracks** menu option, you can click a track name in the **Timeline** to select it, and then in the **Delete Tracks** dialog window, you can choose **Target Track** from the dropdown menu to delete the selected track.

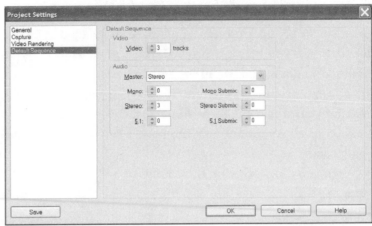

10.4 Setting up a default
     sequence in the Project
     Settings dialog.

If you often work with mono or 5.1 sound, you may get tired of adding new tracks and deleting old ones each time you start a sequence. In this case, you should change the **Default Sequence** options by choosing **Project>Project Settings>Default Sequence** (see Figure 10.4).

In order to know what kind of tracks you're going to need, you need to know whether your imported audio is mono, stereo, or 5.1. You can tell this by selecting any sound file in the Project window (even a video file that contains sound) and looking at the info at the top of the Project window (see Figure 10.5). Check each sound file to see what type it is and add the appropriate types of tracks. Remember, you don't need a track for every sound file you're using—only if you want to use them all at the same time. Sound files can lay one after another in the same track, as long as they're of the same type, mono, stereo, or 5.1.

If you desperately want to place a stereo sound into a mono track, you can select the sound in the **Project** window and choose **Clip>Audio Options>Breakout to Mono Clips** from the menu (see Figure 10.6). Premiere will make two new copies on your original stereo audio clip, each one a mono version of half the stereo sound. You can then drag one of the copies to a mono track in the **Timeline**. Or you can go the opposite way and select a mono clip and choose **Clip>Audio Options>Treat as Stereo**. This will double the mono sound within the file, making it act like a stereo clip. You can then drag it to a stereo track.

The final mix of all of your sounds, the **Master Track**, can also be mono, stereo, or 5.1. Because you won't be placing any clips directly on the master tracks—rather, the clips from all the other audio tracks will filter down to the master—it's fine to set the **Master** to **mono**, even if all of your sound files are stereo or vice versa. The **Master** controls the final output, so if you want to output the sound as 5.1, you need to make sure you have a 5.1

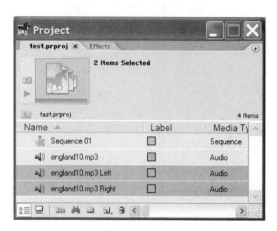

10.5 You can determine if a sound is mono, stereo, or 5.1 by selecting it in the Project window.

10.6 Stereo sound broken into two mono sounds.

master. The default master type is stereo. When you create a new project, you can specify a default master track type (in the **Custom Settings** tab of the **New Project** window, select **Default Sequence** from the list on the left side of the window). Once you're working in a sequence, you won't be able to change the master. But you can change the master type for any new sequences, by choosing **Project>Project Settings>Default Sequence** from the menu. To choose an initial default when you create a new project, switch to the **Custom Settings** tab at the top of the **New Project** dialog. In the **Audio** section, choose the **Master** type from the dropdown menu.

Importing audio from a CD

Importing and capturing is covered in Chapter 3. Note that you can import virtually every popular sound file type, including AIFF, WMA, MP3, and WAV. One thing you can't do is to import sound directly from an audio CD. If you want to bring in CD audio, you'll have to first record the CD into your computer as standard sound files, i.e., MP3s, or WAVs. This process is called ripping, and there are a number of third-party programs that will allow you to do it. One example is Apple's iTunes, which works on PCs a well as Macs. It's free, and you can download it from http://www.iTunes.com. In addition to ripping CDs, iTunes also allows you to buy music from a huge online store, but you won't be able to use any of that music in Premiere. It's in a protected format called AAC, which Premiere can't currently import.

To rip a CD in iTunes:

1. Start iTunes and choose **Edit>Preferences** from iTunes's menu.

2. In the **Preferences** dialog, click the Importing tab. From the **Import Using** dropdown, choose **WAV Encoder.**

3. From the **Setting** dropdown, choose **Custom.**

4. In the **WAV Encoder** dialog, choose:

   • **48.000 kHz** for the **Sample Rate** (see Figure 10.7)

   • **16-bit** for the **Sample Size**

   • **Stereo** for the **Channels**

5. To choose a location for the ripped files, first click the **Advanced** tab in the **Preferences** dialog, and then the **Change** button under **iTunes Music Folder Location.**

6. Insert a CD into your computer's CD drive.

   After a short wait, the tracks on the CD will be listed in iTunes's window. Next to each track, there's a checked checkbox.

7. Uncheck any track that you *don't* want to record.

8. Click the **Import** button.

   After ripping tracks from a video, you can import them into Premiere using the normal **File>Import** option.

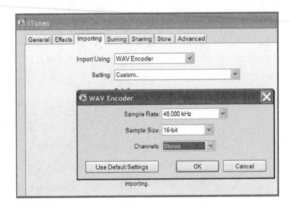

10.7   Setting up iTunes to rip music from a CD.

 **Uncheck All:** To uncheck all tracks in iTunes, **Control**+click a checkbox by any track.

Recording directly to a track

1. To record directly into Premiere, you must first plug a microphone or some other sort of sound-capturing device into your computer's sound card (generally located at the back of your PC).

2. Then, choose **Edit>Preferences>Audio Hardware** from the menu, and make sure your sound card is selected.

3. Bring up the **Audio Mixer** (which we'll explore thoroughly later) by choosing **Windows>Audio Mixer** from the menu (see Figure 10.8).

    In the **Audio Mixer** window, you'll see a column for each track in your **Timeline**. In each column, there's a volume slider for that track, and above the volume sliders are three small icons: a speaker, a bugle, and a microphone.

4. Choose an empty track to record your sound into by clicking the microphone icon in that track's column.

5. Press the red **Record** button at the bottom of the **Audio Mixer** window.

6. To start recording, press the **Play** button in the **Program Monitor** and speak into the microphone.

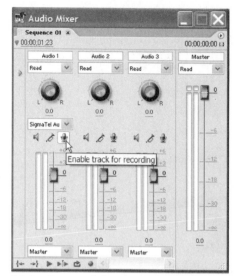

10.8   To record directly to a track, click the Microphone button on one of the tracks in the Audio Mixer window.

7. As you speak, watch the audio levels in the **Audio Mixer** window (the animated vertical lines next to the volume sliders).

    If you see the lines turning orange at their tops, you're speaking too loudly.

8. To finish recording, press the **Record** button a second time.

 Feedback: You may want to turn off your computer's speakers while you record sound, so that you don't create feedback.

When you've finished recording, you'll see a new sound clip in the designated track and also in the **Project** window. Premiere gives these clips default names, but you may want to rename them. To rename a clip, right-click it in the Project window and choose the rename option from the popup menu.

MESSING WITH AUDIO

Unlinking audio and video

When you import or capture video that has associated audio (for instance, if the video and audio were recorded at the same time by your camera), Premiere treats them as a

10.9   If the video and audio tracks
are linked, trimming one trims
both.

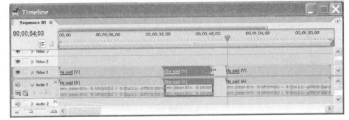

single unit. When you edit them into your sequence, they are linked together, even though
the video lives on a video track and the audio lives on an audio track. If you trim the
video, the audio will become trimmed too, by the same number of frames. If you trim the
audio, the video will become trimmed too, also by the same number of frames (see
Figure 10.9).

But in professionally edited sequences, video and audio do not always stay together.
For instance, you may find that while you're listening to one character speak, it's more
interesting to see the reaction of the listener than to see the speaker speaking. In this case,
you would want to trim in the tail end of the video, making it shorter, so that you can put
the reaction shot after it, while the sound continues to play. This sort of edit is known as
a *split edit,* because the video and audio are split apart, each ending or starting at a different time (see Figure 10.10). Split edits are also commonly used in documentaries, in which
the scene starts with an interview, but as it progresses you only hear the interview while
you see images of what the speaker is talking about. Split edits are also often used as
bridges between scenes. Sometimes you hear the sound from the next scene while the visu-
als are still of the previous scene.

To unlink audio and video, select either clip in the **Timeline** and choose **Clip>Unlink
Audio and Video** from the menu. You can also select this option by right-clicking a clip in
the **Timeline.** You can then trim just the video, or just the audio, and the formerly associated clip will not be trimmed (see Figure 10.11).

10.10 Split edit.

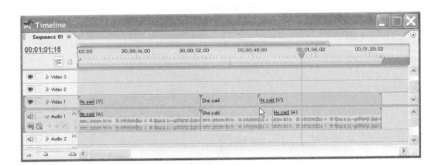

10.11 If you'd like to trim the video clip without trimming the associated audio clip (or vice versa), right-click either the audio or video clip and select the Unlink Audio and Video option.

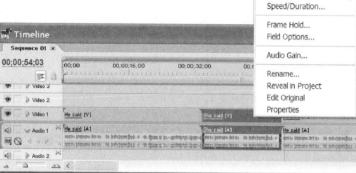

 Deselect after Unlinking: Immediately after you unlink clips, both the audio and the video clip will be selected. So if you try to trim, edit, or move the video clip, the audio clip will follow suit. This isn't because they are still linked. It's just because they are both selected. Deselect both of them by clicking in a gray (empty) area of the **Timeline**. Then select just the one you want to adjust and trim, move, or delete it. The other clip will not be affected.

If you want to relink video and audio, select both clips by **Shift**+clicking them and choose **Clip>Link Audio and Video** from the menu.

Split edits are terrific, but the one risk you take when creating them is moving the video and audio out of sync with each other. To avoid making your sequence look like a badly dubbed Godzilla movie—Is there any other kind?—make sure that you only perform rolling edits on unlinked clips. Remember that ripple edits pull or push all of the subsequent clips away from their original locations. Doing this will move them away from their associated audio clips, or if you're ripple editing audio, it will move the subsequent audio clips away from their associated video clips. Rolling edits, on the other hand, never move clips to different locations. They just reveal or hide handle, so you'll never risk losing sync when you make a rolling edit.

If you do move clips out of sync, Premiere indicates how far off they are by displaying timecode in their upper-right corners. To force Premiere to resync the clips, right-click the timecode and choose **Move Into Sync** from the popup menu (see Figure 10.12).

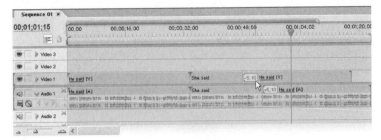

10.12 The timecode indicates these clips are 5 seconds and 10 frames out of sync.

Note

Out of Sync: Premiere will only mark linked clips as being out of sync. Unlinked clips might be out of sync from a human perspective—the speech may not go with the lip movements—but because the clips are unlinked, Premiere doesn't think of them as being related to one another. To fix a sync problem with unlinked clips, you must first link them by selecting them both and choosing **Clip>Link Audio and Video** from the menu. Once they're linked, Premiere will display the out-of-sync timecode.

Because the default smallest unit of measurement on the time ruler is frames, it's possible that two audio clips that appear to be next to each other on the **Timeline** might actually have a gap between them. They would be in adjacent video frames. But there might be an audio-sample gap between them.

The Red Line

You can think of audio samples as sound "frames," but there are many more of them per second than there are video frames. NTSC video runs at approximately 30 frames per second; PAL runs at 24. DV-quality sound runs at 48kHz, which means that there are 48,000 sound "frames" (audio samples) per second.

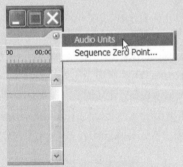

10.13 Changing the time ruler to measure audio units instead of video frames.

As you drag clips in the **Timeline**, a red line at the **Current Time Indicator** means that clips aren't butting against each other. If you see this line while you're dragging video clips, it's easy to close up the gap. Just slam the clip you're dragging up against its neighboring clip until the red line goes away.

To close up audio gaps, switch the time ruler from measuring frames to measuring audio samples. You can do this by selecting the Audio Units option from the **Timeline's** wing menu.

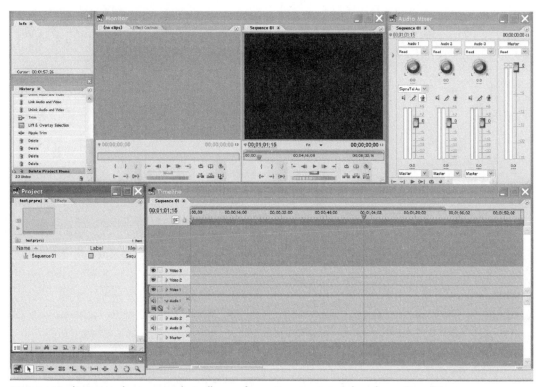

10.14 Windows>Workspace>Audio will reconfigure Premiere's interface for audio editing.

Controlling volume and panning

Many sequences make use of three audio tracks, one for dialog, one for music and one for sound effects. But if you place clips in multiple tracks, they will play simultaneously at their original volumes and drown each other out. Generally, you will want to adjust each track's volume so that the final mix is pleasing and easy to understand.

The easiest way to adjust multiple track's audio levels (volume) is in the **Audio Mixer** window. To bring this up, choose **Windows>Audio Mixer** from the menu. Or you can choose **Windows>Workspace>Audio** to bring up the **Audio Mixer** and switch Premiere's entire interface to one that's convenient for audio editing. When you're finished editing audio, you can return to the normal interface by choosing **Windows>Workspace>Editing** (see Figure 10.14).

As stated earlier, the **Audio Mixer** window contains a **Volume** slider for each track. You can use these sliders to make their associated track's audio louder or softer. To do so, make sure the **Automation State** option, near the top of the window, is set to **Read** for all tracks. Then play the audio using the Play button at the bottom of the **Audio Mixer** window. If one of the tracks sounds too loud or too soft, adjust its volume slider until you're

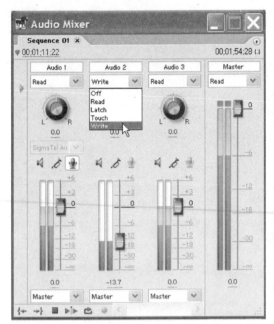

10.15 Set a track's Automation State to Write if you'd like to record new audio levels to that track.

10.16 Click the Bugle button to solo a track.

happy with its new level. This new level won't be set in stone until you change the **Automation** state option from **Read** to **Write**. But when you've found the perfect volume level, leave the sliders at that level, move the **Current Time Indicator** back to the beginning of the **Timeline**, and set the **Automation State** option to **Write**. Then press the **Play** button again. Premiere will record the new volume levels to the track, as long as the **Automation State** is set to **Write** and the sequence is playing (see Figure 10.15). Only set the **Automation State** options to **Write** for the track you want to change (leave the other tracks set to read).

When you get done changing volume levels on one track, you can set them for each subsequent track, one by one. Just remember to set the **Automation State** for the track you're adjusting to **Write**—and all the other tracks to **Read**. When you get done adjusting all the tracks, make sure all of their **Adjustment States** are set to **Read**, so that you don't accidentally record any volume changes.

When writing volume changes, you don't have to just leave the sliders set at a particular volume level. While the sequence is playing, you can drag the sliders up and down, recording changes in volume on the fly.

Sometimes it's difficult to make adjustments when you're listening to all of the tracks at once. You can solo one track (which will silence all of the other tracks) by pressing that **Track's Solo** button, which looks like a bugle (see Figure 10.16). When you want to hear

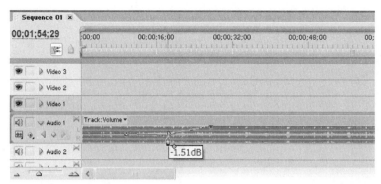

10.17 Adjusting keyframes in the Timeline with the Pen tool.

all of the other tracks again, click the bugle a second time. You can mute tracks individually by clicking their speaker icons. To allow a muted track to play again, click its speaker a second time.

You can also adjust track volume in the **Timeline**. To do so, click the **Show Keyframes** button on the track you want to adjust, and choose **Show Track Volume** from the popup menu. Premiere will draw an orange line across the track, indicating its volume. The higher the line, the louder the volume. To raise or lower the line, drag it up or down with the Pen tool (see Figure 10.17).

In addition to adjusting track volume, you can also adjust track panning. Panning adjusts what percentage of the sound plays in the left and right speakers. To adjust panning, follow the procedures for adjusting volume in the **Audio Mixer** that start on page 245, but instead of dragging the volume level slider, adjust the **Panning** control (see Figure 10.18).

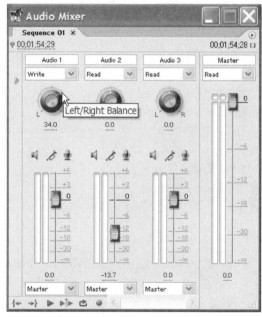

10.18 Rotate the Panning control to move the sound more into the left speaker or the right speaker.

You can adjust panning in the **Timeline** by choosing **Show Track Keyframes** from the track's **Show Keyframes** menu. Then, click the upper-left corner of the first clip on the track to reveal a menu, from which you should choose **Panner>Pan**. The orange line now represents panning. Using the **Pen** tool, drag the line up to pan to the left speaker and down to pan to the right.

Too Many Keyframes

How does Premiere remember all the volume changes you make as you play the sequence? By creating keyframes. In other words, recording volume and other sorts of changes in the audio mixer is simply an automated method of adding keyframes, without having to mess around with stopwatches and the **Effect Controls** panel. You can even view the automatically added key-frames in the **Timeline** window, as described elsewhere.

Unfortunately, the audio mixer tends to add a huge number of keyframes—more than are neces-sary to achieve your volume changes. Extra keyframes make it harder to make changes at a later time, should you want to make manual adjustments to them in the **Timeline**.

Luckily, you can tell Premiere to eliminate unnecessary keyframes by selecting **Edit>Prefer-ences>Audio** and checking either the **Linear Keyframe Thinning** option, which is on by default, or the **Minal Time Interval Thinning** option. Using the latter option, you can instruct Premiere to only place keyframes at specific intervals on the **Timeline**. You can set this interval, in the **Prefer-ences** dialog, to between one and 30 milliseconds.

The default option, **Linear Keyframe Thinning**, removes any superfluous keyframes between two keyframes that define a straight line. This is a little hard to imagine with volume changes, but if you think of an image moving from the left side of the screen to the right side of the screen, that should only require two keyframes. Any keyframes between those two would be superfluous.

 Set Options First: You must set these options *before* recording any volume changes in the Audio Mixer window. Neither option will affect preexisting keyframes.

Clip versus track

So far, all of our adjustments have been to entire tracks. As an alternative, you can adjust volume clip by clip. This method makes sense if you have many different audio clips in the same track, each recorded at a different time, in a different place, using different audio equipment. After adjusting each clip separately, you can still use the methods described previously to set overall levels for the track.

To adjust volume for an individual clip, select the clip and choose **Window>Effect Controls** from the menu. In the **Effect Controls** window, twirl open the **Volume** effect and then twirl open the **Level** property to reveal the slider control (see Figure 10.20). You can drag this slider to the left to lower the volume on the track or to the right to raise it. Notice that the **Level** property's stopwatch is turned on by default. If you leave it on, any level adjustments you make in the **Effect Controls** window will be set as a keyframe for

Off, Read, Latch, Touch, and Write

When adjusting volume and panning, the **Read Automation** state plays back any previously recorded changes but does not record new ones. Any volume or panning changes you hear when you adjust the settings in the audio mixer will just be temporary changes, and you won't hear them next time you play back the sequence. If you want to play back audio without hearing previous adjustments (hearing, instead, the track's original volume levels), set the **Automation** state to **Off**. To record changes, you must use one of the other Automation states: **Latch**, **Touch**, or **Write**.

Latch: This setting will only start recording changes when you click and drag the volume (or panning) control. So if you play your sequence but don't start adjusting the volume until three seconds into it, the changes won't be recorded until three seconds into your sequence. Before that point, Premiere will use earlier changes or the default track volume if you haven't made any earlier changes.

Touch: Like **Latch**, this setting won't start recording changes until you adjust an audio mixer control. When you release the control, the touch setting will return it to its former value for the rest of the sequence's duration.

Write: This setting will start recording immediately (as soon as you play the sequence), regardless of whether or not you're touching any audio mixer controls.

10.19 Automation States.

the current point in time only. You can use this technique to fade the audio in by moving the **Current Time Indicator** (in the **Effect Controls** window, **Timeline,** or **Program Monitor**) to the beginning of the clip and setting a low-volume keyframe. Then you can move the **Current Time Indicator** a little ways into the clip and raise the volume, creating a second keyframe. Premiere will tween between the two keyframes, fading the volume up.

10.20 Adjusting clip volume in the Effect Controls window.

If you just want to raise or lower the volume for the entire clip globally, turn off the stopwatch before making any level adjustments.

You can also adjust clip levels in the **Timeline** by choosing **Show Clip Volume** from the track's **Show Keyframe** menu.

> **Show Clip Volume:** Don't confuse this option with the **Show Track Volume** option, chosen from the same menu. Using the **Pen** tool, you can raise or lower the volume by dragging the yellow line up or down. Or you can add keyframes anywhere along the orange line by **Control+click-ing** with the **Pen** tool.

Finally, you can set clip volume by selecting the clip in the **Timeline** and choose **Clip>Audio Options>Clip Gain** from the menu. In the **Clip Gain** dialog, scrub the gain value up or down to raise or lower the clip's volume.

Audio effects

Clip effects

You can add, adjust, and animate audio effects on individual clips via the same methods used to add, adjust, and animate effects for video clips. These techniques are explored in Chapter 6 beginning on page 133. Note that **Audio Effects** (**Effects window>Audio Effects**) are organized into three subfolders, mono, stereo, and 5.1. Effects from each folder can only be used on clips of their associated type. In other words, you can't use a mono effect on a stereo clip.

Perhaps the most useful audio clip effect is **Constant Power** (**Effects window>Audio Transitions>Crossfade>Constant Power**), which will fade a clip in or out or create a crossfade between two clips.

VST Effects

The audio effects that ship with Premiere conform to the Steinberg VST plug-in standard. VST stands for Virtual Studio Technology. VST effects are standard in the recording industry, and they work in many audio editing applications. If you have other audio tools on your system with their own VST effects, Premiere will detect these effects and allow you to access them from within Premiere too.

Since this is a transition effect, you need to drop in on the crack between two clips in the **Timeline**. If you drop it right on the crack, it will crossfade between the two clips. If you drop it just to the left of the crack, it will fade out the first clip. If you drop it just to right of the crack, it will fade in the second clip. As you drag your mouse across the crack, from left to right, the mouse cursor icon indicates where the effect will land when you drop it. To fade up the first clip in the entire sequence, drop the **Constant Power** effect on the beginning of that clip. Or you can drop the effect on the end of the final clip in the

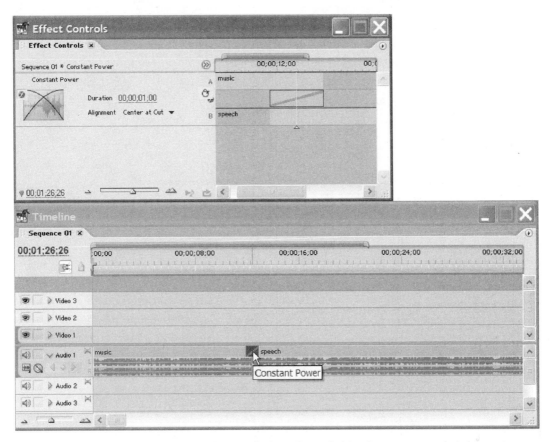

10.21   The Constant Power transition effect can fade a clip in, fade a clip out, or crossfade between two clips.

sequence to fade it out. If you select the effect in the **Timeline** and bring up the **Effect Controls** window, you can adjust the fade's duration.

One subtle but useful application of **Constant Power** is to even out the audio in dialog scenes. Often in such scenes, the sequence cuts between close-ups of two actors as they talk to each other. But because each actor's dialog may have been recorded at a different time, there may be a noticeable pop when the sound switches between them. To fix this problem, apply the **Constant Power** effect to problem cuts using a very short duration, maybe just four frames long. The audience won't hear it as a crossfade. Instead, it will soften the crude transition between the two clips (see Figure 10.21).

Track effects

When working with audio, you have the option to apply effects to an entire track (as opposed to single clips on a track). You do this in the **Audio Mixer** window, inside which you'll find a column for each audio track. In each track's column, there's a large inset area where you can apply up to five effects per track. If you don't see the insets, click the twirly triangle near the upper-left corner of the window to reveal them (see Figure 10.22).

To add a track effect, select one by clicking the dropdown arrow in the upper-right corner of an inset area (see Figure 10.23).

Once you've added an effect, Premiere will display its adjustable properties at the bottom of the inset. If there's more than one adjustable property, you can switch between them by choosing them from the dropdown menu at the

10.22 Click the twirly to reveal an area where you can apply track effects.

bottom of the currently displayed property. To add a second effect, click the dropdown arrow in the row below the first effect. To display properties for an individual effect, after you've applied multiple effects, click the effect's name to select it (see Figure 10.24).

To remove an effect, click the dropdown menu by its name and choose None. To disable an effect, select it and then click the *f* icon in the upper-right corner of its properties area. To re-enable the effect, click the *f* icon a second time.

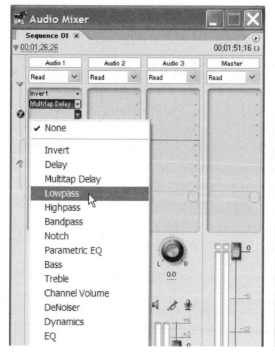

10.23 Select effects from the dropdown menus in the inset area. *(left)*

10.24 To display effect properties, click the effect name to select it. *(below)*

Adjusting on the Fly: If you set a track's **Adjustment State** to **Write**, **Latch**, or **Touch** and then press the **Play** button at the bottom of the **Audio Mixer** window, you can adjust audio effect controls in the **Audio Mixer** window while the audio is playing. As with volume and panning, Premiere will save any effect changes to the specific time you made the adjustment during playback. Remember to set the **Adjustment State** to **Read** when you're done recording effect-property changes, so that you don't accidentally record over your changes next time you play your sequence.

Mixing audio

No matter how many audio tracks you've added to your sequence, they ultimately all mix together in the **Master Track**. But you can send one, some or all of them to intermediary weigh stations before they get there. These rest stops are called *submix tracks*.

When making cakes, you sometimes throw all the ingredients into a big bowl and mix them all together. More often, though, you mix the dry ingredients together in one bowl (submix) and the wet ingredients together in another bowl (submix). Only then do you combine them all together in a single bowl (master).

Submixes serve a similar purpose. They allow you to mix tracks together before they reach the Master Track. You might want to do this, for instance, if your have tracks of wind, crickets, lapping surf, and a conversation. The first three tracks (wind, crickets, and surf) are meant to be the background ambience—the night scene that quietly plays under the conversation. You may find that the easiest way to create a pleasing mix is to send the conversation directly to the **Master** but to stop the crickets, wind, and surf at a submix track first, adjust their levels, and apply any effects there, and then send them as a unit to the **Master Track**.

To create a submix track, choose **Sequence>Add Tracks** from the menu. At the bottom of the **Add Tracks** dialog, enter the number of submix tracks you want to add and their types: mono, stereo, or 5.1 (see Figure 10.25).

10.25 Adding a submix track.

Multiple Types: You *can* send a track of one type to a submix track of another type. For instance, you can send mono tracks into stereo submixes and vice versa.

Once you've added a submix track, you can route any normal track to it (rather than to the **Master Track**) in the **Audio Mixer**. In the **Audio Mixer** window, each track lists its destination at the very bottom of its column. By default, each track is routed to the **Master Track**. To reroute a track to a submix track, choose the submix track from the drop-down menu at the bottom of its column (see Figure 10.26). You can route as many tracks as you want to a single submix track.

Then you can manipulate a submix track in the **Audio Mixer** as if it was a normal track. You can add effects to it (which will affect all the tracks routed to it), adjust its level or its pan, and you can even route a submix track to another submix track if you want (though to stop infinite loops, you can only route a submix track to another submix track to its right in the **Audio Mixer** window).

If you've adjusted audio levels or set effects in the original track, before it was routed to a submix, but its original levels and effects and the ones it gains in the submix track will be added together to create the final mix.

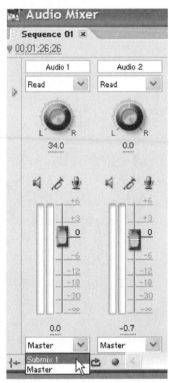

10.26 Routing a normal track to a submix track.

WRAPPING UP

As you can see, though Premiere isn't a dedicated audio editor, its control over sound is pretty sophisticated. You can adjust volume, panning, and audio effects on a clip-by-clip or track-by-track basis. Using submix tracks, you can create audio composites as easily as you can create video composites. Combining the two, you can generate multileveled, multilayered stories that will thrill your viewers. But once you've layered video on top of audio, you may find that you need one more layer: titles. Titles are the subject of the next chapter.

Chapter 11

Titles

Since it has nothing to do with video editing, you might expect Premiere's titler to be a simplistic tool. If so, you'll be pleasantly surprised by its depth and power. It will allow you to style text in almost any imaginable way, import graphic logos, create new graphic shapes, and even make rolling or crawling credits. Just about the only thing it can't do, alas, is create animated tiles, other than rolls and crawls. If you want to make your text move around the screen, you'll have to first create it in the **Title** window and then apply the Motion Effect to your title. If you want to animate your text letter by letter, you'll have to use a dedicated animation package like Adobe After Effects. Strictly speaking, you *could* animate text letter by letter in Premiere. To do this, you'd have to save each letter as a separate title and place each title in a different track, applying the **Motion** effects to each. But this may be more trouble that it's worth, when there are animation programs waiting on the sidelines, just dying to get their hands on your text.

Premiere saves your titles as external files, separate from your project. This allows you to import the same title into many projects. You can also save title templates and generate many titles from the same template.

If you want to create an extreme text effect—for instance, one in which each letter is warped and morphed into an odd shape—you might need to design your titles in an external application like Adobe Photoshop or Adobe Illustrator and then import them into Premiere. But the benefit of creating titles in Premiere is that you can also edit them in

11.1   Press F9 to bring up the Title Designer window, click, and start Typing. Note that the Type tool (the T icon) is turned on by default.

11.2   To move text, switch to the Selection tool.

Premiere when you need to make changes. So don't write off Premiere's titler until you see all that it can do.

NEW TITLE

When you choose **File>New>Title** or press the keyboard shortcut **F9**, the **Title Designer** window appears (see Figure 11.1). At the left side of the window, you'll notice a tool palette. On this palette, the default **Type** tool is already selected. So just click anywhere in the drawing area (the big rectangular area in the center of the **Title Designer** window) and type some text. You should just click and start typing. Don't try to drag a rectangular text box before you type.

When you finish typing, switch from the **Type** tool to the **Selection** tool, which looks like a black arrow (see Figure 11.2). Use it to drag your text to a new location in the drawing area. (Drag from within the boundary around the text, not from one of the little squares around the boundary, or you'll risk resizing or rotating your text.) If you need to modify the text itself (e.g., to correct a spelling error), select the **Type** tool again (the **T**) and click somewhere in your text to see a type cursor. If you need to move your text again, reselect the **Selection** tool and use it to drag your text elsewhere.

Notice the new menu item at top of the screen: **Title** (see Figure 11.3). Within this item, which only appears while you're working in the **Title Designer**, you'll find options to change all sorts text properties, such as font, size, and text alignment. These options will only work if your text is selected.

One you've finished typing and moving your text, save your title by choosing **File>Save** from the menu. Premiere assumes that you're trying to save the title—not the

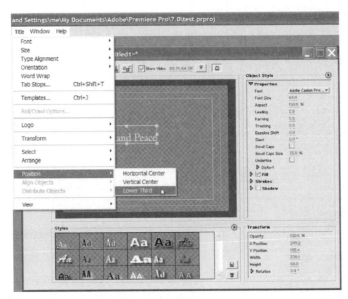

11.3   A new menu option called
Title appears when the Title
Designer window is activated.

entire Premiere project—because you're currently working in the **Title Designer** and its window is activated. If you deactivate the **Title** window—say, by clicking one of the monitors or the **Timeline**—**File>Save** will save the project instead of the title. So make sure the **Title Designer** window is active before saving. If necessary, click anywhere in the window to activate it. You can tell that it's the active window by noting the color of its title bar (the horizontal strip at the top of the window that is labeled "**Adobe Title Designer**" in its upper-left corner). If the title bar is grayed out, the window is deactivated.

After you choose **File>Save**, Premiere displays the **Save** dialog window. Choose a location for the title on your hard drive. You can later import this title into any other Premiere project by choosing **File>Import** and bringing it in, just as you would with any other graphic file. Premiere automatically imports in into the current project file, so you'll see it in the **Project** window as soon as you finish saving.

Now you can close out of the title design window and add the title to your sequence. You do this the same way you add any other item to your sequence, by dragging it to the **Timeline**. Because titles are static, with the exception of rolls and crawls, you may want to bypass the **Source** monitor and drag them directly from the Project window to the **Timeline**. You may want to drag your titles to the **Video 2** track, assuming the rest of your video footage is in **Video 1**. This way, Premiere will superimpose them over your video footage in the lower track (see Figure 11.4).

To make the title last for a longer or shorter length of time, trim its head or tail using any trimming tool or by choosing **Clip>Duration** from the menu.

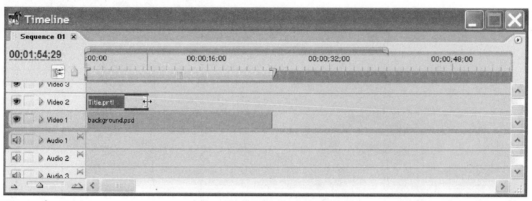

11.4   If you want to superimpose a title over Video 1, drag it to Video 2. Trim it out to make it last for a longer time.

If you want to edit the title—even after you've added it to the **Timeline**—just double-click it, either in the **Timeline** or in the Project window. It will reopen in the **Title Designer** for editing. When you're done making changes, choose **File>Save** and then close the **Title Designer**. Premiere will automatically update any instances of that title in the sequence.

DISPLAY OPTIONS

As you work in the **Title Designer,** it can help to see the title superimposed over the video that will eventually be underneath it, once you edit it into the sequence. If you check the **Show Video** option (top center of the **Title Designer** window), you can see a frame from your **Timeline** in the drawing area's background as you work on your title. You can choose a specific frame by clicking the timecode to the right of the **Show Video** option and typing in the timecode of the frame you want to display. Or you can scrub the timecode to interactively move to a specific frame. Or you can move the **Current Time Indicator** in the **Timeline** and then click the **Sync to Timeline Timecode** button in the **Title Designer** window (to the right of the timecode). When you click this button, Premiere will display the current **Timeline** frame in the **Title Designer.**

Displaying a frame in the drawing area can help you correctly position your text (using the **Selection** tool to move it) so that it doesn't cover any important aspects of your video. It can also help you choose text colors that are easy to read over a specific background and don't clash with the colors of in your sequence.

Notice that the background image is not part of the title and is not saved with the title. If you uncheck the **Show Video** option, the image will disappear from the **Title Designer** window (see Figure 11.5). There are ways to import an image into your title (see "Importing Graphics" on page 287), but this isn't one of them. And when you finally edit

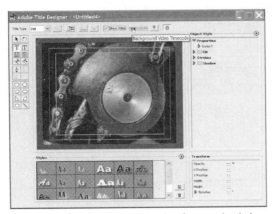

11.5   To see a background video frame, check the Show Video option and then scrub the timecode to select a frame.

11.6   A title in Video 2 is composited over an image in Video 1.

your title into the sequence, you can place the title anywhere—even over footage that has no resemblance to the frame you used while you were creating the title (see Figure 11.6).

A common mistake involves editing a title into the sequence and then creating a new title. The **Show Video** option is checked by default. Also by default, the frame that displays is the frame that you're currently parked on in the **Timeline**. If before invoking the **Title Designer,** you left the **Current Time Indicator** parked on a frame that shows part of your original title, you'll see that original title in the background of the **Title Designer.** This might lead you to believe that you're somehow editing that original title. You're not. It's just a background image, and you may want to choose a less confusing frame to display (see Figure 11.7).

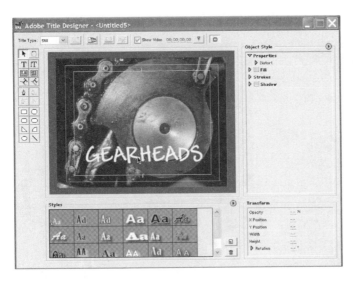

11.7   If you press F9 to create a new title, you'll see the composite in the Title Designer. You can't select the text, because it's not really in the Title Designer. The text is part of the composite in the Timeline. You're seeing it in the Title Designer because the Show Video option is selected.

11.8   To view your title in an external monitor, click the Send frame to External Monitor button.

In addition to displaying a frame of your video in the **Title Designer**, you can also display the title itself in an external TV monitor, assuming one is hooked up to your computer. To do so, click the **Send Frame to External Monitor** button in the **Title Designer** window (see Figure 11.8). This is useful because colors (and other visual aspects) on a TV don't always match colors on your computer monitor. You can look at the title on the external monitor to see what it will really look like when it's broadcast or shown on a video monitor. For more about setting up an external monitor, see Chapters 1 and 2.

The two rectangles that you see in the drawing area are additional guides to help you make sure that your title looks right on TV. TVs often crop off the parts of the image closest to the edge of the screen. If you align a title right at an edge, some of it will likely be cut off. Tom Cruise probably won't be too happy if his name appears as "om Cruise." To make sure this doesn't happen, create or move all of your text within the inner rectangle, which is called the **Title Safe Area**. The outer rectangle is called the **Action Safe Area**. The rectangles are just for display within the **Title Designer** and never become a part of your title. Titles that span all the way into the **Action Safe Area** will probably display on most TVs, but the letters near the edge may be distorted. To be really safe, stay within the **Title Safe Area** (see Figure 11.9).

On the other hand, if you're producing video for the web or CD, you don't need to worry about the edges—only TVs cut them off—so you can safely ignore the rectangles. If

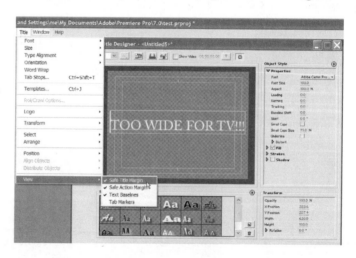

11.9   Keep your text within the Title Safe Margin.

they bother you, you can even turn them off by choosing either or both of the following menu options: **Title>View>Safe Title Margin** and **Title>View Safe Action Margin**. Choosing these same options again will turn the rectangles back on.

TYPE TOOLS

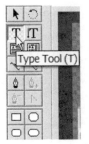

The **Title Designer** boasts six type tools (see Figure 11.10):

- One for normal horizontal text
- One for normal vertical text
- One for large blocks of horizontal text (paragraphs)
- One for vertical paragraphs
- One for horizontal text on a path
- One for vertical text on a path

11.10 Type tool.

The horizontal and vertical versions of the tools work the same way, expect one flows text from left to right while the other flows text from up to down.

Type tool and Vertical Type tool

This is the click-and-type tool that's selected by default when you first enter the **Type Designer** window. Once you've finished using it, you can format your text in a couple of ways. If you select your text with the **Selection** tool, any formatting adjustments you make (e.g., changing font size) will affect all of the characters at once (see Figure 11.11). For instance, if you change the font size from 10 to 25, all of the characters will change from 10 to 25.

If you want individual control over each letter, use the **Type** tool to make a selection before formatting: switch to the **Type** tool if it's not already selected, then highlight one, some, or all of the characters just as you would in a word processor, by dragging the cursor across the characters you want to change. The highlighted characters are the only ones that will by affected by subsequent formatting changes. So if you type the word "catapult" and select just the first three characters, changing the font to a bigger size will result in catapult (see Figure 11.12).

Highlighting tips and tricks

There are a few useful highlighting tricks worth memorizing. They will work in Premiere, Photoshop, Illustrator, Microsoft Word, and almost any other program that lets you highlight text. For instance, to highlight without dragging, click to place a cursor before the first character you want to change. Then **Shift+click** after the last character you want to

11.11 If text is selected with the Selection tool, any formatting changes will affect all of the text.

11.12 If characters are highlighted with the Type tool, any formatting will affect only the highlighted text.

change. Both characters and all characters in between will become highlighted. This is sometimes useful when you want to select a really large amount of text, which can be hard to select by dragging and dragging and dragging the mouse. Just click, move, and **Shift**+click.

When highlighting, it's all too easy to highlight a little too much or a little too little. For instance, if you're trying to highlight the word "fang," you can easily let up on the mouse button a little too early and only highlight "fan." To fix this problem, use **Shift**+an arrow key. The **Left** and **Right Arrows** will highlight one fewer character or one more character, respectively, each time you press them. So to turn "fan" into "fang," press **Shift+Right Arrow** once. Each time you press **Shift+Down Arrow**, you'll include one additional line of text (assuming your text spans more than one line). Each time you press **Shift+Up Arrow**, you'll remove one line from the already highlighted text.

If you double-click a word, the entire word will instantly become highlighted. If you type text on the keyboard, the text you type will instantly replace any selected text. So if you want to change the word "Clinton" to the word "Bush," don't use the backspace key first to delete "Clinton." That's a waste of time. Just double-click "Clinton," which will select it, and then type "Bush." You'll see history repeat itself!

Note that **Type** tool type doesn't automatically wrap around to the next line. So if you keep typing and typing, your text will eventually bleed off the edge of the drawing area. To move to the next line, you have to manually press the **Enter** key (see Figure 11.13). If you'd rather work with wrapping text, choose **Title>Word Wrap** from the menu. Then your text will wrap around to the next line when it hits the **Title Safe Area** boundary (see Figure 11.14).

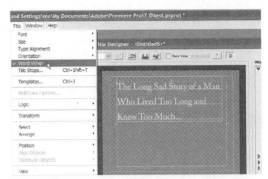

11.13 By default, text typed with the Type tool won't wrap around to the next line when you reach the edge of the screen. To move to the next line, you'll have to press Enter.

11.14 However, if you select Title>Word Wrap from the menu, text will wrap around to the next line when it hits the Title Safe Margin.

You can highlight with any of the following text tools, exactly the same way as you do it with the **Type** tool.

Area Type and Vertical Area Type tool

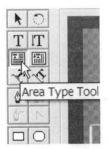

11.15 Area Type tool.

If you need to type a large amount of text, and you want to make sure that the text fits within a specific area, you might want to use this tool(see Figure 11.15). It works similarly to the **Type** tool, but you have to define an area before you start typing (see Figure 11.16). You do this by selecting the tool and then dragging diagonally, as if you were moving from the upper-left corner of an invisible rectangle to the lower-right corner. You can also drag from the lower-right to the upper-left corner.

Once you're done creating the boundary, you can type within it, still using the **Area Type** tool. Text within boundaries always wraps around to the next line when it hits a boundary wall, even if you have the **Word Wrap** option turned off in the **Type** menu.

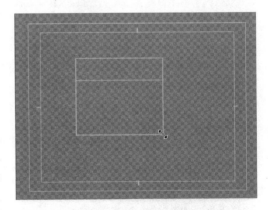

1.16 Drag diagonally with the Area Type tool to define a text boundary.

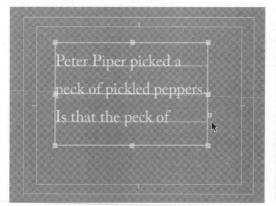

11.17 The tiny plus sign indicates hidden text.

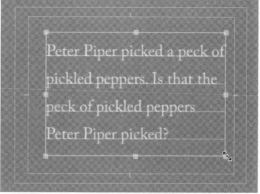

11.18 You can reveal hidden text by using the Selection tool to drag the boundary wider from one of its scale handles.

You can type more text than will fit in the boundary, but the boundary won't resize to fit it. Instead, when you run out of room, you won't be able to see any of the extra type. Premiere displays a tiny-plus-sign-in-a-square icon to indicate that there's unseen text (see Figure 11.17).

If you switch to the **Selection** tool, you can, as usual, drag the text to a new position, or, if you point to one of the little squares around the edge of the text, you can resize the boundary. If you make the boundary bigger, you'll see text that previously didn't display because it was too big to fit within the old boundary. If you make the boundary smaller than the text within it, you'll hide some of the text (see Figure 11.18).

Path Type tool and Vertical Path Type tool

11.19 Path Type tool.

The most confusing thing about the **Path Type** tool is that you create both the text *and* the path with this tool (see Figure 11.19). This is different from some other programs that have text-on-path options, in which you make a path with some other tool and then use a text tool to position text on that path. In a sense, the **Path Type** tool is similar to the **Area Type** tool in that when you use it, you define where you want the text to go before you type the text (see Figure 11.20).

When you select the **Path Type** tool and hover your mouse above the drawing area, you will see a pen icon. This is Premiere's way of telling you that you can now draw a path using pen-tool techniques. If you've never used a pen tool, you might want to skip ahead to the section that describes it on page 281. After completing your path, press **Esc** on your keyboard and click the path to get a text cursor. Then type your text. When you

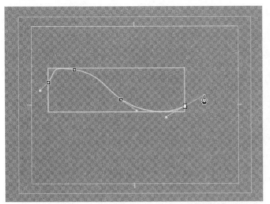

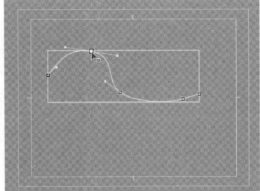

11.20 Using the Path Type tool (not the Pen tool), draw the path you'd like your text to follow. Press Esc when you're done drawing the path. *(above)*

11.21 To adjust the path, keep the Path Type tool selected, point to one of the path points, and drag the point to a new location. *(above right)*

11.22 To add text along the path, keep the Path Type tool selected and click the path in-between two of the path points. *(right)*

click to type, make sure that you click in between the path points, rather than on them. On the other hand, if you want to adjust the path, drag the path points to new locations. You do all of this—creating the path, typing the text, and moving the path points—with the **Path Type** tool selected (see Figures 11.20–11.22).

Although the **Path Type** tool is similar to the **Pen** tool, you can't use the **Pen** tool to draw a text path. Putting this another way, you can't place text on any path drawn with the **Pen** tool. Only **Path Type** tool paths can hold text. Conversely, **Path Type** tool paths are invisible in the final title. If you want to draw a visible path or shape, you must use the **Pen** tool.

Another drawback: You can't animate text moving along the path. If you're interested in doing animations of text along a path, you will have to use programs such as Adobe After Effects, Macromedia Flash, or Boris Graffiti.

After placing text on a path, if you switch to the **Selection** tool and use it to drag the little square handles around your text, the path will get bigger or smaller, but the text on it will stay the same size.

Switching between typing and selecting

As you work in the **Type Designer**, you will frequently need to switch back and forth between a type tool, to type and edit your text, and the **Selection** tool, to move or resize your text. You can save time by pressing the **Esc** key on your keyboard when you finish typing. This will automatically switch you from any type tool to the **Selection** tool, with the text you just typed selected.

You can switch from the **Selection** tool to the appropriate type tool by double-clicking any text in the drawing area.

Suppose you've just finished typing the text "Barbarella" with the **Type** tool and you want to move it up higher in the drawing area. Press **Esc** and then drag it there. Then double-click just after the final "a," and you'll get a cursor. Press **Return** and type "Queen of the Galaxy" on the next line. Then press **Esc** and move your text over a bit to the right. Double-click between the words "the" and "Galaxy" and add the word "known," so that the bottom line of text reads, "Queen of the known Galaxy."

Adjusting text with the Selection tool

In addition to moving text, you can also use the **Selection** tool to resize or rotate. You can make these adjustments to text or to graphics. In either case, to resize, drag one of the little square handles. If you drag a handle towards the center of the text, it will get smaller (see Figure 11.23). Dragging a handle away from the center will make it grow larger. Dragging a top-center handle or bottom-center handle will just resize vertically. Dragging a left-center handle or right-center handle will just resize horizontally. Dragging a corner handle will resize horizontally and vertically at the same time.

If you hold down the **Shift** key as you drag, you'll ensure that the text always stays in proportion as you drag it. It will get bigger or smaller, but it will never look distorted. If you hold down the **Alt** key as you drag, you'll resize from the center, rather than from the handle you're dragging. You can hold down both the **Shift** and **Alt** keys while you drag to constrain proportions *and* drag from the center at the same time.

If you drag a handle so far into the center than the text resizes to nothing and then keep dragging, you'll flip the text to face the opposite direction from the way it was facing before you started dragging.

Only resizing text typed with the **Type** tool actually changes the size of the text itself. **Resizing Area Text** changes the size of the boundary around the text. **Resizing Path Text** changes the size of the path that the text is on. To resize the actual text within boundaries or on paths, you have to change the font size (see "Adjusting Text Properties" on page 268).

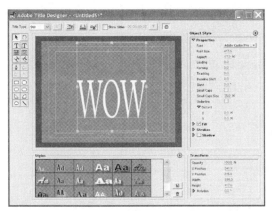 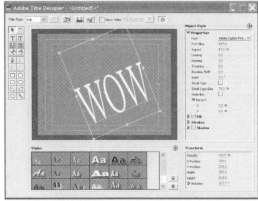

11.23 Drag a sizing handle to scale the text. *(above left)*

11.24 To rotate text, move the mouse cursor a short distance away from a handle and drag. *(above right)*

11.25 Transform area: an alternative to moving and sizing with the selection tool. *(right)*

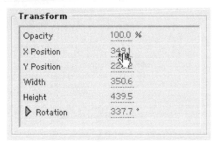

To rotate the text, move the mouse pointer just slightly away from any one of the handles (on the outside of the boundary) until you see a curved, double-headed arrow symbol (see Figure 11.24). Once you see this symbol, simply drag the mouse to rotate the text. **Shift+dragging** will constrain the rotation to 45° increments.

There is a rotate tool (to the right of the **Selection** tool), but **Selection** tool rotating is generally quicker.

As you know, dragging from within the text boundary (not on a handle) allows you to move the text. While the **Selection** tool is active, you can also move the text by pressing the arrow keys on the keyboard. Each time you press one of these keys, you'll nudge the text one pixel in that key's direction, which is great for precise positioning. **Shift+clicking** one of the arrow keys (with the **Selection** tool active) will nudge the text five pixels in the key's direction.

When you read the section about **Shapes** on page 279, remember that all **Selection** tool manipulations (moving, rotating, resizing, etc.) work on them too.

Instead of using the **Selection** tool to make adjustments to text or shapes, you can scrub the values in the **Transform** area at the bottom right of the **Title Designer** window, where you can also adjust opacity—to make your text or shapes partially transparent— which you can't do with the **Selection** tool (see Figure 11.25).

ADJUSTING TEXT PROPERTIES

You can adjust type properties, such as text color and font size, as you type or after you finish typing. If you adjust as you type, the change will take place for the next character you type, after making the adjustment. If you adjust after you're done typing, the adjustment will only affect highlighted characters (see "Highlighting tips and tricks" on page 261). Or, if the text is selected with the **Selection** tool, adjustments will affect all of the characters.

In addition to making adjustments on the **Title** menu's submenus, such as **Font** and **Size,** you can also make adjustments by using the **Object Style** area, on the right side of the **Title Designer** window. Within this area, Premiere lists dozens of adjustable properties, organized into broad categories. To each category's left, there's a small triangle icon. If the triangle is facing right, that means you're only seeing the category name. Click it, and the triangle will twirl so that it faces down. Premiere will then display all of the adjustable properties within that category (see Figure 11.26).

When you're done adjusting properties in that category, you can click the triangle again to collapse that category back to name-only display. If too many categories are fully expanded, you may have to scroll up or down in the **Object Style** area to find the property you want to adjust (see Figure 11.27).

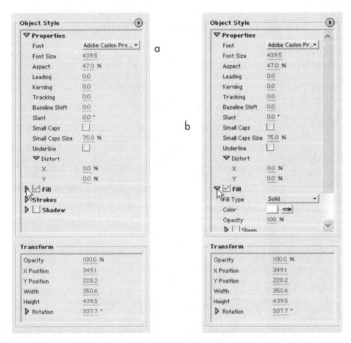

11.26 Twirl open a category to view its properties.

11.27 Scroll to view additional properties.

When you adjust a property, if it seems to have no effect, make sure you've selected (or highlighted) some text. Unfortunately, Premiere can't read your mind. It has no way of knowing which specific character or characters you want to adjust, unless you tell it.

Confusingly, the topmost category of properties is called **Properties**. Within it, you'll find all of the standard, word-processor text properties, like **Font** and **Font Size**. Different properties are adjusted different ways. For instance, to choose a font for the selected text, you have to click the dropdown menu to the right of the property name **Font**. To change a font size, you can either click the current size and type in a new value—or you can scrub the font-size value. Premiere doesn't embed fonts within the title, so if you move the title file onto another computer, remember to move the font with it. It should be stored in the **Windows>Fonts** folder on your main hard drive.

Next is some info on some of the important or lesser-known properties. For a complete list and description of all properties, see the Premiere online help or user manual—or just try adjusting property to see what happens.

Leading: Named after lead strips that printers used to place between lines of type in the old printing-press days, this properties adjusts what most people call "line spacing," or how much space there is between each line. Unless you're trying to achieve some specific, unusual effect, it's customary to set leading to slightly larger than font size. So if your font size is 20, you might want to set leading to 22 (see Figure 11.28).

Kerning: If there's one property that makes amateurs look like amateurs and pros look like pros, it's kerning, which adjusts the amount of space between any two letters. Amateurs tend not to touch this property, and their text winds up looking bad. So if you want to create professional titles, take a look at your text when you're done typing it and note any letters that look like they're too far from or too near to the letter next to them. Then

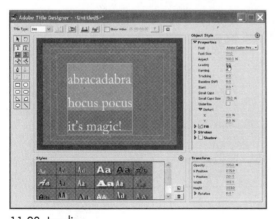

11.28 Leading.

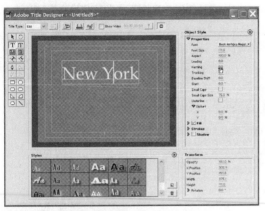
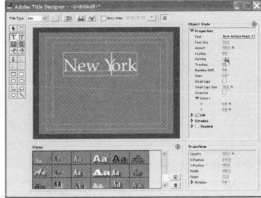

11.29 Kerning.

park the text cursor between those two letters and scrub kerning until the spacing looks right (see Figure 11.29).

Tracking: This is similar to kerning, but it adds (or removes) space between all of the selected characters—not just between two characters (see Figure 11.30).

Baseline Shift: The baseline is the line that characters rest on. Some characters, such as the lower-case y (in most fonts) have descenders that extend below the baseline. To move the selected characters above or below the baseline, adjust the **Baseline Shift** property. You might use this to make a subscript, such as the 2 in H_2O or a superscript such as the asterisk after footnote text. When making superscripts and subscripts, you must adjust both **Baseline Shift** and **Font Size** (see Figure 11.31).

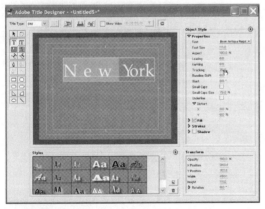

11.30 Tracking.

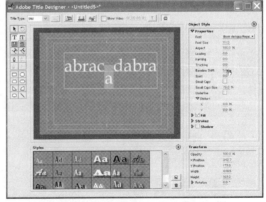

11.31 Baseline Shift.

Where Are All My Fonts?

When you click the **Font** property dropdown, you may be surprised to see only a some of your fonts listed. Never fear, you can see more of them by selecting the **More** option near the top of the dropdown list. As new lists of fonts appear, each list will have a **More** option near its top, which you can click to reveal even more fonts.

As an alternative, click the **Browse** option at the top of the list. Premiere will open a **Font Browser**, in which you'll see have access to all of your installed fonts in a single list. The **Font Browser** displays sample text swatches, so that you can see what a font looks like before clicking to select it.

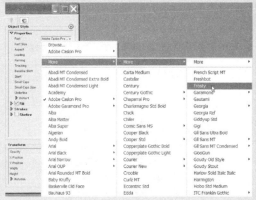

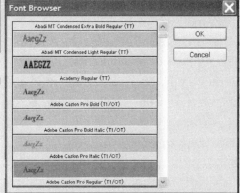

11.32 If you don't see all of your fonts listed, click the More option.

11.33 To open the Font Browser, click the Browse button at the top of the Title Designer window.

Alignment: If you want to center text within its own textbox—or if you want text to be right aligned or left aligned, click the left, right, or center alignment buttons at the top of the **Title Designer** window. These will align text within the boundaries of their own bounding boxes. If you want to align text to the center of the screen, select it with the **Selection** tool, and then choose **Title>Position>Horizontal Center** or **Title>Position>Vertical Center** from the menu. Or choose both options, to place text in both the horizontal and vertical center of the screen.

At the bottom of the **Properties** category, there's a subcategory called **Distort**. If you twirl open the triangle to its left, you can adjust the *X* and *Y* properties to warp text along its horizontal or vertical axis.

Fill Properties: From the drop down next to the **Fill Type** property, you can choose a specific style of fill. The default, solid, fills your selected text with one color. You can choose the fill color by clicking the small swatch next to the **Color** property or by using the eyedropper, with which you can sample a color from anywhere on the screen. This is useful when you want to set text color to one of the colors in the video. Just check the **Show Video** option at the top center of the **Title Designer** window and scrub the timecode to display the frame that contains the color you want to sample. Then use the eyedropper tool to click that color. Any selected text will change to the color you clicked with the eyedropper tool (see Figure 11.34).

If you choose the **Linear** or **Radial Gradient** fill types, Premiere will display two color stops, because a gradient is a gradual blend of one color into another color. To set the two colors, click one of the two stops to select it and then set its color by clicking the color swatch next to the **Color Stop Color** property—or by using the eyedropper by the same property. Then repeat the same steps with the other stop, this time choosing a different color (see Figures 11.35–11.38). You can also click either or both stops and adjust the **Color Stop Opacity** property, to make the stop partially or completely transparent.

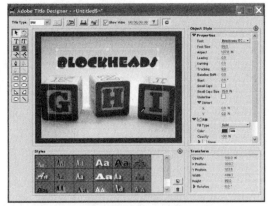

11.34 If you want to set the text's fill color to a color found somewhere on your screen (even outside of the Title Designer window), click the Eyedropper button (in the Fill category), hold down the mouse button, roll over the color you want to use, and then release the mouse button.

You can create text that fades to transparent at the bottom by setting the leftmost color stop to a color and then setting the rightmost color stop's opacity to 0%. Next, set the **Angle** property to 90°, which will move the first stop color to the top of the text and the second stop color to the bottom of the text, so the bottom is transparent. Finally, slide the first stop color to the right until more of the text is colored and less is transparent (see Figure 11.39).

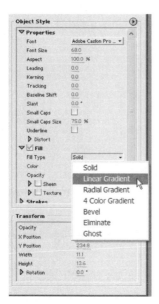

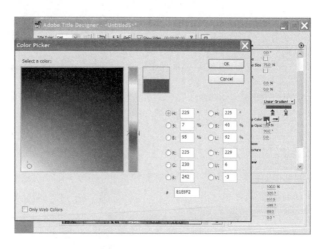

11.35 Selecting the Linear Gradient fill. *(left)*

11.36 Choosing a starting color. *(above right)*

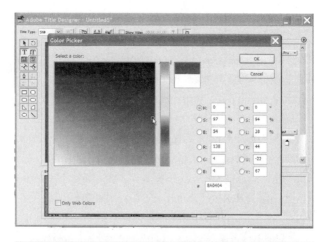

11.37 Selecting the ending color stop. *(above)*

11.38 Choosing an ending color. *(above right, middle)*

11.39 Creating text that fades out along the bottom. *(right)*

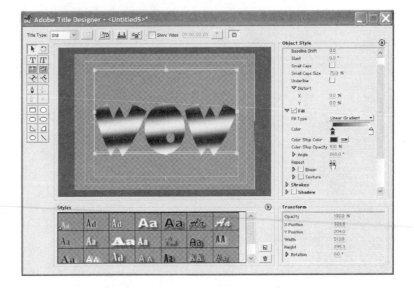

11.40 Creating Stripes.

If you want to make striped text, choose two stripe colors by setting your stops to those colors. Then adjust the **Repeat** property until the stripes are a size that you like. Finally, adjust the **Angle** property to slant the stripes in any direction you want (see Figure 11.40). If you make one of the stop colors transparent, you will have colored stripes alternating with transparent stripes, through which you'll be able to see the underlying video.

The **Four Color Gradient Fill Type** is similar to the **Linear** or **Radial** gradient, except that it gives you four color stops. If you don't see all four stops, point to the right edge of the **Title Designer** window until you see a double-headed arrow and then drag to make the window wider. Then window needs to be of a certain width in order for it to have room to display all four stops.

The **Bevel Fill** type gives you a new set of properties that you can use to make your text looked like it's raised a bit above its surface. The secret to getting **Bevel** to work is to set **Highlight** and **Shadow** to two different colors, and to check the **Lit** property. Then adjust the **Size** property until you see a bevel appear around the text. You won't see much of anything unless you work with fairly large text, so bump up the font size. Play with the other properties to adjust the bevel to your liking (see Figure 11.41).

Eliminate turns off the fill altogether, leaving you with invisible text unless you set a **Stroke** (see page 277). **Eliminate** will also turn off shadows (see page 278), so if you've added a shadow and don't see it anymore, check to see if you've accidentally set the **Fill** type to **Eliminate**. If you want to get rid of fills and keep shadows, choose the **Ghost** type, because that's exactly what it does (see Figure 11.42).

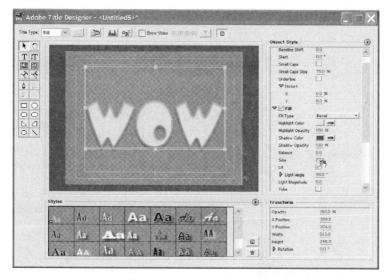

11.41 The Bevel Fill. *(above)*   11.42 The Ghost fill type turns off the fill, but displays shadows. This won't
work unless you've added shadows. *(below)*

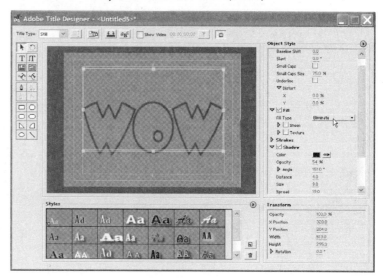

Sheen: This property simulates a beam of light falling across your text. After turning it on, twirl open the property to see some subproperties that you can adjust. You won't see the sheen at all until you set **Size** to something greater than zero. Once you see the sheen, you can use **Color** and **Opacity** to change the sheen's color and to make it solid or semi-transparent. You can also adjust the sheen's **Angle**, so that the light beam cuts across the letters diagonally, vertically, or horizontally. Adjust offset to relocate the sheen to a different part of your text (see Figure 11.43).

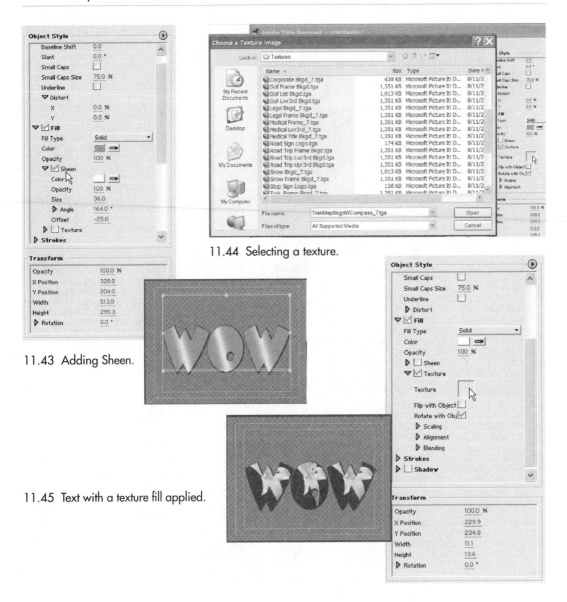

11.44 Selecting a texture.

11.43 Adding Sheen.

11.45 Text with a texture fill applied.

Texture: After checking this property, you can twirl it open and then click the gray square next to the **Texture** subproperty to select a texture. Premiere will display a file browser window, set by default to *Program Files\Adobe\Premiere Pro\Presets\Textures*, a folder on your hard drive containing many textures that come with Premiere. But you can navigate to any other folder on your hard drive and select another graphic file for the texture. Virtually any kind of graphic can fill text. Use the subproperty categories **Scaling, Alignment,** and **Blending** to style the texture once you add it to your text (see Figures 11.44–11.45).

Strokes: Strokes are outlines around your text characters. Specifically, inner strokes are outlines that run just inside the character borders (so if your text is very small, the stroke could take over the entire interior of the characters), and outer strokes are outlines that run just outside the text boarders, making your letters a little bigger than they were before you added the outer stroke. By default, text has fills turned on and strokes turned off.

To add strokes, twirl open the **Strokes** category and click the word **Add** next to the kind of stroke you want to add. Then twirl open the stroke type that you added (inner or outer) to adjust its color and other properties. You can add up to 12 strokes around any selected text (outlines around outlines around outlines...) by clicking **Add** repeatedly. When you twirl open the stroke type, you'll see a separate subcategory for each stroke you added. You can then twirl open these subcategories to format the strokes. Premiere will draw the strokes in the order you add them, so if you add a red outer stroke and then a green outer stroke, your text will be surrounded by a red outline and the red outline will be surrounded by a green outline (see Figure 11.46).

If you want to change the stroke order, select a stroke by clicking on its subcategory name (which will be **inner:** or **outer:**), and then choose **Movie Stroke Up** or **Move Stroke Down** from the **Object Style** wing menu, which you can access by clicking the small triangle to the right of the words **Object Style**, near the upper-right corner of the **Type Designer** window. You'll also notice that from this menu you can delete a stroke. Or you can disable a stroke by unchecking the checkbox by its subcategory name (see Figure 11.47).

You can select multiple strokes by **Shift**+clicking or **Control**+clicking them in the **Object Style** area. If you select a group of strokes, options in the wing menu (such as **Delete Stroke**) will apply to all of the selected strokes.

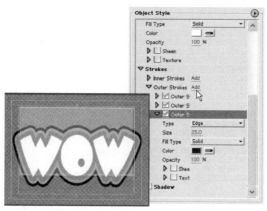

11.46 Adding strokes.

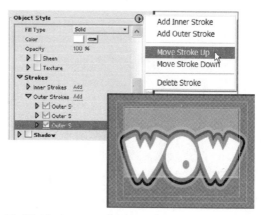

11.47 Moving a stroke up or down.

Shadow: To add a drop shadow to your text, check the box next to the **Shadow** category and then twirl open the category to adjust the properties. Distance will move the shadow further from the text; **Angle** will cast the shadow in any direction; **Spread** will blur the shadow (see Figure 11.48).

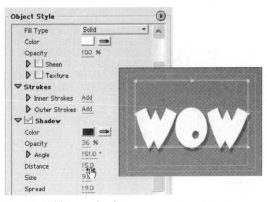

11.48 Adding a shadow.

TAB STOPS

If you want to make evenly spaced columns of text, you should use **Tab Stops.** As you type text, each time you press the **Tab** key on your keyboard your text cursor will pop to a specific location, further to the right. You can set these locations by clicking the **Tab Stops** button at the top of the **Title Designer** window. Premiere will then open a smaller window, containing a ruler and three buttons(see Figure 11.49). From left to right, these buttons set left-aligned, center-aligned, and right-aligned tab stops, respectively. If you press **Tab** and type your text at a center-aligned tab stop, your text will be centered around that stop. Similarly, your text will be left-aligned or right-aligned around left- and right-aligned stops (see Figure 11.50).

Select the tab type you want to add by clicking one of the three buttons and then click anywhere on the ruler to place a tab stop of that type. After placing it, you can drag it right or left along the ruler to move it to another location. Or you can drag it up or down, off the ruler, to remove it. Add as many of these stops as you want and then press the **OK** button. Now each time you press the **Tab** key, your cursor will pop to one of the tab stops

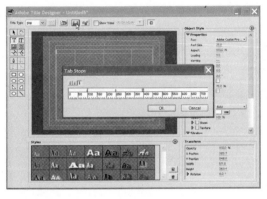

11.49 Setting tab stops.

11.50 Text aligned at tap stops.

you set earlier. If you want to see the tab stops in the drawing area, select **Title>View>Tab Markers** from the menu. Premier will then display tab stops as yellow vertical lines.

ROLLS AND CRAWLS

To make rolling or crawling credits—or other text that rolls or crawls—choose **Roll** or **Crawl** from the **Title Type** dropdown near the upper-left corner of the **Title Designer** window (see Figure 11.51). **Rolls** animate text from the bottom of the screen upwards; **Crawls** animate text left to right or right to left, like the famous news displays in Times Square.

11.51 Selecting the Roll option for rolling credits.

You can't control the speed of the roll or crawl in the **Title Designer**. That's totally dependent on the duration of your title in the **Timeline**. Once you've added the rolling or crawling title to your sequence, you can make it animate more slowly by trimming it out until it covers a longer span in the **Timeline**. To make it run faster, trim it in (shorter). If the title covers 20 seconds of your timeline, the animation will take 20 seconds to finish.

After selecting **Roll** or **Crawl**, type your text as usual with the **Type** tool (not the **Area** or **Path Type** tool). For rolls, you should turn on the **Word Wrap** option on the **Type Menu** or press Enter after each line. Leave the **Word Wrap** option off for crawls.

After you select **Roll** or **Crawl**, Premiere adds a scroll bar to the drawing area (vertical for rolls; horizontal for crawls). To see the animation in the **Type Designer** window, drag in the scroll bar. When you finally edit your title into the sequence, the scroll will animate automatically (see Figure 11.52).

Click the **Roll/Crawl Options** button to change the timing or direction of your scroll. For instance you can set **Preroll** and/or **Postroll** options to add pauses before and after the scroll. Select **Start Off Screen** and **End Off Screen** to ensure that text rolls or crawls from all the way off one side to all the way off the other (see Figures 11.53–11.54).

SHAPES

Although it's not a full-featured drawing application, like Photoshop or Illustrator, you can draw simple shapes in the **Title Designer** window which can act as backdrops behind your text or as other decorative elements.

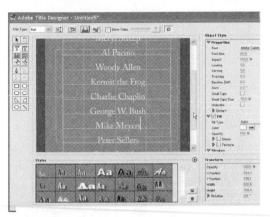

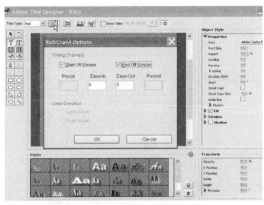

11.52 Using the Horizontal Scroll Bar to scroll through rolling credits.

11.53 Click the Roll/Crawl Options button to change the timing or direction of your rolling or crawling title.

11.54 Trimming rolling credits in the Timeline to make them run slower.

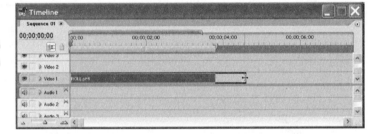

To draw a shape, select one of the shape tools along the left side of the **Title Designer** window and drag diagonally in the drawing area (see Figure 11.55). After you've drawn the shape, switch to the **Selection** tool to move, scale, or rotate the shape, using the same techniques you use when adjusting text with the **Selection** tool.

Also similar to text, you can adjust shape properties in the **Object Styles** area. Make sure that the shape you want to adjust is selected before changing any of the properties. Most of the shape properties, such as **Stroke, Fill,** and **Shadow,** work exactly the same way as their text counterparts. One unique property to some shapes is **Fillet** (see Figure 11.56). You can use the **Fillet** property on the rounded-corner rectangle to make the corners more rounded or less rounded.

Also note that you can change a shape to a completely different shape, by selecting a new shape from the **Graphic Type** property popup. This is a great timesaver if you've already spent a long time styling, say, a rectangle—choosing fills, strokes, etc.—and then you realize that it should really be a rounded-corner rectangle (see Figure 11.57).

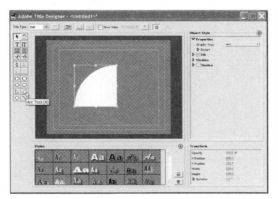

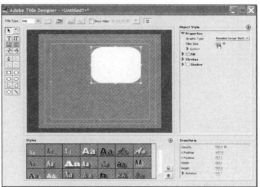

11.55 Drawing a shape with one of the shape tools.

11.56 Adjusting the Fillet property to make rounder corners on a rounded-corner rectangle.

PEN TOOL

If none of the simple shapes suffice, you can create a custom shape with the **Pen** tool. Many people avoid pen tools for years, because they are a little counter-intuitive when you first use them. But they are extremely powerful and definitely worth learning. Once you learn to use one pen tool, you can easily use similar ones in Photoshop, Illustrator, After Effects, Flash, Freehand, Fireworks, and dozens of other graphics programs.

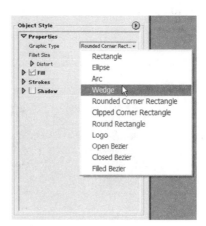

11.57 Changing a shape to a different shape, chosen from the Graphic Type popup.

What confuses most people about the **Pen** tool is the fact that it's *not* a freehand drawing tool. In other words, you can't just select it, hold down the mouse and then drag around. Such a technique will work with tools such as Photoshop's paintbrush or pencil, but not with a pen tool.

The easiest way to use the pen is to make only straight lines. It's a bit more complicated to make curves, so make sure you've mastered straight lines first. To draw a straight line, select the **Pen** tool, click anywhere in the drawing area where you'd like the line to start, then release the mouse button. Premiere will place a tiny point where you clicked. *Without* holding the mouse button down, move the mouse to a new location and click again. Premiere will place another point at the location of your second click and draw a line between the two points (see Figures 11.58–11.61).

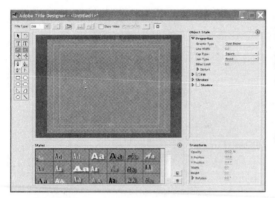

11.58 Click with the Pen tool to create a starting point.

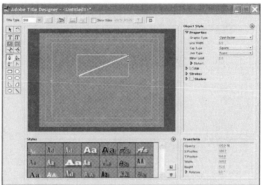

11.59 Click somewhere else to place a second point. Premiere will connect your two points with a line.

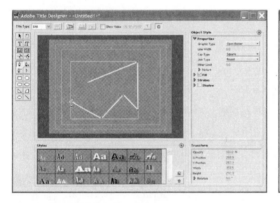

11.60 Keep clicking to place more points. Premiere will connect your points with lines. Switch to the Selection tool to quit drawing and create an open shape.

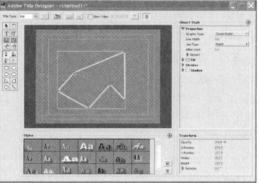

11.61 If you want to create a closed, fillable shape, reclick the first point you created.

If you want to end your drawing now while it's just a single straight line, switch to the Selection Tool (so that the **Pen** tool is no longer active) or hold down the **Control** key on the keyboard and click anywhere in the drawing area with the **Pen** tool. This will end the shape but keep the **Pen** tool active, so that you can start a new shape somewhere else.

If you want to keep drawing, simply click in a third location, and Premiere will lay down yet another point, connecting your second point to it with a line. Keep clicking new locations. Each time you click, Premiere will draw a line from your previous click location to the place you just clicked. It's sort of like playing connect-the-dots, only you're laying down the dots and Premiere is connecting them. When you're done playing, you have two options: as described previously, you can switch to the **Selection Tool** or **Control**+click to

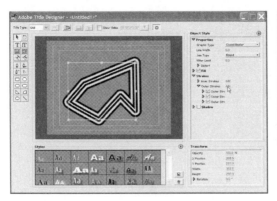
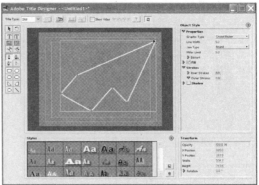

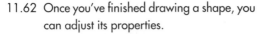

11.62 Once you've finished drawing a shape, you can adjust its properties.

11.63 Drag shape points to move them with the Pen tool.

end the shape as an open path. Or you can click a second time on the starting point (the first point you laid down) to close the shape, so that it can be filled with a solid color, gradient, or texture.

Once you've finished drawing a shape with the **Pen** tool, you can select it with the **Selection Tool** and adjust its properties the same ways you'd adjust any other shape or text properties (see Figures 11.62–11.63).

Or you can keep the **Pen** tool selected and drag the shape's points (the tiny icons Premiere placed at each location you clicked) to change the shape to a different shape.

You can switch to the **Add Anchor Point Tool** (the **Pen** with the plus sign next to it) to add new points anywhere along the shape's path, except where a point already exists (see Figure 11.64). Once you've added a point, you can drag it to a new location with the **Pen** tool.

Note: In the **Title Designer,** the points you create with the **Pen** tool are called anchor points. Don't confuse these with the **Anchor Point** property of the **Motion** effect. **Pen** tool anchor points are similar to the vertices you can manipulate in the **Program Monitor** when animating an object moving along a path. See Chapter 9 for more information about path animation.

Or you can click an existing point with the **Delete Anchor Point Tool** (the **Pen** with the minus sign next to it) to remove a point, simplifying your shape (see Figure 11.65).

In Premiere, you move points with the **Pen** tool. This is different from the way you move points in most other programs that have pen tools. In most of those programs, such as Illustrator or Flash, you move points with a selection tool—sometimes a white arrow tool. Premiere only has a black arrow tool (the **Selection Tool**). This tool moves the entire shape, not individual points.

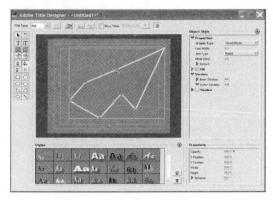

11.64 Click anywhere on the path with the Add Anchor Point Tool to add a new, movable point.

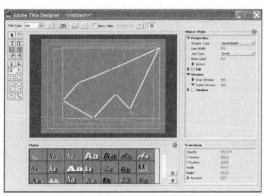

11.65 To remove a point, click the point with the Delete Anchor Point Tool.

To draw curves, you first have to understand that a curve is controlled by two points—its two anchor points—which specify where the curve starts from and where the curve ends up. And it's also controlled by two direction lines, one which specifies the direction of the curve as it leaves the first anchor point and the other which specifies the direction of the curve as it approaches the second anchor point (see Figure 11.66).

You can think of each anchor point as a planet, and the curve as the path of a rocket that blasts off from one planet and lands on the other. The direction line pointing away from the first planet indicates the direction that the rocket is heading when it blasts off. If the other planet didn't exist, the rocket would fly straight in that direction (see Figure 11.67).

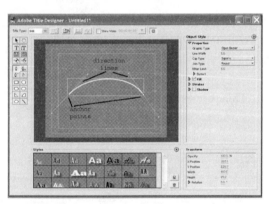

11.66 Each curve is controlled by two anchor points and two direction lines.

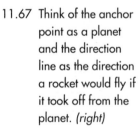

11.67 Think of the anchor point as a planet and the direction line as the direction a rocket would fly if it took off from the planet. *(right)*

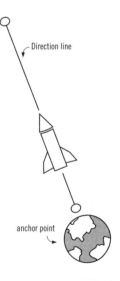

Direction line

anchor point

11.68 The gravity of the second planet (anchor point) affects the trajectory of the rocket so it can't completely follow the direction of the first planet's direction line.

11.69 If you pull one direction line out so that it's very long, it's as if you've given its associated planet (anchor point) a much heavier mass than the other planet. So it exerts the greatest influence over the rocket.

But the other planet *does* exist, and its gravity affects the path of the rocket, not allowing it to exactly follow its original trajectory. When the rocket finally gets near the second planet, its direction line guides the rocket in for a safe landing. By rotating the direction lines, you can change the direction the rocket leaves one planet and arrives at the next (see Figure 11.68).

In addition to rotating direction lines, you can also drag them out longer or shorter. The longer a direction line is, the more *influence* it has over the entire curve. You can imagine that the direction line's length corresponds to the strength of its planet's gravity. If the two direction lines are equally long, both planets exert the same pull on the rocket (the both have the same amount of influence). You can clearly see that at the halfway point, the rocket stops heading away from the first planet and starts heading towards the second planet.

If the first planet's direction line is short and the second planet's direction line is long, that means the second planet exerts a stronger gravitational pull than the first planet. So its direction line will take over the rocket's trajectory pretty soon after the rocket blasts off (see Figure 11.69).

To make your own planets and rockets—a.k.a. curves—select the **Pen** tool and then hold down and drag somewhere in the drawing area. At the place where you originally clicked, Premiere will place the first planet (anchor point). As you drag, Premiere will extend a direction line out from the planet, which you can rotate and lengthen as you drag. When you're done configuring the direction line, release the mouse button and roll the mouse (without holding down the mouse button) to a new location, wherever you

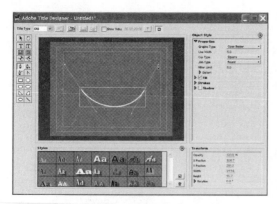

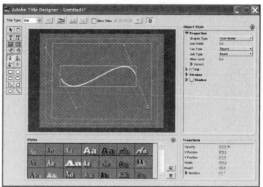

11.70 If you drag down from the first anchor point and up from the second anchor point, you'll get a u-shaped curve.

11.71 If you drag down from the first anchor point and down from the second anchor point too, you'll get an S-shaped curve.

want to place the second planet (anchor point). Once your mouse is in place, hold down the button to place the planet and drag away from it to create that planet's direction line.

If you drag in the opposite the direction from as first-planet drag, you'll end up with a U-shaped curve. If you drag in the same direction as your first-planet drag, you'll make an S-shaped curve (see Figures 11.70–11.71).

Once you've finished creating the curve, you can switch to the **Selection Tool** or **Control**+click with the **Pen** tool to finish the shape. Or you can keep clicking and dragging in new locations to make more curves, connected to your first curve. When you're finished laying down curves, you can leave the path open by choosing the **Selecting Tool** or **Contol**+clicking with the **Pen** tool. Or you can click the starting planet to close the shape, so that it can be filled.

Because it's difficult to make a specific shape when you're laying down curves, a good strategy is to ballpark it and then, when you're done, adjust curve points to get the exact shape you want. For instance, you can move anchor points (planets) to new locations by dragging them with the **Pen** tool. Similarly, you can rotate the ends of the direction lines with the **Pen** tool to change curve directions. You can even lengthen or shorten direction lines—by dragging their ends with the **Pen** tool—to enlarge or reduce influence (how much gravitational pull each planet exerts on the rocket).

As with straight lines, you can click anywhere except on an existing anchor point with the **Add Anchor Point** tool to make a new anchor point along the path. You can then drag the new point to a new location with the **Pen** tool. Or you can delete a point by clicking it with the **Delete Anchor Point** tool.

To change a curve point into a straight-line point (also known as a corner point), click it with the **Convert Anchor Point** tool. To change a straight-line point to a curve point, drag direction lines out from it with the **Convert Anchor Point** tool. In fact, if you're uncomfortable drawing curves, make an approximation of the curvy shape you want using just straight lines. Then when you're done, convert each corner point into a curve point by dragging out from in with the **Convert Anchor Point** tool (see Figure 11.72).

Notice that when you drag a direction-line point with the **Pen** tool, the opposite point also moves, and the two direction lines pivot like a teeter-totter, one end goes down while the other end goes up (and vice versa). This ensures

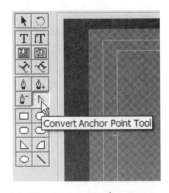

11.72   Convert Anchor Point tool.

that the curve stays smooth. If you don't want a smooth curve, drag the ends of a direction line with the **Convert Anchor Point** tool rather than the **Pen** tool. This allows you to adjust one direction line without affecting the other.

IMPORTING GRAPHICS

When all the drawing tools inside the **Title Designer** tool are just not good enough, you can import a graphic created in an external program, such as Photoshop or Illustrator. You can import graphics in two different ways: as standalone, freely positional pictures, or as a text element. If you import the graphic as a text element, it acts as if it was a character in one of your text boxes, and it flows with the text. To do this, you must be using a type tool. With the type tool selected, place a text cursor where you want the graphic to go and then choose **Title>Logo>Insert Logo Into Text** from the menu. Premiere will open up a file-browser window. Select a graphic file on your hard drive and then click the **Open** button (see Figure 11.73). Premiere will insert the graphic as if it was a character that you just typed.

Or, you can choose **Title>Logo>Insert Logo** to import a graphic as a standalone element, just like a shape you create inside the **Title Designer**. Once you import a graphic, you can select it with the **Selection Tool** and adjust it just as you'd adjust any other shape or text box (see Figure 11.74).

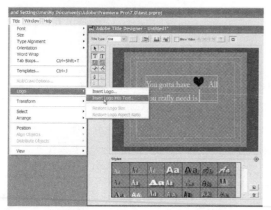

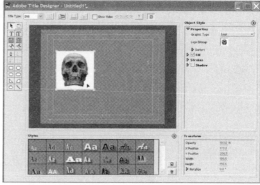

11.73 If you have the Type tool selected, you can insert a graphic at the cursor point so that it flows with the text.

11.74 Or you can import a graphic as a standalone element.

LAYOUT

Arranging the stacking order

As you add multiple elements to the drawing area—text, shapes, etc.—Premiere will stack them on top of each other. The stacking order won't be obvious unless you position two or more objects so that they overlap. Once you do this, you'll notice that the default positioning places the first object you created on the bottom and each object after that higher and higher in the stack. Sometimes the default stacking order works against your design. For instance, you may be trying to place red text in front of a blue square. But if you create the text *before* the square, it will stay behind the square.

To solve this problem, select the square and choose **Title>Arrange>Send To Back** from the menu (or you can select the square and choose **Title>Arrange>Bring to Front**.

If you're overlapping three objects—a square, a circle, and a triangle—and you want to move the triangle from the top to the middle position (between the square and the circle), don't choose the **Send To Back** option. This will send the triangle to the very bottom of the stack(see Figure 11.75). Instead, choose **Tile>Arrange>Send Backwards** from the menu. Each time you choose this option, the selected object will move down one level in the stacking order. Similarly, the **Send Forwards** option will move the object one level up in the stacking order.

Aligning objects

It's difficult to place multiple objects along a straight line by dragging them and eyeballing their positions (see Figure 11.76).

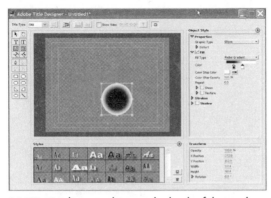

11.75 Sending an object to the back of the stack.

For precise placement, select all of the objects you want to line up and then choose one of the options from the **Title>Align Objects** menu or click one of the alignment buttons along the lower left edge of the **Title Designer** window (see Figure 11.77).

To select multiple objects, **Shift**+click each object you want to add to the group. Or you can use the selection tool to drag a marquee around multiple objects you want to include in a group. To select all objects in the drawing area, you can use the keyboard shortcut **Control+A**. If you **Shift**+click an already selected object, Premiere will remove it from the selection group.

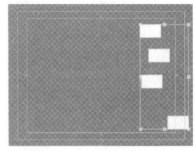

11.76 Objects out of alignment.

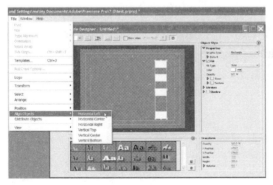
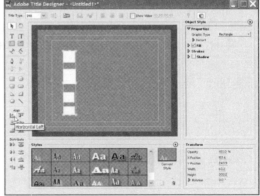

11.77 You an align objects by selecting them and then choosing an option from the Title>Align Objects menu or clicking one of the alignment buttons in the Title Designer window.

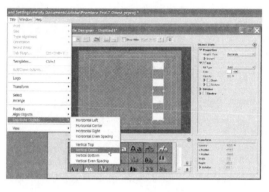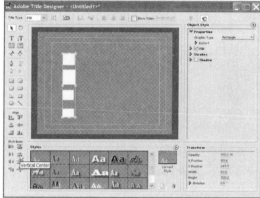

11.78 You can distribute objects evenly by selecting them and choosing an option from the Title>Distribute Objects menu or clicking one of the distribution buttons in the Title Designer window.

Once you've selected the objects you want to line up, click the **Align Left** button or choose **File>Align Objects>Horizontal Left** to line all of the select objects up with the left edge of the leftmost object in the selection group. Since all the objects will be lined up with the leftmost object, it makes sense to position that object before forming the selection group and choosing the **Horizontal Left** option. Similarly, you can **Align Objects** by their horizontal right edges or centers, or by their vertical left edges, right edges, or centers.

Distributing objects

If you want to evenly space objects within the drawing area, select all the objects you want to adjust and then click on of the distribution buttons along the bottom-left edge of the **Title Designer** window or choose one of the options under the **Title>Distribute Objects** menu, such as **Vertical Centers**. This will distribute all objects so that there's an equal amount of space between the vertical center of one object and the vertical center of the objects above and below it. The furthest-apart objects will be used as boundaries (and those objects won't be moved at all), so you may want to place these objects before using distribute commands (see Figure 11.78).

REUSING TITLE STYLES

Saving and using styles

If you've spent a long time styling text or other objects, you can save all style attributes as a thumbnail in the bottom area of the **Title Designer** window (see Figure 11.79). Then

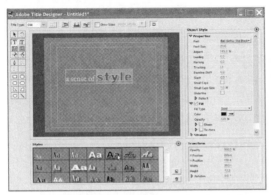

11.79 Select some text and then style it by clicking one of the style thumbnails at the bottom of the Title Designer window.

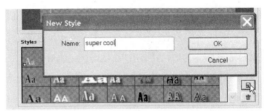

11.80 To create a new style thumbnail, select some styled text and then click the New Style button.

you can easily reuse these styles (or any of the default styles), by selecting an object (or objects) and then clicking on one of the thumbnails. When you click the thumbnail, its style attributes will be added to the selected object or objects. If you **Alt**+click a thumbnail, all style attributes will be added to the selected object, except for font properties, which is great if you want to quickly change text files, strokes, etc. without altering font choice, font size, kerning, etc.

To create a new style thumbnail, select text or a graphic that displays the style you want to save, and click the **New Style** button to the right of the thumbnails (see Figure 11.80). In the dialog window that appears, type a name for your style, and then click the **OK** button. To delete a style, click its thumbnail to select it and then click the **Trash Can** button to the right of the thumbnails.

Options in the wing menu to the right of the **Style** thumbnail area allow you to save all the thumbnails into a library, a single file that you can backup or share with a friend, if he or she has the appropriate fonts installed (see Figure 11.81). You can also replace the current group of thumbnails with a library file that you saved earlier or restore the thumbnails to Premiere's default set.

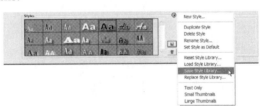

11.81 The wing menu contains additional style options.

Creating and using templates

You can save any title as a template and then generate multiple titles from that template. Suppose you're editing a series called *The Amazing Adventures of Turtleman*. Each episode might start with a title that looks exactly the same, except for the name of the episode. So the first one says, *The Amazing Adventures of Turtleman, episode 1: the Origin of Turtleman,* and the second one says, *The Amazing Adventures of Turtleman, episode 2: Turtleman meets Slothwoman,* and so on.

Once you create your first title, you can save it as a template and then generate your second title from the first one, changing only the text that differs between the two but keeping the same font, colors, and style treatments.

To save a title as a template:

1. Click the **Templates** button at the top of the **Title Designer** window (see Figure 11.82).

11.82 Click the Templates button to save a title as a template (or to apply an old template to a new title).

2. In the **Templates** dialog window, click the little wing menu in the upper-right corner, and choose the **Save As Template** option, which is the first option in the menu (see Figure 11.83).

3. Give the template a name and click **OK**.

4. Later, when you want to create the episode 2 title, choose **File>New>Title**, and when the Title Designer window appears, click the **Templates** button. In the **Templates** window, choose your template from the **User Templates** category.

In the **Title Designer Presets** category, you'll find all sorts of cool, premade templates.

Regardless of which category you choose a template from, Premiere will open a *copy* of the template in the drawing area, complete with all of its text and graphics. Alter whatever you want to

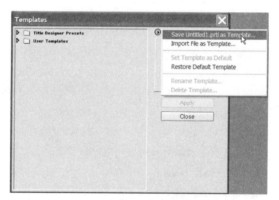

11.83 To save a template, click the wing menu inside the Templates dialog and choose the Save As Template option.

alter and save the title. You will *not* alter the template. Instead, you'll save a copy based on the template file.

WRAPPING UP

Titles are the final icing on a video and audio cake. In Premiere, you can manipulate all of these elements into a complex, evocative mix. But unless your work is seen, no one will ever appreciate all of your hard work. This is why the next chapter, where we explore output, is so important.

Chapter 12

Output

So you've finished editing your Great American Movie. (Great European Movie? Great Asian Movie?) But if it's only on your computer, how are people going to see it? Rather than asking the entire world to crowd around your computer screen, or lugging your computer from festival to festival, you'll ultimately want to output your video in a format that can be viewed outside of your computer.

The most common way to output your work is to record it onto videotape. But with the proliferation of new media technologies, outputting may also include exporting a QuickTime file for the Web or for CD-ROM, creating an MPEG2 file for DVD authoring, or exporting a video frame as an image file for printing onto paper or for posting on your website. Since there are so many possible ways to output your work with a wide variety of settings, this chapter will only discuss the most popular methods. Additional documentation can be found on Adobe's website and in online help.

RECORDING TO VIDEOTAPE

There are two ways to output your sequence onto videotape: a crash record, a manual process, and **Export to Tape,** which is automated. But before you can do either of these, you have to set up your equipment.

Setup

To record your program onto videotape, you'll have to first connect your deck or camcorder to your computer. Typically, this should be done before launching Adobe Premiere. For a reminder on how to properly configure your video equipment for Adobe Premiere, refer to Chapter 1.

Once your device is connected, you'll need to tell Adobe Premiere to send your video signal to it. Choose **Project>Project Settings>General,** and confirm that your **Editing Mode** is set to the **DV Playback** option.

Click the **Playback Settings** button (see Figure 12.1). In the **Playback Settings** dialog, select the **Play Video on DV Hardware** option and the **Play Audio on DV Hardware** option. Then click **OK** to close the **Project Settings**. If your video device is also connected to a television or to a video monitor with speakers, you will see and hear your sequence play on that screen.

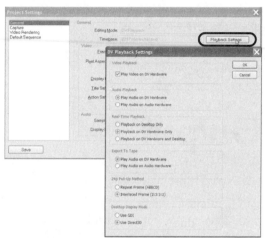

Crash record

Now that your equipment is properly connected and configured, you could record your sequence onto videotape, a process commonly referred to as a *crash record.*

12.1   After choosing Project>Project Settings>General from the menu, click the Playback Settings button and ensure that the Play Video on DV Hardware and Play Audio on DV Hardware options are checked.

1. On your video device, cue your tape to where you want your recording to begin.

2. Park the **Current Time Indicator** at the beginning of the sequence (see Figure 12.2).

3. On your video device, press the **Record** button.

12.2   Park the Current Time Indicator at the beginning of the sequence.

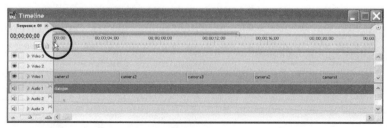

12.3 Press the spacebar or click the Play button in the Program Monitor.

You should notice the tape's timecode advancing when recording has begun.

4. In Adobe Premiere, play your sequence by pressing the **Spacebar** or clicking the **Play** button in the **Program Monitor** (see Figure 12.3).

5. When your show finishes playing, press the **Stop** button on your video device.

> **The Effect of Effects:** Because this method records a sequence playing from the **Timeline**, complex effects or transitions might slow the recording down. If you don't want the recording to suddenly shift to slow motion, make sure that *before* recording, you create preview files for each part of the sequence that contains effects. To learn how to generate preview files, see "Generating Previews" on page 166 in Chapter 6.

Export to Tape

A crash record will get the job done, and if you need to output a one-hour show that's due to air in one hour and five minutes, then a crash record will probably be your method of choice. But for something a bit more elegant and automated, you can choose to export to tape instead.

1. Make sure your sequence is active by clicking in the **Timeline** or **Program Monitor,** and choose **File>Export>Export to Tape** (see Figure 12.4).

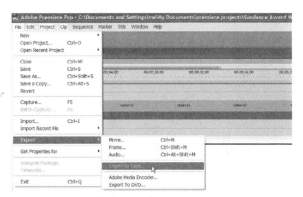

12.4 Click inside the Timeline or Program Monitor; then choose File>Export>Export to Tape.

2. To allow Adobe Premiere to perform the recording for you, select the **Activate Recording Device** option.

3. If you want to specify exactly where on your videotape to begin recording, enable the **Assemble at timecode** option, and type in the timecode for when you'd like recording to begin on your videotape.

This allows your recording to be frame accurate. Otherwise, the computer will simply record from wherever the tape is cued. Note that this option refers to videotape time-code, not sequence timecode. In other words, if you want the sequence to record five minutes into the tape, select this option. If your video device doesn't support timecode, you'll be better off using the crash record method explained previously.

Other options include:

- **Delay movie start:** This setting allows you to create a delay between the video on your computer and the video recorded on your tape. The default setting should suffice.

- **Preroll:** If the computer is going to automate your recording, it will need a few seconds of video to already exist on the tape so that the computer has enough time to synchronize with your equipment. This time is determined by the amount of preroll, and the default setting of 150 frames (or 5 seconds) should suffice. If you know that your videotape doesn't have at least 5 seconds of video before your recording point, then you can type a different number.

12.5   The Export to Tape dialog window.

4. In the **Options**, you can choose to have the system abort and warn you if it could not successfully record every frame of your show onto videotape (see Figure 12.5).

    This is usually a good idea. If your computer cannot properly output your video, you'll probably want to know about it immediately in order to track down the problem and try again.

5. Choose the **Render Audio Before Export** option to ensure that audio is ready to record properly before it's dumped onto tape.

6. On your computer screen, click the **Record** button, and your computer will automatically record your show to videotape.

7. You can stop the recording process by clicking the **Stop** button (see Figure 12.6). Otherwise,

12.6   To cancel recording, press the Stop button.

when the recording is finished, you should receive a **Recording Successful** confirmation.

EXPORT TO DVD

If you have a DVD burner, Premiere can output your sequence to a DVD video format that will play on most consumer DVD players (see Figure 12.7). With the **File>Export>Export to DVD** command, Premiere can burn a simple DVD that plays your program from beginning to end, but with no menus or buttons. This method will produce a DVD with no advanced features, such as menus or buttons, it will at least provide you with an easy way to output to the popular DVD video format without having to use another application.

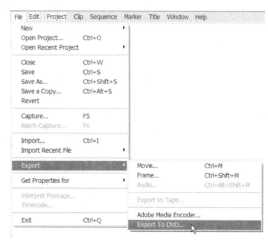

12.7 To Export a DVD, choose File>Export>Export to DVD from the menu.

For a more sophisticated DVD, you can use the **Adobe Media Encoder** to export your sequence as an MPEG2 file so that a DVD authoring application, such as Adobe Encore DVD, can process it. The **Adobe Media Encoder** will be discussed in the next section on page 302.

To record you sequence to a DVD:

1. With your sequence active, choose **File>Export>Export to DVD**.

2. Modify the **General** settings as you see fit (see Figure 12.8).

   • **Disc Name:** Enter a name for the DVD.

   • **Chapter Points At:** Choose this option if you want to specify timeline markers as chapters on the DVD. This will allow viewers to skip to different parts of your

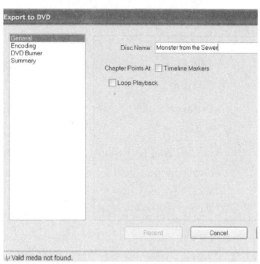

12.8 Export to DVD General settings.

DVD by using the **Previous** and **Next** buttons on common DVD player remote controls.

- **Loop Playback:** Choose this if you want a DVD player to repeat your show when it reaches the end.

3. Customize the **Encoding** settings to suit your needs.

- **Preset:** The preset you choose will depend on your source material and how good you want the DVD to look (see Figure 12.9). In most cases, you'll want to set this to **NTSC DV 4×3 High Quality 7Mb VBR 2 Pass SurCode for Dolby Digital 5.1**, which is optimized for a wide variety of programs. Choose the PAL equivalent if your project is PAL. For 16×9 projects, choose the **VBR 2 Pass** setting with the highest MB. When you choose a preset, Premiere will fill out the rest of the **Encoding** settings for you.

12.9 Choose a preset from the dropdown menu.

- **Comment:** This area displays any comments that were saved with the preset.

- **Edit:** Here, you can choose to modify the current preset, save a preset, or import an existing one.

- **Export Range:** Specify whether to export the entire sequence or just the **Work Area**.

- **Fields:** This setting allows you to override the field ordering of the preset. Each NTSC or PAL video frames are made up of two images, called *fields*. Each field contains one-half of the images. Premiere joins the two fields together to create a single frame.

  Some cameras or video-capturing systems capture the upper field first; others capture the lower field first. If you're not finishing your video in Premiere—if you're going to output it from Premiere but then open it up in some other editor—you might need to switch the field order. Some systems like the lower field to be displayed first. Others like the upper field to be displayed first. All DV cameras capture the lower field first, and most programs built to work with DV display the lower field first. In all likelihood, you'll want to leave this setting at its default of **Lower.**

If you are bringing the video into another program, check that program's manual to see if it prefers lower field first video or upper field first video. Adobe After Effects works equally well with either.

- **Maximize Bitrate:** Select this option if you want Adobe Premiere to use all of the available space on the blank DVD to produce the best possible image quality. This setting will override any bitrate setting of the current preset. While this may sound like a great setting, keep in mind that many DVD players may have difficulty with bit rates that are too high. To use an analogy, your car may be able to go as fast as 200 mph, but that's not always a good idea. For greater compatibility without the risk of overstressing your bitrate, do not enable **Maximize Bitrate.**

- **Force Variable Bitrate:** When **Maximize Bitrate** is selected, this setting will vary the bitrate of the DVD based on the content of your sequence. For example, a scene of an interview consisting mostly of talking-head footage doesn't contain a lot of motion, so the computer doesn't need to allocate a lot of data to maintain the image quality of the scene. While a scene of a car chase will probably contain lots of motion, and will require more data to maintain its image quality. So **Force Variable Bitrate** may reduce some of the stress described previously, and it's probably something you'll want to enable if you decide to you **Maximize Bitrate.**

4. Specify the settings for DVD Burner (see Figure 12.10).

   - **DVD Burner:** Select your name of your DVD burner.

   - **Rescan:** Click this button if your computer doesn't recognize your DVD burner. If you have an external DVD burner, the computer will only recognize it if it was connected and turned on before launching Adobe Premiere. So, if your DVD burner still won't

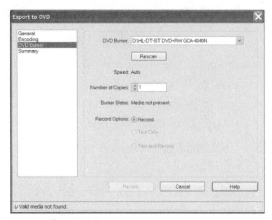

12.10 The DVD Burner settings.

appear, you may need to quit and relaunch Adobe Premiere, and try again.

- **Number of Copies:** If you know ahead of time how many DVDs you want to make, you can specify that number here. It's usually a good idea to set this so that you don't have to go through this entire process for each disc.

- **Burner Status:**

Message	Meaning
Ready	The computer is ready to burn the disc.
None Detected	The computer doesn't recognize a burner.
Media Not Present	The computer recognizes the burner, but doesn't see a disc.
Unrecognized Disc	The DVD burner doesn't like the disc.
Disc Full	There's not enough blank space on the disc to output your sequence.

- **Record Options:**

Setting	Result
Record	The computer will immediately initiate the output process when you click the Record button.
Test Only	Will not actually burn the disc, but instead test your media and report any possible problems.
Test and Record	Will perform a test first and then immediately initiate the output process if the text was successful.

Your choice will depend on how much time you have to spend on this process, and how concerned you are about the possibility of wasting a blank disc. As blank DVDs continue to drop in price, you may choose to skip the test in order to speed up the burning process.

5. Click the **Record** button at bottom of the window, and take a long break.

MPEG2 FILE WITH ADOBE MEDIA ENCODER

If you want to produce a DVD with more sophisticated features, such as menus and buttons, you'll need to use a DVD authoring application such as Adobe Encore DVD (see Figure 12.11). Typically, these DVD apps require your video elements to be converted to the MPEG2 format. Adobe Premiere includes a feature called the **Adobe Media Encoder**, which allows you to export your sequence in a variety of formats, including MPEG2.

1. Activate your sequence, and choose **File>Export>Adobe Media Encoder**. The first time you choose this feature, you may be asked to activate or register it. Simply follow the on-screen instructions, and continue.

2. Choose the appropriate format. For creating an MPEG2 file for DVD authoring, choose MPEG2-DVD (see Figure 12.12).

3. Choose the appropriate preset. Set this to **NTSC DV High quality 4Mb VBR 2 Pass** or the PAL equivalent, if the video is intended for European viewers. It is optimized for a wide variety of programs.

4. Click **OK**. Adobe Premiere should produce an MPEG2 file suitable for a DVD authoring program.

SELF-CONTAINED MEDIA FILE

After completing a sequence, you may wish to export it as a self-contained movie, which is a media file that no longer references the original source files. Experienced video editors refer to this process as a *video mixdown*. (If you're an Adobe Photoshop user, this is similar to "flattening" the video.) You may also want to export a self-contained movie file so that you have it in a format that can be used in other applications, such as Adobe After Effects, Discreet's cleaner, or Sorenson Squeeze.

To export a sequence as a media file:

1. Activate the sequence, and choose **File>Export>Movie** (**Control+M**).

2. Click on the **Settings** button.

12.11 To export using the Adobe Media Encoder, choose File>Export>Adobe Media Encoder from the menu.

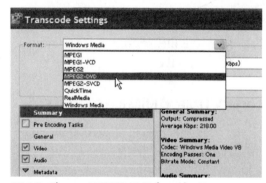

12.12 Choose MPEG2-DVD from the Format dropdown menu.

12.13 From the menu, choose File>Export Movie; then click the Settings button.

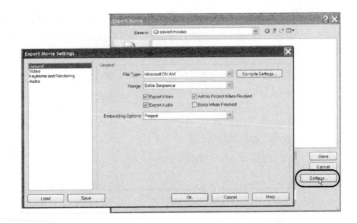

3. Choose a format. To maintain DV quality, set this to **Microsoft DV AVI**. Choose to export the entire sequence or only the **Work Area,** and choose to include video, audio, or both. You can also check the **Add to Project When Finished** option if you'd like Premiere to import the saved video file into your current project. All of the other settings can be left at their defaults.

Note **Work Area:** The **Work Area** is the bar at the top of the **Timeline**, which is also used to preview effects (see Figure 12.14). It's discussed in Chapter 6 on page 168.

4. Click **OK** to close the settings.
5. Name the file, choose its destination, and click **Save.**

QuickTime Animation File

If you want to export a media file and preserve its transparent areas, such as with an animated title you want to reuse over other clips, you can output it as a QuickTime file. This process will produce

12.14 The Work Area.

a high-quality media file with transparency data stored in an alpha channel.

1. Activate the sequence, and choose **File>Export>Movie** (**Control+M**) (see Figure 12.13).
2. Click the **Settings** button.

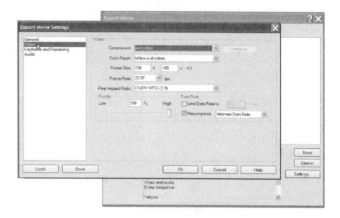

12.15 In the Video Settings, choose Animation for Compressor and Millions+ for Color Depth. Uncheck Recompress.

3. Choose **QuickTime** for your file type. Choose to export the entire sequence or only the **Work Area,** and choose to include video, audio, or both. If you'd like Premiere to automatically import the QuickTime file into the currently open project, choose **Add to Project When Finished.**

4. In the **Video** settings, choose **Animation for Compressor** and **Millions+** of colors for **Color Depth.** Uncheck **Recompress** (see Figure 12.15). All the other settings can be left at their defaults.

5. Click **OK** to close the settings, name the file, choose its destination, and click **Save.**

QUICKTIME FILE FOR WEB OR CD-ROM

The **Adobe Media Encoder** allows you to export your sequence in a wide variety of formats, and its QuickTime options are very good. You may be asking yourself why you would want to use the QuickTime format when many PC users might not even have QuickTime installed. With QuickTime you have the ability to use the Sorenson Video 3 compression scheme (a.k.a. codec), which is capable of producing very high-quality files at very small sizes. This is why QuickTime is a great format for delivering movie trailers on the web; when you're trying to sell a blockbuster movie, you want your audience to see a great-looking trailer without having to wait too long to download it. Fortunately, all of the QuickTime presets in the **Adobe Media Encoder** use the Sorenson Video 3 codec.

The only drawback, as mentioned earlier, is that many Windows users don't have QuickTime installed on their computers. This is resolved simply by including a link to the QuickTime download page, http://www.apple.com/quicktime/download/.

The movie industry feels that if users want to see high-quality trailers, then they will take the time to download and install the latest version of QuickTime onto their machines. Historically, they have been correct. Every time there is a new trailer for a popular franchise, like *Star Wars* or *Lord of the Rings*, the number of QuickTime downloads skyrockets to record numbers. So if your intended web audience consists of Internet mediaphiles, then they will probably be QuickTime users as well. QuickTime is also part of the installation of iTunes, which increases the likelihood that music enthusiasts may already have it.

To export your sequence as a QuickTime file for the web or CD-ROM:

1. Activate your sequence, and choose **File>Export>Adobe Media Encoder.**

2. Choose **QuickTime** as your format.

3. Choose the appropriate preset.

   As mentioned earlier, these are all good. The challenge is finding the right balance between file size and quality, and the main determining factors are frame size, frame rate, and data rate. If you toggle the different presets, you'll see that they are all different combinations of these three settings. Feel free to experiment with each preset to see the difference. If you're feeling advantageous, try starting with QT alternate NTSC download or the PAL equivalent if the video is intended for European viewers. In the **Video** settings, experiment with modifying **Frame Rate** and **Datarate**. While a frame rate of 15 will produce jerkier motion, you'll notice a large drop in file size. Increase the frame rate for smoother motion, but anything greater than 30 will probably only produce a larger file with no visual difference. To improve the quality of the image (while increasing file size), experiment with different datarates and spatial qualities. Modifying the **Audio** settings can also help to reduce file sizes. Choosing to output your audio as **Mono** and reducing your sample rate frequency to 22 kHz usually compresses the audio at acceptable amounts for a decrease in file size.

4. Click **OK**, and see your results.

MPEG1, QuickTime, RealMedia, and Windows Media

In addition to QuickTime and MPEG2, the **Adobe Media Encoder** also supports MPEG1, RealMedia, and Windows Media formats. As with QuickTime, the presets have been fine-tuned to produce good results for a wide variety of material, so feel free to experiment with each one in order to see the difference. While QuickTime with Sorenson Video 3 is the best-looking option, you may prefer to export as one of these other formats to accommodate the non-QuickTime audience. In fact, you may have noticed that many popular media sites offer their content in different formats simply so that users don't have to bother to download additional software before they can see anything. So if you want to please as many people as possible, offer as many formats as your server can support.

What's the difference between them? Table 12.1 gives a quick reference to their features and drawbacks.

Table 12.1   Video format comparison

Format	Pro	Con
MPEG1	Based on a standard, so almost every player on both Mac and Windows supports it.	Comparatively poor quality.
QuickTime	Very good quality with Sorenson Video 3 codec.	While every Mac already has it built in, many Windows users may not have the QuickTime Player installed.
RealMedia	Works on both Mac and Windows.	Mediocre quality, and all users have to download RealOne Player to see it.
Windows Media	Built into the Windows operating system, so many users won't have to download anything to see it.	Mediocre quality, Mac users have to download the Windows Media Player, and some codecs don't work on Mac.

EXPORTING A STILL IMAGE

To export a video frame as a still image file:

1. Park the **Current Time Indicator** on the desired frame, and choose **File>Export>Frame (Control+Shift+M)** (see Figure 12.16).

2. Click on the **Settings** button (see Figure 12.17).

3. Choose an image format. The most compatible uncompressed format is TIFF. You can choose to **Add to Project When Finished,** but if you just need this image for print or for the Web, leave this option unchecked.

4. In the **Video** options, set your image specifications. For best results, choose **None for Compressor.** If you want to maintain any transparency in your video frame, choose

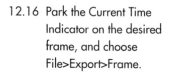
12.16 Park the Current Time Indicator on the desired frame, and choose File>Export>Frame.

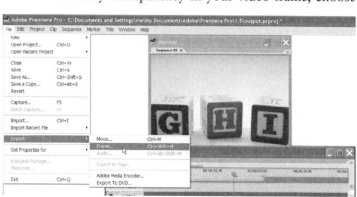

12.18 Check the
Deinterlace option.

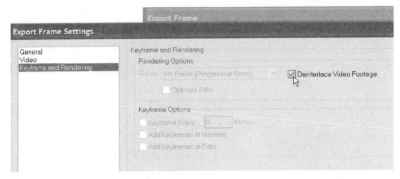

Millions+ of colors, and transparent areas of the image will be stored in an alpha channel. Otherwise, **Millions** of colors (without the **+**) will suffice. If you plan to use this still image in a DV program, you'll want to have the **Frame Size** set to 720×480 and the **Pixel Aspect Ratio** to D1/DV NTSC (0.9) or the PAL equivalent if the video is intended for European viewers. If you plan to use this image for print or for the Web, set this however you wish, but a **Frame Size** of 640×480 is the largest size that maintains the original resolution, and set the **Pixel Aspect Ratio** to **Square Pixels** (1.0).

5. In the **Keyframe** and **Rendering** options, turn on the checkbox for **Deinterlace Video Footage** (see Figure 12.18).

6. Click **OK** to close the settings.

7. Name the file, choose its destination, and click **Save**.

Other Formats: You can also export AAF, OMF, and EDL files from Premiere by clicking the **Note** Project window and then choosing **Project>Export Project As** (AAF/OMF or EDL) from the menu. Each of these file types allows other editing applications, such as Final Cut Pro or Avid Xpress DV to open your project, though Premiere-only features won't survive the translation. To learn more about these formats, see Premiere's online help.

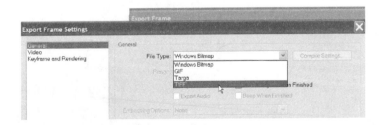

12.17 Click the Settings
button and choose a
file format, like TIFF.

Importing into After Effects

You can import a Premiere project file directly into Adobe After Effects by selecting **File>Import > File** for After Effect's menu. Then browse to the project file's location and select it for import. Each Premiere sequence in the project will import as a separate After Effects composition, and all of the Premiere footage files will import in as AE footage. Sequence tracks will become composition layers.

Some Premiere-only effects and transitions will not translate into After Effects. AE will add placeholders for any transitions it can't duplicate.

When you're done working in AE, you'll have to render the project out as a Quicktime file or some other kind of video file if you want to import back into Premiere. This is because though you can import Premiere projects into After Effects, you can't import After Effects projects into Premiere.

You can also copy and paste selected clips between Premiere and After Effects.

WRAPPING UP

Whether you use Premiere to create QuickTime video files for the web, AVIs to insert into PowerPoint presentations, or video for television or DVDs, once you've gone through the export procedure, you've completed a long journey that began way back when you captured video.

Congratulations. You've now milked Premiere for all its worth, especially if you've used Appendix A to customize it to your way of working. You've created a rough draft using three-point editing techniques. You've trimmed your draft into a polished sequence. You've added effects and transitions. You've done some color correction. You've sweetened the audio. And you've even added some titles.

You're now a storyteller and a filmmaker.

Appendix A

Customizing Premiere

Now that you know how to use Premiere, it's time to turn it into *your* application. You can do this by adjusting all sorts of customizable options, including creating your own keyboard shortcuts for frequently used commands, creating your own arrangements of the various windows and palettes that populate Premiere's interface. You can even change the way clips display in the **Timeline** and **Project** windows.

KEYBOARD SHORTCUTS

To customize keyboard shortcuts in Premiere, choose **Edit>Keyboard Customization** from the menu. Premiere will display the **Keyboard Customization** window (see Figure A.1).

If you're coming to Premiere from Avid Xpress DV or Final Cut Pro, and you're used to the keyboard shortcuts in either of those applications, you can force Premiere to use the same shortcuts by choosing **Shortcuts for Avid Xpress DV 3.5** or **Shortcuts for Final Cut Pro 4.0** from **Set** dropdown menu. Of course, most Avid and Final Cut users customize keyboard shortcuts within those applications. Premiere can only be set to the default Avid and Final Cut shortcuts. To return to the default Premiere shortcuts, choose Adobe Premiere Factory Defaults from the Set dropdown menu (see Figure A.2).

Below the Set dropdown menu is a second dropdown menu, from which you can pick shortcut categories, including **Application, Windows,** and **Tools.** The **Application** category includes shortcuts that allow you to access Premiere's menu options **Control+Shift+Z** for **Edit>Redo.** If you want to change the shortcut for **Edit>Redo** to

311

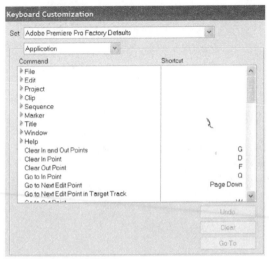

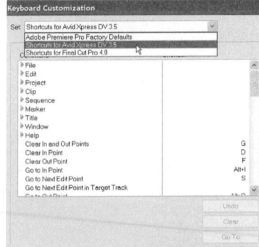

A.1 To make up your own keyboard shortcuts, choose Edit>Keyboard Customization from the menu.

A.2 If you'd like to use Avid or Final Cut Pro shortcuts, choose the appropriate application from the Set dropdown menu.

Control+Y, you need to first choose the **Application** category. The **Windows** category allows you to adjust shortcuts that are active in individual windows, such as the **Effect Controls** window or the **Audio Mixer**. The **Tools** category allows you to adjust the keyboard shortcuts that select tools on the **Tools** palette. For instance, the default shortcut that selects the **Razor** tool is **C**. If you think **R** makes more sense, you can make that change, but you need to first choose the **Tools** category (see Figure A.3).

Once you've chosen a category, find the command to which you'd like to add or change a shortcut. Many commands are in subcategories that you'll have to twirl open before you'll be able to find the command. Double-click in the right column, either on an existing shortcut or in the black space where the shortcut would be if it existed. Type the new keyboard shortcut (see Figure A.4).

For instance, if you set the category to **Application**, you'll find the keyboard shortcuts for clearing **In** and **Out** points below the lowest subcategory (**Help**). By default, **D** is the shortcut for clearing the **In** point and **F** is the shortcut for clearing the **Out** point. You might want to change these shortcuts to **Alt+I** and **Alt+O**, respectively, so that you can set **In** and **Out** points using **I** and **O** and clear them using **Alt+I** and **Alt+O**. Double-click the letter **D** to the right of **Clear In Point**; then click **Alt+I** on the keyboard. Click the **F** across from **Clear Out Point** (once you double-click the first shortcut, you only need to single click others); then press **Alt+O** on the keyboard. When you're done customizing shortcuts, you can save your changes by clicking the **OK** button.

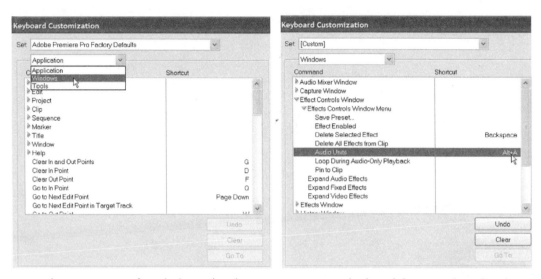

A.3 Choose a category from the lower dropdown menu.

A.4 Type a keyboard shortcut in the right column.

Or you can save an entire set of changes by clicking the **Save As** button (see Figure A.5). Premiere will prompt you to name your set, and from then on you'll be able to select it from the **Set** dropdown at the top of the **Keyboard Customization** window (see Figure A.6). If you want to return to the Premiere defaults, choose **Adobe Premiere Factory Defaults** from the **Set** dropdown menu.

Table A.1 shows some shortcut suggestions, but this is a personal matter, so by all means feel free to ignore them and choose your own.

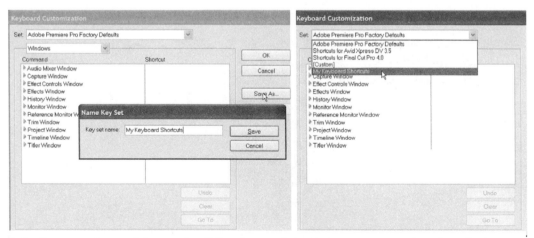

A.5 Save an entire set of shortcuts by clicking the Save As button.

A.6 You can access saved sets from the Set dropdown menu.

Table A.1   Suggested Customized Shortcuts

Category	Shortcut	Comment
Application>Clip>Link Audio and Video	Alt+L	This will also become the shortcut for **Unlink Audio and Video**, so if you want to create a split edit, you'll now only need to select either the audio or video portion of linked clips and click **Alt+L** to unlink them.
Application>Window>Effect Controls	F2	**F2** brings up the **Effect Controls** window in Adobe After Effects, so if you're an AE user, this will help you feel at home in Premiere.
Window>Capture Window>Log Clip	Shift+O	This way you can use **I** and **O** to mark in and out points and then just add in the **Shift** key and click **O** again to log a clip for batch capturing.

WORKSPACES

If you select **Window>Workspace** from the menu, you'll find Premiere's four default workspaces: **Editing, Effects, Audio,** and **Color Correction** (see Figure A.7). Selecting any one of these options reconfigures the screen, opening certain windows, closing others, resizing windows, moving windows to specific screen locations and docking windows as tabbed groups.

You can create your own workspaces and save them to the **Window>Workspace** menu. To do so, configure your screen so that windows are displayed in a useful way, and then choose **Window>Workspace>Save Workspace** from the menu. Premiere will prompt you to name your new workspace. After doing so, click the **Save** button. Now, if you choose **Window>Workspace,** you'll see your new workspace has been added to the list (see Figure A.8). Try toggling back and forth between your new workspace and **Window>Workspace>Editing** to see how Premiere reconfigures your screen each time you make a workspace selection.

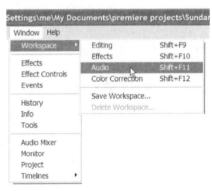

A.7   Choose from one of four default workspaces in the Window>Workspace menu.

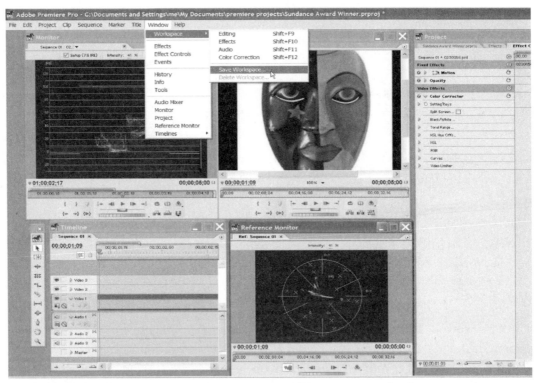

A.8   After arranging windows to your liking, you can save the arrangement by choosing Window>Workspace>Save Workspace from the menu.

Once you've added a workspace, you can create a keyboard shortcut to toggle to it (see the previous section on customizing keyboard shortcuts). To do so, choose **Edit>Keyboard Customization** and choose the **Application** category in the **Keyboard Customization** window. Down below the last subcategory (help), you'll find commands to toggle to the user workspaces. They are listed as **User Workspace 0, User Workspace 1,** etc. **User Workspace 0** is the first custom workspace listed in the **Window>Workspace** menu, **User Workspace 1** is the second, and so on. None of them have default keyboard shortcuts, but you can add your own (see Figure A.10).

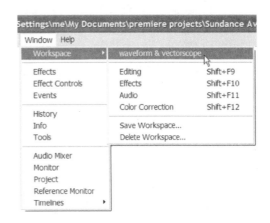

A.9   Saved workspaces are available on the Window>Workspace menu.

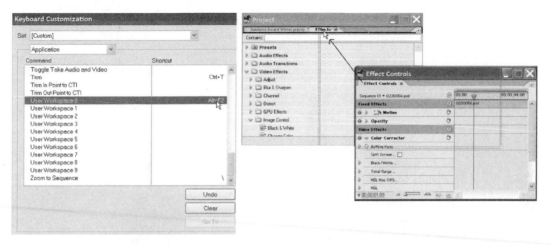

A.10 You can set a keyboard shortcut to display your workspace in the Keyboard Customization dialog window.

A.11 To group and ungroup windows, drag them by their tabs.

Before you set up your own workspace, you should know a little bit about the way windows work in Premiere. For instance, you can group similar windows together by placing them in tabbed groups (see Figure A.11). For instance, you can group the **Effects** window and the **Project** window together by opening the **Effects** window and dragging it by its tab onto the top of the **Project** window. When you see a black outline appear at the top of the **Project** window, release the mouse button and the two windows will be grouped together. To ungroup the windows, drag either tab away from the group.

You can close windows by clicking the small x icons on their tabs. To open a closed window, choose its name from the **Window** menu.

To resize a window, point to one of its edges. When you see a double-headed arrow, hold down the mouse button and drag to resize.

The **Tools** palette has the unique ability to lie vertically (the default) or horizontally (like a traditional toolbar in Microsoft Word). To switch its layout between these two options, right-click the **Tools** palette on a gray pixel, not directly on any of its tools (see Figure A.12).

A.12 To toggle the Tools palette between a horizontal row and a vertical column, right-click it on a gray area where there aren't any buttons.

You can drag a window to a new location by dragging its title bar.

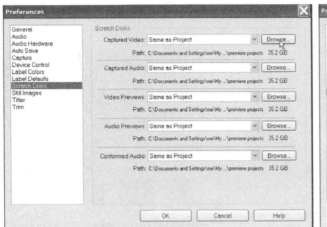

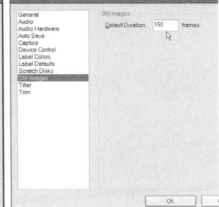

A.13 To choose where Premiere saves files, select Scratch Disks from the Edit>Preferences menu.

A.14 You can choose a default duration for still images by choosing Edit>Preferences>Still Images from the menu.

PREFERENCES

As with most programs, you can adjust all sorts of user preferences by choosing **Edit>Preferences** from the menu. Two adjustments you might want to make are to scratch disks and still images (see Figures A.13 and A.14).

Edit>Preferences>Scratch Disks lets you choose where you want Premiere to save captures and preview files. You make have bought expensive hard drives for your video, but Premiere won't use them unless you tell the scratch disk preferences about them.

In the **Scratch Disks** preferences, **Video** and **Audio** previews refer to temporary files that Premiere generates while you scrub around in the **Timeline** and apply effects. **Conformed Audio** refers to audio files that Premiere automatically generates when you import audio with a different kHz rate than you set in your project settings. If you're project is set to 32kHz and you import 48kHz audio, Premiere has to downsample it, which means it will create new, downgraded audio files that are copies of the original audio files you're trying to import. It needs to store these files somewhere.

For best results, set all of your **Scratch Disks** preferences to hard drives *other* than your root drive (usually your C drive on the PC). Your root drive is where the Windows operating system lives, and if the computer has to access the operating system at the same time as its capturing video, on the same drive, you'll force the playhead on that drive to jump back and forth, slowing things down and possibly causing dropped frames in your capture.

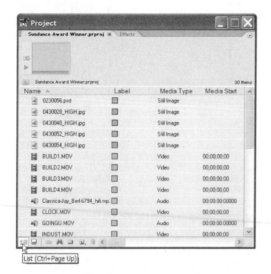

A.15 You can toggle between List View and Icon View by clicking the two leftmost buttons at the bottom of the Project window.

A.16 You arrange clips in sequence order by dragging them into thumbnail-view slots.

If you choose **Edit>Preferences>Still Images**, you can set the default duration of any still images you import into Premiere. Of course, you can always make images last for a longer or shorter time, once you've added them to the **Timeline**, by trimming them.

PROJECT WINDOW VIEW

You can view the items in the **Project** window in two different ways: **List View** and **Icon View**. You can toggle between these two views by clicking the first two buttons in the **Project** window's lower-left corner (see Figure A.15). In **Icon View**, each footage item appears as a thumbnail. This view is especially useful for creating storyboards. To drag a clip between two other clips, select the clip you want to move and then drag it to the crack between two other clips. When you see a dark black line in the crack, drop the clip you're dragging. You can drag each thumbnail into its own slot, placing the clips in the order you'd like them to appear in the sequence (see Figure A.16). But if you want to see detailed information about each item, select **List View** and then drag the right edge of the project window out as far as you can (see Figure A.17). When the **Project** window is extended wider and the display style is **List View**, you can see many columns of information.

Columns include **Media Start and End** (starting and ending timecodes for each clip), **Media Duration, In and Out Points, Video Info** (width and height), and **Audio Info.** You can double-click in blank columns—such as **Comments, Description,** and **Log Note**—to

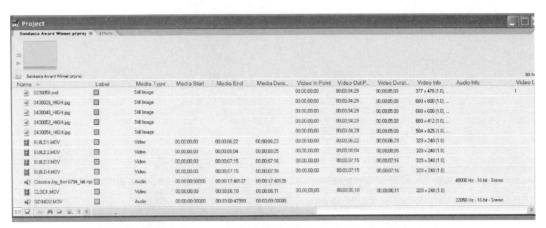

A.17 In List View, you can widen the Project window to see many columns of information.

enter any text you want, information you'd like stored with each clip (see Figure A.18). If a column isn't wide enough for you to view your whole comment, you can drag the edge of its heading to the right to widen it (see Figure A.19).

To sort the items by a particular column, click the column heading (the name of the column)(see Figure A.24). Click a column heading a second time to sort in reversed order (e.g., z to a or longest duration to shortest duration). You can also drag columns around by their headings to change their order from left to right in the Project window (see Figures A.20 and A.21).

The columns you see by default are not all the possible columns. Choose **Edit Columns** from the **Project** window's wing menu (the triangle in its upper-right corner) to see a complete list of displayable columns(see Figure A.22). Check a column to add it to the **Project** window. Uncheck a column to remove it from the **Project** window (see Figure A.23).

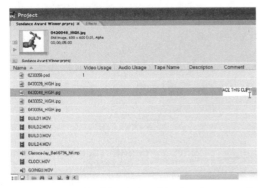

A.18 You can double-click in blank columns and type notes.

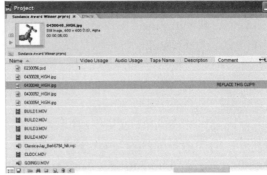

A.19 Widen a column by dragging the edge of its heading to the right.

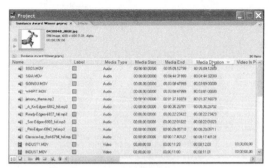

A.20 Click a column heading to sort by that column.

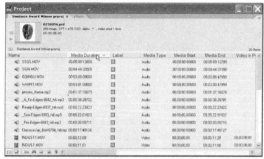

A.21 Drag column headings to rearrange column order.

A.22 To see a list of all available columns, choose Edit Columns from the Project window's wing menu.

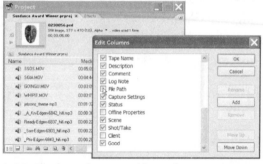

A.23 Check a column to add it to the Project window. Uncheck a column to remove it.

Or you can click the **Add** button to add your own custom column. Premiere will prompt you to name it and choose a column type, **Text** or **Boolean. Boolean** columns contain checkboxes; text columns contain cells which you can click to add text. For instance, you could add a column called **Quality**, and choose text for its type. Then, you could click each **Quality** cell in the Project window and add one two or three asterisks. Finally, you could click the column heading,

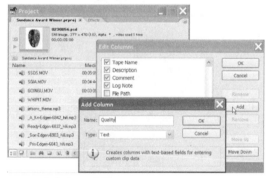

A.24 Click the Add button to create a custom column.

Quality, to sort from low quality (*) to high quality (***). Or you could click the column heading a second time to sort from high quality to low quality.

The most unique of the default columns is **Label**, which contains a color swatch for each clip. Premiere labels each type of clip—video, audio, still, etc.—with a different

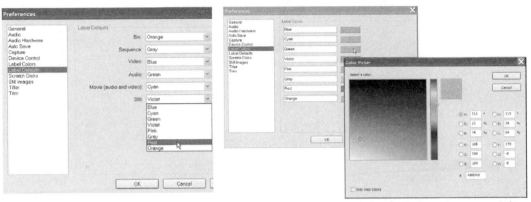

A.25 To change the default color clip types, choose Edit>Preferences>Label Defaults from the menu. *(left)*

A.26 To pick completely new colors, choose Edit>Preferences>Label Colors. *(right)*

color. You can change the default color for each type of clip by choosing **Edit>Preferences>Label Defaults** from the menu (see Figure A.25). If you don't like Premiere's color choices, you can pick new ones by choosing **Edit>Preferences>Label Colors** from the menu (see Figure A.26). This will allow you to select basic colors used by Premiere. You can then assign these colors to specific footage types in the **Label Defaults** preferences. You can even override a specific clip's label by selecting that clip in the **Project** window, and choosing **Edit>Label** from the menu and then choosing a new color (see Figure A.27).

Once you're happy with your clip labels, you can sort your clips by clicking the **Label** heading in the **Project** window. Even more useful, you can select one clip in the project window and then choose **Edit>Label>Select Label Group** to force Premiere to select all clips labeled in the same color (see Figure A.28).

Label colors also display in the **Timeline**, running along the tops of the clips (see Figure A.29).

TIMELINE VIEW

Speaking of the **Timeline**, you can customize it too. By clicking the **Set Display Style** button, located immediately below the eyeball at the left edge of each track, you can choose a track display (see Figure A.30). Options include **Show Head and Tail, Show Head Only, Show Frames,** and **Show Name Only.** The final option will only the name of each clip along its duration in the **Timeline.** The other options all show clip thumbnails. **Show Head and Tail** displays thumbnails at the beginning and end of each clip in the track, whereas **Show Head Only** shows thumbnails only at the beginning of each clip. If you choose **Show Frames** and zoom in all the way, you'll see a thumbnail of each clip. Regardless of which view you pick, you must have the track twirled open to see the thumbnails.

A.27 To override the color for a specific clip, select the clip in the Project window and choose Edit>Label from the menu.

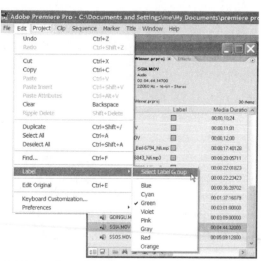

A.28 To select all clips of a specific type, choose Edit>Label>Select Label Group.

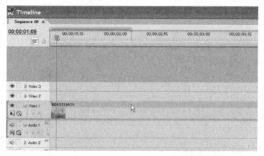

A.29 Label colors also display in the Timeline, running along the tops of clips.

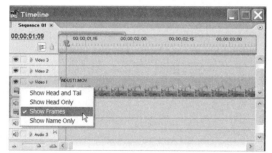

A.30 Choose a track display option by clicking the Set Display button by any track in the Timeline.

You can make a track higher by pointing to the dividing line between it and the track above it (if it's a video track) or it and the track below it (if it's an audio track), as shown in Figure A.31. Place your mouse cursor on the line above the track's name, not in the clip section of the **Timeline**. When your mouse cursor is in place, it should change to a double-headed arrow. You can then drag upwards to make tracks taller and downwards to make them shorter.

If you hold the **Shift** key down while you're dragging, all expanded tracks of the same type (video or audio) will also resize. Audio tracks are especially worth resizing, because the bigger they are, the more details of their waveform you can see. You may also want to resize track when adjusting Bezier curves in the **Timeline**.

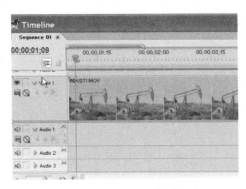

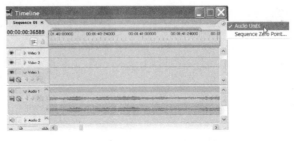

A.32 To change the time ruler's units from frames to audio units or vice versa, click the Timeline's wing menu.

A.31 You can make tracks taller by dragging their boundaries.

Note **Resizing Tracks:** You can only resize expanded tracks. If you want to expand a track, twirl open the triangle to the left of its name.

You can also customize the **Timeline** by renaming tracks. To rename a track, right-click its current name and choose the rename option. For instance, you could rename **Video 1** "Footage" and **Video 2** "Titles." You could rename **Audio 1** "Dialog," **Audio 2** "Music," and **Audio 3,** "Sound FX."

AUDIO SAMPLES

Normally, the tick marks in the time ruler at the top of the **Timeline** indicate timecode increments. If you zoom in as far as you can go by dragging the slider in the **Timeline's** lower-left corner to the right, each tick mark represents a frame. You can't zoom in any further than that, because frames are the atomic units of video.

But not audio.

Audio "frames," which are really called *audio samples,* break at much finer increments than video frames. If you are editing audio (see Chapter 10), it's often useful to zoom deep into audio samples, rather than content yourself with moving frame by frame. After all, you might want to adjust audio when an actor says a specific word, and he might start to say that word halfway through a frame.

To change the **Timeline's** ruler to display audio samples instead of frames, click the **Timeline's** wing menu (the triangle in its upper-right corner) and choose **Audio Units** from the popup menu. Choose **Audio Units** a second time to switch back to frames (see Figure A.32).

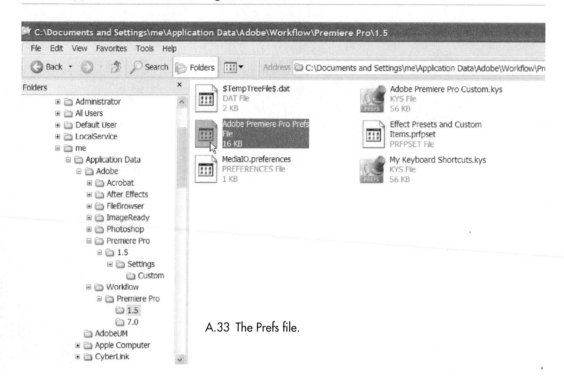

A.33 The Prefs file.

You can also view audio units in both monitors, the **Effects Control** window and (of course) the **Audio Mixer.** In any of these cases, you can switch to viewing audio units by choosing the **Audio Units** option in the specific window's wing menu.

PREFERENCES FILE

The various customizations you have learned to create in this chapter are stored in a file called *Adobe Premiere Pro Prefs* (see Figure A.33). If you ever want to return the program to its factory defaults (the way it looked and acted when you first installed it), just delete or rename this file. Then restart Premiere. If Premiere can't find its *Prefs* file, it will create a fresh one from scratch.

It's a good idea to back this file up on a floppy disk or CD. That way, if you have to reinstall Premiere, you can get all of your preferences back.

If you ever find that Premiere isn't working right, the *Prefs* file might have become corrupted. To fix Premiere, delete the current *Prefs* file and reinstall your backup in its place. If you haven't backed up the file, you can always just delete the current one and let Premiere create a new one—but you'll lose all your customizations.

Here's the path to the Prefs file: *C:\Documents and Settings\YOUR USER NAME\Application Data\Adobe\Workflow\Premiere Pro\1.5\Adobe Premiere Pro Prefs*. On any specific computer, the text "YOUR USER NAME" should be replaced with the specific user on that system. PC user settings can get complicated, especially when there are multiple users, which can make it difficult to find the *Prefs* file. But you can always find it by choosing **Search** from your PC's **Start** button menu. In the left pane of the **Search** window, select the **All Files and Folders** option. Then type *Adobe Premiere Pro Prefs* in the text field labeled **All or part of the filename**. From the **Lookin** dropdown, choose **My Computer**. Then click the text **More Advanced Options** and check the **Search Hidden Files and Folders** option. Finally, click the **Search** button (see Figure A.34).

A.34 Searching for the Prefs file.

THIRD-PARTY PLUG-INS

If you find yourself getting bored with the effects that ship with Premiere, you can buy dozens of third-party plug-ins. Most plug-ins come with their own install programs, but if you ever need to install a plug-in by hand, just drag it in into the plug-ins folder *C:\Program Files\Adobe\Premiere Pro\Plug-ins* (see Figure A.35). When you next start Premiere, there will be a new effect listed in the **Effects** window.

Adobe maintains a list of Premiere third-party plugins at http://www.adobe.com/store/products/plugins/view_by_application.jhtml?id=catPluginsForPremiere.

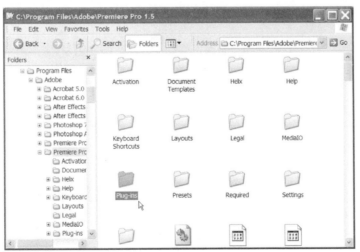

A.35 Install plug-ins in this folder.

WRAPPING UP

You should customize Premiere, because ultimately the way you work in an editing application is a reflection of who you are. Each editor works in his or her own unique way. You should work *your* way. Your work will be imprinted with your own style and personality. You will produce videos that are communications from your brain and fingertips to the world. And having pushed your video out into the world, you will have changed the world a little.

Index

THE AUTHORITY ON DIGITAL VIDEO TECHNOLOGY

00:21:25:03

00:15:32:03

PROD. NO.

SCENE

TAKE.

ROLL

DATE

PROD. C

TOR

MAN

DV
MAGAZINE

DV
EXPO AND
CONFERENCES

DV
QUARTERLY

DV
QUARTERLY

DV
.com

DV
FILM FESTIVAL

DV
EXPERT SERIES
(A DIVISION
OF CMP BOOKS)

INSPIRING AND EMPOWERING CREATIVITY

FOR PRODUCT DETAILS, GO TO **WWW.DV.COM**

Digital Video
DV
Media Group

Designing Menus with Encore DVD

John Skidgel

Create engaging, well-structured menus with the latest version of Encore DVD. This full-color book guides you through all of the essential DVD authoring concepts and shows how to plan and manage projects and inter-application workflows. The companion DVD contains tutorial media and plug-ins.

$49.95, 4-Color, Softcover with DVD, 240 pp, ISBN 1-57820-235-3

Using Audition

Ron Dabbs

Finish your projects with compelling audio tracks. Practical examples and tutorials demonstrate all the techniques you need—whether you are adding narration, getting out the hum, or using loops to create custom, royalty-free, music tracks. The CD includes third-party DirectX and VST plug-ins, filters, encoding software, and utilities.

$44.95, Softcover with CD-ROM, 352 pp, ISBN 1-57820-240-X

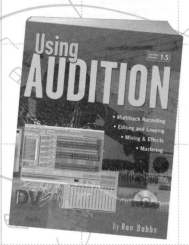

Creative Titling Premiere Pro

Ed Gaskell

Create compelling title sequences using Premiere Pro. Packed with four-color illustrations, explanations, instructions, and step-by-step tutorials, this book teaches and inspires editors to produce work that is a cut above the rest. Covers conceptualization, design, methodology, and the mechanics of successful title sequences.

$44.95, 4-Color Softcover, 198 pp, ISBN 1-57820-233-7

CMP**Books**

Instant Encore DVD

Douglas Spotted Eagle

Get working with Encore DVD in an instant. This accessible and thorough orientation features detailed screen shots and step-by-step directions. You learn the full range of functions as well as professional techniques for efficient workflow and polish.

$19.95, Softcover, 208pp, ISBN 1-57820-245-0, **June 2004**

Nonlinear Editing

Bryce Button

Build your aesthetic muscles with this application-agnostic guide to digital editing so you can make better decisions in the edit bay and in your career. CD-ROM includes a treasure trove of valuable software, image files, tools, utilities, fonts, filters, and sounds.

$49.95, Softcover with CD-ROM, 523pp, ISBN 1-57820-096-2

Windows Media 9 Series by Example

Nels Johnson

Deliver a first-class presentation to your Web, home theater, and desktop video audience with proven strategies for reliable performance and positive user experiences. You'll find tutorials and complete instructions on how to capture, edit, compress, serve, and otherwise present WM 9 Series video files.

$44.95, Softcover, 383pp, ISBN 1-57820-204-3

CMP**Books**

Creating Motion Graphics with After Effects
Volume 1: The Essentials, 3rd Edtion
Trish Meyer & Chris Meyer

Master the core concepts and tools you need to tackle virtually every job, including keyframe animation, masking, mattes, and plug-in effects. New chapters demystify Parenting, 3D Space, and features of the latest software version. **Available September, 2004**

$59.95, 4-Color, Softcover with CD-ROM, 448 pp, ISBN 1-57820-249-3

Photoshop CS for Nonlinear Editors
2nd Edition
Richard Harrington

Use Photoshop CS to generate characters, correct colors, and animate graphics for digital video. You'll grasp the fundamental concepts and master the complete range of Photoshop tools through lively discourse, full-color presentations, and hands-on tutorials. The companion DVD contains tutorial media and plug-ins.

$54.95, 4-Color, Softcover with DVD, 336 pp, ISBN 1-57820-237-X

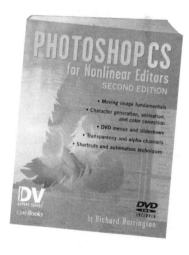

After Effects On the Spot
Richard Harrington, Rachel Max, & Marcus Geduld

Packed with more than 400 expert techniques, this book clearly illustrates all the essential methods that pros use to get the job done with After Effects. Experienced editors and novices alike discover an invaluable reference filled with ways to improve efficiency and creativity.

$27.95, Softcover, 256 pp, ISBN 1-57820-239-6

CMP **Books**

On the DVD-ROM

- Five project files, each with an ad for the American Diabetes Association (ADA) at a later stage of completion.

- A PDF (Adobe Acrobat) document, outlining the steps used in completing the ADA spot.

- A text file *(script.txt)* containing the script for the ADA spot.

- Six low-quality AVI video files: raw footage for the ADA spot.

- A folder called *demos* containing four videos, in which the author demonstrates how he edited the ADA spot.

- A folder called *hi res videos* with good-quality copies of the ADA raw-footage in Quick-Time format.

- This readme document.

Copy the contents of the DVD onto your hard drive before using the project files. Premiere will run slowly if it has to continually access the DVD for files.

Footage courtesy of the American Diabetes Association (www.diabetes.org).

Production by RHED Pixel (www.rhedpixel.com).

Updates

Want to receive e-mail news updates for Premiere Pro Editing Workshop? Send a blank e-mail to premiereworkshop@news.cmpbooks.com. We will do our best to keep you informed of software updates and enhancements, new tips, and other Premiere Pro resources. Further, if you would like to contribute to the effort by reporting any errors or by posting your own tips, please contact the author at mgeduld@hotmail.com.

Made in the USA
Monee, IL
28 November 2020

49831080R00059

DATE: _____

_____

_____

_____

_____

NAME: _____

DATE: _____

_____

_____

_____

_____

NAME: _____

DATE: _____

_____

_____

_____

_____

NAME: _____

"

DATE: _____

_____

_____

_____

_____

NAME: _____

"

MEMORIES

_____

_____

_____

_____

_____

_____

_____

_____

_____

_____

_____

DATE: _____

_____

_____

_____

_____

NAME: _____

DATE: _____

_____

_____

_____

_____

NAME: _____

DATE: _____

_____

_____

_____

_____

NAME: _____

DATE: _____

_____

_____

_____

_____

NAME: _____

MEMORIES

_____

_____

_____

_____

_____

_____

_____

_____

_____

_____

_____

DATE: _____

_____

_____

_____

_____

NAME: _____

DATE: _____

_____

_____

_____

_____

NAME: _____

DATE: _____

_____

_____

_____

_____

NAME: _____

DATE: _____

_____

_____

_____

_____

NAME: _____

MEMORIES

_____

_____

_____

_____

_____

_____

_____

_____

_____

_____

DATE: _____

_____

_____

_____

_____

NAME: _____

MEMORIES

_____

_____

_____

_____

_____

_____

_____

_____

_____

_____

_____

DATE: _____

_____

_____

_____

_____

NAME: _____

DATE: _____

_____

_____

_____

_____

NAME: _____

DATE: _____

_____

_____

_____

_____

NAME: _____

DATE: _____

_____

_____

_____

_____

NAME: _____

DATE: _____

_____

_____

_____

_____

NAME: _____

DATE: _____

_____

_____

_____

_____

NAME: _____

DATE: _____

_____

_____

_____

_____

NAME: _____

MEMORIES

_____

_____

_____

_____

_____

_____

_____

_____

_____

_____

"

DATE: _____

_____

_____

_____

_____

NAME: _____ **""**

"

DATE: _____

_____

_____

_____

_____

NAME: _____ **""**

"

DATE: _____

_____

_____

_____

_____

NAME: _____ **""**

DATE: _____

_____

_____

_____

_____

NAME: _____

MEMORIES

_____

_____

_____

_____

_____

_____

_____

_____

_____

_____

" DATE: _____

_____

_____

_____

_____

NAME: _____ **"**

" DATE: _____

_____

_____

_____

_____

NAME: _____ **"**

" DATE: _____

_____

_____

_____

_____

NAME: _____ **"**

DATE: _____

_____

_____

_____

_____

NAME: _____

MEMORIES

_____

_____

_____

_____

_____

_____

_____

_____

_____

_____

_____

DATE: _____

_____

_____

_____

_____

NAME: _____

DATE: _____

_____

_____

_____

_____

NAME: _____

DATE: _____

_____

_____

_____

_____

NAME: _____

66

DATE: _____

_____

_____

_____

_____

NAME: _____ 99

MEMORIES

_____

_____

_____

_____

_____

_____

_____

_____

_____

_____

DATE: _____

_____

_____

_____

_____

NAME: _____

DATE: _____

_____

_____

_____

_____

NAME: _____

DATE: _____

_____

_____

_____

_____

NAME: _____

DATE: _____

_____

_____

_____

_____

NAME: _____

MEMORIES

_____

_____

_____

_____

_____

_____

_____

_____

_____

_____

66

DATE: _____

_____

_____

_____

_____

NAME: _____   99

66

DATE: _____

_____

_____

_____

_____

NAME: _____   99

66

DATE: _____

_____

_____

_____

_____

NAME: _____   99

DATE: _____

_____

_____

_____

_____

NAME: _____

MEMORIES

_____

_____

_____

_____

_____

_____

_____

_____

_____

_____

_____

"

DATE: _____

_____

_____

_____

_____

NAME: _____

""

"

DATE: _____

_____

_____

_____

_____

NAME: _____

""

"

DATE: _____

_____

_____

_____

_____

NAME: _____

""

DATE: _____

_____

_____

_____

_____

NAME: _____

MEMORIES

_____

_____

_____

_____

_____

_____

_____

_____

_____

_____

_____

DATE: _____

_____

_____

_____

_____

NAME: _____

DATE: _____

_____

_____

_____

_____

NAME: _____

DATE: _____

_____

_____

_____

_____

NAME: _____

DATE: _____

_____

_____

_____

_____

NAME: _____

MEMORIES

_____

_____

_____

_____

_____

_____

_____

_____

_____

_____

" DATE: _____

_____

_____

_____

_____

NAME: _____ **"**

" DATE: _____

_____

_____

_____

_____

NAME: _____ **"**

" DATE: _____

_____

_____

_____

_____

NAME: _____ **"**

DATE: _____

_____

_____

_____

_____

NAME: _____

MEMORIES

_____

_____

_____

_____

_____

_____

_____

_____

_____

_____

"

DATE: _____

_____

_____

_____

_____

NAME: _____ **"**

"

DATE: _____

_____

_____

_____

_____

NAME: _____ **"**

"

DATE: _____

_____

_____

_____

_____

NAME: _____ **"**

DATE: _____

_____

_____

_____

_____

NAME: _____

MEMORIES

_____

_____

_____

_____

_____

_____

_____

_____

_____

_____

DATE: _____

_____

_____

_____

_____

NAME: _____

DATE: _____

_____

_____

_____

_____

NAME: _____

DATE: _____

_____

_____

_____

_____

NAME: _____

DATE: _____

_____

_____

_____

_____

NAME: _____

MEMORIES

_____

_____

_____

_____

_____

_____

_____

_____

_____

_____

_____

DATE: _____

_____

_____

_____

_____

NAME: _____

DATE: _____

_____

_____

_____

_____

NAME: _____

DATE: _____

_____

_____

_____

_____

NAME: _____

DATE: _____

_____

_____

_____

_____

NAME: _____

MEMORIES

_____

_____

_____

_____

_____

_____

_____

_____

_____

_____

66

DATE: _____

_____

_____

_____

_____

NAME: _____ 99

66

DATE: _____

_____

_____

_____

_____

NAME: _____ 99

66

DATE: _____

_____

_____

_____

_____

NAME: _____ 99

66

DATE: _____

_____

_____

_____

_____

NAME: _____

99

MEMORIES

_____

_____

_____

_____

_____

_____

_____

_____

_____

_____

NAME: _____

_____

_____

_____

_____

DATE: _____

NAME: _____

_____

_____

_____

_____

DATE: _____

NAME: _____

_____

_____

_____

_____

DATE: _____

DATE: _____

_____

_____

_____

_____

NAME: _____

MEMORIES

_____

_____

_____

_____

_____

_____

_____

_____

_____

_____

" DATE: _____

_____

_____

_____

_____

_____

NAME: _____ **"**

" DATE: _____

_____

_____

_____

_____

_____

NAME: _____ **"**

" DATE: _____

_____

_____

_____

_____

_____

NAME: _____ **"**

DATE: _____

_____

_____

_____

_____

NAME: _____

MEMORIES

_____

_____

_____

_____

_____

_____

_____

_____

_____

_____

_____

DATE: _____

_____

_____

_____

_____

NAME: _____

DATE: _____

_____

_____

_____

_____

NAME: _____

DATE: _____

_____

_____

_____

_____

NAME: _____

DATE: _____

_____

_____

_____

_____

NAME: _____

MEMORIES

_____

_____

_____

_____

_____

_____

_____

_____

_____

_____

DATE: _____

_____

_____

_____

_____

NAME: _____

DATE: _____

_____

_____

_____

_____

NAME: _____

DATE: _____

_____

_____

_____

_____

NAME: _____

DATE: _____

_____

_____

_____

_____

NAME: _____

MEMORIES

_____

_____

_____

_____

_____

_____

_____

_____

_____

_____

_____

NAME: _____

_____

_____

_____

_____

DATE: _____

NAME: _____

_____

_____

_____

_____

DATE: _____

NAME: _____

_____

_____

_____

_____

DATE: _____

_____

_____

_____

_____

_____

_____

_____

_____

_____

_____

MEMORIES

NAME: _____

_____

_____

_____

DATE: _____

NAME: _____

_____

_____

_____

_____

DATE: _____

NAME: _____

_____

_____

_____

_____

DATE: _____

NAME: _____

_____

_____

_____

_____

DATE: _____

MEMORIES

_____

_____

_____

_____

_____

_____

_____

_____

_____

NAME: _____

_____

_____

_____

DATE: _____

NAME: _____

_____

_____

_____

_____

_____

DATE: _____

NAME: _____

_____

_____

_____

_____

_____

DATE: _____

NAME: _____

_____

_____

_____

_____

_____

DATE: _____

MEMORIES

NAME: _____

_____

_____

_____

_____

DATE: _____

NAME:

DATE:

"

NAME:

DATE:

"

NAME:

DATE:

"

_____

_____

_____

_____

_____

_____

_____

_____

_____

_____

MEMORIES

NAME: _____

_____

_____

_____

DATE: _____

NAME:

DATE:

NAME:

DATE:

NAME:

DATE:

_____
_____
_____
_____
_____
_____
_____
_____
_____
_____

MEMORIES

NAME: _____

_____

_____

_____

DATE: _____

NAME:

DATE:

NAME:

DATE:

NAME:

DATE:

MEMORIES

NAME:

DATE:

NAME: _____

_____

_____

_____

_____

DATE: _____

NAME: _____

_____

_____

_____

_____

DATE: _____

NAME: _____

_____

_____

_____

_____

DATE: _____

_____

_____

_____

_____

_____

_____

_____

_____

_____

_____

MEMORIES

NAME: _____

_____

_____

_____

_____

DATE: _____

NAME:

DATE:

NAME:

DATE:

NAME:

DATE:

MEMORIES

NAME:

DATE:

NAME:

DATE:

NAME:

DATE:

NAME:

DATE:

MEMORIES

NAME:

DATE:

NAME: _____

_____

_____

_____

_____

DATE: _____

NAME: _____

_____

_____

_____

_____

DATE: _____

NAME: _____

_____

_____

_____

_____

DATE: _____

_____

_____

_____

_____

_____

_____

_____

_____

_____

_____

MEMORIES

NAME: _____

_____

_____

_____

DATE: _____

NAME: _____

_____

_____

_____

_____

DATE: _____

NAME: _____

_____

_____

_____

_____

DATE: _____

NAME: _____

_____

_____

_____

_____

DATE: _____

MEMORIES

NAME:

DATE:

"

NAME: _____

_____

_____

_____

_____

DATE: _____

"

"

NAME: _____

_____

_____

_____

_____

DATE: _____

"

"

NAME: _____

_____

_____

_____

_____

DATE: _____

"

MEMORIES

NAME:

DATE:

NAME: _____

_____

_____

_____

_____

DATE: _____

NAME: _____

_____

_____

_____

_____

DATE: _____

NAME: _____

_____

_____

_____

_____

DATE: _____

MEMORIES

NAME: _____

DATE: _____

NAME: _____

_____

_____

_____

_____

DATE: _____

NAME: _____

_____

_____

_____

_____

DATE: _____

NAME: _____

_____

_____

_____

_____

DATE: _____

_____

_____

_____

_____

_____

_____

_____

_____

_____

_____

MEMORIES

NAME: _____

_____

_____

_____

DATE: _____

NAME: _____

_____

_____

_____

_____

DATE: _____

NAME: _____

_____

_____

_____

_____

DATE: _____

NAME: _____

_____

_____

_____

_____

DATE: _____

_____

_____

_____

_____

_____

_____

_____

_____

_____

_____

_____

MEMORIES

NAME: _____

_____

_____

_____

DATE: _____

NAME: _____

_____

_____

_____

_____

DATE: _____

NAME: _____

_____

_____

_____

_____

DATE: _____

NAME: _____

_____

_____

_____

_____

DATE: _____

MEMORIES

NAME:

DATE:

NAME:

DATE:

NAME:

DATE:

NAME:

DATE:

MEMORIES

NAME:

DATE:

NAME: _____

_____

_____

_____

_____

DATE: _____

NAME: _____

_____

_____

_____

_____

DATE: _____

NAME: _____

_____

_____

_____

_____

DATE: _____

MEMORIES

NAME:

DATE:

NAME:

DATE:

NAME:

DATE:

NAME:

DATE:

MEMORIES

NAME: _____

DATE: _____

NAME: _____

_____

_____

_____

_____

DATE: _____

NAME: _____

_____

_____

_____

_____

DATE: _____

NAME: _____

_____

_____

_____

_____

DATE: _____

MEMORIES

NAME:

DATE:

NAME: _____

_____

_____

_____

_____

DATE: _____

NAME: _____

_____

_____

_____

_____

DATE: _____

NAME: _____

_____

_____

_____

_____

DATE: _____

MEMORIES

NAME:

DATE:

NAME:

DATE:

NAME:

DATE:

NAME:

DATE:

_____
_____
_____
_____
_____
_____
_____
_____
_____
_____

MEMORIES

NAME: _____
_____
_____
_____
DATE: _____

NAME: _____

_____

_____

_____

_____

DATE: _____

NAME: _____

_____

_____

_____

_____

DATE: _____

NAME: _____

_____

_____

_____

_____

DATE: _____

MEMORIES

NAME:

DATE:

"

NAME: _____

_____

_____

_____

_____

DATE: _____

"

"

NAME: _____

_____

_____

_____

_____

DATE: _____

"

"

NAME: _____

_____

_____

_____

_____

DATE: _____

"

_____

_____

_____

_____

_____

_____

_____

_____

_____

_____

MEMORIES

NAME: _____

_____

_____

_____

DATE: _____

NAME:

DATE:

NAME:

DATE:

NAME:

DATE:

MEMORIES

NAME:

DATE:

NAME: _____

_____

_____

_____

_____

DATE: _____

NAME: _____

_____

_____

_____

_____

DATE: _____

NAME: _____

_____

_____

_____

_____

DATE: _____

MEMORIES

NAME:

DATE:

NAME: _____

_____
_____
_____
_____

DATE: _____

NAME: _____

_____
_____
_____
_____

DATE: _____

NAME: _____

_____
_____
_____
_____

DATE: _____

_____

_____

_____

_____

_____

_____

_____

_____

_____

_____

MEMORIES

NAME: _____

DATE: _____

NAME: _____

_____

_____

_____

_____

DATE: _____

"

NAME: _____

_____

_____

_____

_____

DATE: _____

"

NAME: _____

_____

_____

_____

_____

DATE: _____

"

THIS BOOK
BELONGS TO:

S0-BYN-495